Actors'
Handbook
2009-10

Edited by Andrew Chapman

a  directory

© Casting Call Pro 2009

This edition first published 2009 by

Casting Call Pro
Unit 1, Waterloo Gardens
Milner Square
London N1 1TY

www.uk.castingcallpro.com

A CIP catalogue record for this book is available from the British Library

ISBN 978-0-9556273-1-6

Set in Frutiger & Serifa
Designed and edited by Andrew Chapman (www.awrc.co.uk)

Printed in Britain by
Wheatons, Exeter

/continues...

4: Sources of work 161

5: Fringe & comedy 189

6: Living as an actor 211

7: Organisations & resources 221

Introduction

Acting can be one of the most rewarding and frustrating of professions. This guide is intended to make your professional life just that little bit easier. With useful introductions to some of the key areas for establishing oneself as a professional actor, and comprehensive listings for agents, service providers, theatre companies and venues, and all the UK's major acting organisations and drama schools, Actors' Handbook is designed to help you pick a path through the ever changing landscape of the professional actor.

Whether you are considering entering the profession, have just taken your first steps, or are already established as an actor, Actors' Handbook is both a useful guide to the industry and an invaluable resource to help further your career development, covering topics such as: choosing a drama school; finding work and marketing yourself; auditioning; further training, and industry related jobs for those times when you're between roles.

Actors' Handbook is brought to you by the people behind Casting Call Pro, one of the leading resources for professional UK actors. The information in this book is updated regularly, more recent information can always be found at **www.uk.castingcallpro.com**. This 2009-10 edition has been fully revised, with many extra listings.

If you have any questions about this book or feel an organisation or company ought to be included in future editions please send details to info@castingcallpro.com.

Acknowledgements

We are extremely grateful to the following people for their contributions. Each of the contributors bring a fresh and informative insight into what can, at times, seem a daunting and impenetrable industry. Many thanks are due to:

- The National Council for Drama Training (NCDT) – **www.ncdt.co.uk**
- James Berersford, co-director of The Actor's Studio – **www.actorsstudio.co.uk**
- Claire Grogan, highly respected headshot photographer – **www.clairegrogan.co.uk**
- Chantal Ellul, director of the Actor's One–Stop Shop, one of the UK's leading showreel providers for both edited clips and shot from scratch – **www.actorsonestopshop.com**
- Kerry Mitchell, director of Cut Glass Productions, specialists in Voice Overs and voicereel production – **www.cutglassproductions.com**
- James Bonallack, director of Foreign Voices, the UK's foremost agency for native foreign language voice over artists and in-house voice over production – **www.foreignvoices.co.uk**
- James Aylett, performer and co-author of the entertaining and informative Fringe – **www.fridaybooks.co.uk/ www.tartarus.org/james**
- Hils Barker, acclaimed stand up comic and comedy writer for Radio 4 – **www.hilsbarker.com**.

Section 1
Drama schools & training

Choosing a drama school

Do I need to go to drama school?

Training at a reputable drama school is the best route into professional acting. Not only does it afford you an actual grounding in acting and an opportunity to practise your craft, it also gives you credibility in the eyes of casting professionals. (There are a fortunate few who have found success without studying at drama school. They have perhaps been spotted by an agent in an amateur production, but this is a lottery and not to be relied upon if you are serious about making a long-term career in acting.) Attending drama school demonstrates ongoing commitment to your calling and, as long as the school is reputable and you demonstrate a willingness to learn, you'll be better placed at the end of the course to succeed as an actor.

Choosing a course

When selecting a drama course, it is important to realise that not all drama institutions are equal. With several drama courses nationwide to choose from, it is vital to do some serious research before applying. When narrowing your options, start by looking at the institution itself: is it a university or college dedicated to drama, media or stage craft? or a private collection of teachers operating out of rented premises? Investigate how long the institution has been established and how long it has been offering a drama course. It is also important to look at who is teaching the course: do the teachers have the experience required to teach you what you need to succeed? Take time to review what facilities the institution offers: do they have their own theatre and dedicated stage staff? Finally, check the institution's pedigree by talking to past students about their experience, and check out their alumni – where are they now?

Along with your choice of institution, your course selection is also pivotal. Many courses will offer a broad cross-section of acting disciplines, while others are more specific, eg dedicated to screen acting or stage acting. A school's website should give you a good idea of the courses they offer – look thoroughly at the course outline and

THE BENEFITS OF TRAINING
In these sections throughout this chapter Nicole Hay, projects manager at the National Council for Drama Training (NCDT), explains the advantages and process of finding a suitable course:

Acting is an increasingly competitive career. Equity – the actors' union – calculates that a high percentage of its members are unemployed at any given time, with actors working professionally an average of 11.3 weeks of the year. Except for those at the top of the profession, actors earn comparatively low salaries and most have to undertake temporary periods of alternative employment between engagements. To succeed, an actor needs to be intelligent, sensitive, observant and imaginative. Equally important are physical and mental resilience and self-discipline.

For those who do aspire to an acting career it is not all bad news. Despite the gloomy statistics, the personal rewards involved can be immense – how many people can claim they are making a living doing something they really want to do?

There are no formal entry requirements for becoming an actor; it is possible for untrained people to enter the profession. However, in such a competitive industry it makes sense to have as many advantages as possible including vocational training on a course accredited by the NCDT. A report carried out by the Institute of Manpower Studies on behalf of the Arts Council of England found that 86% of actors working in the profession had received formal professional training, and that the vast majority were satisfied with their preparation for working, the careers advice and guidance they had received and the overall quality of their training.

The benefits of vocational training are numerous. NCDT accredited courses provide not only the discipline, practical skills and intellectual understanding necessary for building a lasting career, but also opportunities to be seen by agents, casting directors, theatres and television companies, so vital in securing that all-important first job.

if you have any questions give the school a call; they'll be happy to help with your enquiries. When choosing a course, there are a number of factors to consider. Your research should include finding out about a course's reputation by talking to people and gleaning what you can from industry publications and the internet (don't just go by the school's website which might have an inherent bias). Remember, the reputation of any particular course will fluctuate over time depending on its output of actors and its current teaching staff.

Entry is based mainly on auditions, for which you will usually be expected to select two speeches (one modern, one classical) and for which you may well be charged an audition fee (usually around £30 to £40). You will be expected to cover your own travel and accommodation costs to attend auditions.

With so many competing factors to weigh up, choosing the right drama school can be a daunting process. The National Council for Drama Training (NCDT) accredits those courses which it feels offer the highest levels of vocational training (see opposite). While competition for places on NDCT-accredited courses is fierce, their graduates do tend to be better prepared for the real world of acting; in this tough, competitive environment, every advantage you can acquire is an asset.

HOW & WHEN TO GO TO DRAMA SCHOOL

Drama school courses vary from three-year degree or diploma courses to one-year postgraduate courses for people who have already attended university or have comparable prior experience. Entry is by audition – talent being the principal requirement for securing a place. For three-year courses, applicants must be 18 years and above. Many drama schools prefer to take students who are older as they are looking for people with the maturity to cope with the demands of actor training. For one-year courses, the minimum age is 21. Some students have a lot of prior experience of performing, others very little, but you must demonstrate a genuine commitment.

DIFFERENT TYPES OF COURSE

While all drama school courses aim to prepare students to enter the profession, the philosophy of actor training varies from school to school. Some place great emphasis on classical theatre training, others focus more broadly. Certain courses are specifically targeted at those who wish to make a career in musical theatre. Anyone considering applying to drama school should research their options carefully and consider the sort of career to which they are aspiring. The NCDT website (**www.ncdt.co.uk**) has links to the websites of drama schools with accredited courses and the Conference of Drama Schools website (**www.drama.ac.uk**) has a downloadable guide to professional training in drama and technical theatre.

It is important to make a distinction between vocational training courses and the vast number of performing arts courses on offer at UK universities. The Higher Education Funding Council for England funds more than 2,100 degree courses with 'drama' or 'theatre' in the title. University courses are generally more academic and may not aim to train people as actors. A one-year course accredited by NCDT may be a suitable choice for those who have already completed a drama or theatre studies degree.

What is NCDT accreditation?

NCDT accreditation aims to give students confidence that they courses they choose are recognised by the drama profession as being relevant to the purpose of their employment; and that the profession has confidence that the people they employ who have completed these courses have the skills and attributes required for the continuing health of the industry.

Students studying on an accredited course have student membership of Equity. On successful completion of the course they have automatic qualification for Equity membership provided that they are entitled to work in the UK.

What if I've had no other training or acting experience?

There are no formal criteria you must meet in order apply to a drama school. Fundamentally, what the schools are looking for is genuine talent and commitment. Though you are not required to have acted at school or in local amateur theatre, it certainly won't do you any harm in the eyes of casting directors, and amateur theatre can be a good way of learning more about the craft and gaining valuable experience.

Schools are generally very receptive to older applicants as they can bring life experience to bear in the acting process. As Sartre said, "Acting is a question of absorbing other people's personalities and adding some of your own experience." No bad thing, then, to have a bit of life experience under your belt.

One thing is for sure: if you don't apply, you won't be considered by the drama school, so if you have that burning passion it's time to start knocking on doors.

What about training for under 18s?

For those too young to be eligible for three-year drama school courses, the traditional route is stage school, where a range of acting, singing and dance skills is likely to be taught. Most of these are private and therefore there will be considerable fees to meet, although there may be some scholarship options. There are a few publicly funded stage schools and a number of part-time options.

Another option for younger children to discover whether acting is really for them is to attend a drama workshop. The National Association of Youth Theatres (**www.nayt.org.uk**) and the National Youth Theatre (**www.nyt.org.uk**) will help you track down suitable workshops and youth theatre groups.

What about older actors?

As with any degree-level course, most people taking it are likely to be in their late teens or twenties – but that doesn't mean there aren't opening for mature students (ie anyone into their thirties!). Check with the drama school, though – some do have age limits. Even if they don't, steel yourself for being thrown into the society of people considerably younger than yourself. If you can't find a suitable full-time course, a part-time one may be worth considering, though these are less likely to lead to career openings afterwards.

Having said that, many young actors leave the profession in the first few years for one reason or another, so there may be a little less competition for work. Actors of all ages are needed for stage and screen alike, so there's always hope – but proper training will stand you in much better stead than simply being a keen member of the local Gilbert and Sullivan society.

What about training for actors with disabilities?

There's a growing demand for actors from a broader and more inclusive spectrum of society, so disability need not be an inherent barrier to an acting career (though opportunities may still be fewer). Check with the main drama schools what their policy is – and of course what the facilities there are like for disabled people, such as hearing loops for deaf people in auditoria or rehearsal spaces, ramps for wheelchairs and so on.

The National Disability Arts Forum (**www.ndaf.org**) may be able to help with general advice, both on finding training and work as well as overcoming any potential discrimination.

There are numerous theatre companies which either welcome or specialise in employing actors with disabilities. Some of these – such as Graeae (**www.graeae.org**) and Mind the Gap (**www.mind-the-gap.org.uk**) – run some training courses themselves and are building links with drama schools to improve access to training for disabled people.

Joining a course

Applying for a course entails contacting the school, via its website, by telephone or in writing, in order to get your hands on an application form and prospectus. A standard application form will ask for your basic details, your acting experience to date and your reasons for wanting to attend the course. Check the deadline for applications as these vary from course to course and school to school. Don't leave it until the last minute – get the application in as early as you can. There's nothing to stop you from applying for more than one course, though if you've received a place on one it's polite to let the other(s) know. There should be no fees for applying, but you should bear in mind that if you're called for an audition a school will usually charge an audition fee, as explained on p10. (For general advice on auditions see p157.)

The course itself

Once you've secured your place on a course you can give yourself a pat on the back, and then get ready for the hard work: fame costs. Okay, so you might not be looking for fame, but you get the point. If you're going to get the most out of the course (for which you'll be paying either directly or indirectly), you can't rest on your laurels. This isn't the quick route to celebrity and the paparazzi.

You will be expected to attend classes, prepare, rehearse, study, and to exercise self-discipline, commitment and organisation. You'll be working with respected teachers and alongside other talented actors who will go on to work in the industry and whose path you will cross time and time again in the coming years. So take the time to look, listen and learn.

Acting courses emphasise the practical exploration of theatre, with classes revolving around physical exercises, roleplays and scenarios leading to full productions, though every course will be backed up with lectures about the history and theory of acting.

Foundation courses

Some schools and a growing number of organisations offer foundation or 'taster' courses. These can be short-term, part-time or intensive courses designed to give you an introduction to acting. It can help to have completed a foundation course before applying for drama school but they shouldn't be viewed as a substitute for a full-time drama course. You should be wary of courses promising too much for a short investment of your time and a large investment of your money. As with all other courses, check out the credibility of the institution, teachers and facilities before parting with any money.

Courses: Useful links & organisations

NATIONAL COUNCIL FOR DRAMA TRAINING (NCDT)
{T} 020 7387 3650
Visit the NCDT's website for a full list of accredited drama courses and to download a copy of their Applicants' Guide to Auditioning and Interviewing at Dance and Drama School or the Guide to Vocational Training in Dance and Drama.
WWW.NCDT.CO.UK

CONFERENCE OF DRAMA SCHOOLS (CDS)
WWW.DRAMA.AC.UK

COURSES, CAREERS – WHY CHOOSE DRAMA SCHOOL?
WWW.HE.COURSES-CAREERS.COM/DRAMA.HTM

PART-TIME COURSES
WWW.NCDT.CO.UK/PARTTIME.ASP

LEARN DIRECT – ACTORS
WWW.LEARNDIRECT-ADVICE.CO.UK

Drama school funding

Drama school training doesn't come cheap. Standard course fees will usually start at around £3,000 per year. In addition to tuition fees you'll also have to fund course materials, accommodation, travel and living expenses. If the course is in London, as most are, you should factor in additional costs for day-to-day living expenses. Rent, in particular, is more expensive in London than other regions.

Remember, on graduation you won't be guaranteed a lucrative West End contact, and even if you get an agent from your end of year showcase you could find yourself facing considerable ongoing costs. Headshots can cost up to £300, putting together a showreel may cost an additional £300, putting on a showcase can cost another £300 and finding out about jobs through The Stage, PCR, Casting Call Pro and other services can cost you an additional £500 per year, not to mention the cost of Spotlight and Equity. That's not to say you will need to bear all these costs, but it's worth building some flexibility into your finances to ensure you can survive those tough first months after graduation.

Student Loans

Student Loans are indexed to the rate of inflation and do not have to be paid back until you have graduated and your income is over £15,000 pa. They are available to eligible full-time higher education students; two types of loan cover fees and maintenance respectively.

For maintenance loans, for the year 2009/10 the maximum loan is £4,950 for students living away from home outside London, and more for those living away from home and based in London. Eligible students are automatically entitled to 75% of the maximum, with the remainder dependent on an assessment of the student's and their household's income. The amounts are reduced in the final year of study to take into account the shorter year. For up-to-date details check the government's student finance information pages at **www.direct.gov.uk/en/EducationAndLearning/UniversityAnd HigherEducation/StudentFinance/**.

WHAT DOES IT COST TO GO TO DRAMA SCHOOL?

Drama school training is intensive and expensive. There are three main ways drama school courses are funded.

The majority of accredited three-year courses in acting, musical theatre, stage management and technical theatre are degree programmes in higher education (HE) and government state-funded. Most drama schools now offer the three-year degree courses funded by means of a parent HE institution which usually awards the qualification.

Some accredited courses are in independent drama schools which are part of the Dance and Drama Awards (DaDA) scheme, a scholarship programme funded by the Department for Education and Skills. These courses offer professional diplomas awarded by Trinity College London. The awards were introduced in 1999 to increase access to dance, drama and stage management training from all sectors of the community and provide help with fees and maintenance for talented students wishing to attend approved vocational courses at independent dance and drama schools.

It is important to be aware that the awards provide scholarships to only a percentage of students on a course and the remaining students have to fund their own places similar to full-cost courses. Each drama school is responsible for allocating its DaDA scholarships, which are given to those students who show the most talent and potential at audition. The students' financial circumstances may also be taken into consideration when an award is given, but only as a secondary factor.

A relatively small number of accredited courses are full cost or independent courses, and do not attract any government funding. The students are responsible for full fees (which average £9,000) and living costs while studying.

Maintenance grants

If you're from a low income household you may also be eligible for a maintenance grant from the government. These are worth up to £2,906 for the 2009/10 academic year and do not have to be paid back. Again, see **www.direct.gov.uk** for more information about these and other possible sources of funding.

Bursaries and scholarships

Many schools have their own bursary and scholarship schemes which will vary from full course fees and some help towards living expenses to smaller awards which will go some but not all the way to covering your costs. There will only be a limited number of bursaries/scholarships given out each year, and competition will be tough, so you certainly can't rely on, or expect to receive, this kind of financial support. Check out the funding policy and opportunities for each establishment thoroughly before applying.

Charities and other sources

It is also possible to raise funds from charities, trusts and foundations – a list of these is available in a factsheet at the NCDT website (**www.ncdt.co.uk/facts.asp**).

If you are going down this route, make sure you target suitable sources of funding carefully and avoid simply sending out a standard letter to as many organisations as you can get addresses for. Your application will stand much more of a chance if you've tailored it to an appropriate body, and in an individual manner. Another route might be to think of local businesses who have shown evidence of supporting the arts – check out local newspapers and theatres to see which sponsors' logos appear, and make contact with them.

ENTERING THE PROFESSION

For graduates entering the profession the opportunities for work are many and varied. Traditionally actors gained early experience by working in regional repertory theatres, though today they are just as likely to secure their first job in television. An actor's career may also involve work in film, corporate training videos, radio, commercials, voice-overs, cruise ship entertainment, small-scale theatre touring, theatre-in-education, and West End productions. An actor's life may include employment at some point in nearly all of these areas.

Funding: Useful links & organisations

STUDENT LOANS COMPANY
{T} 0800 40 50 10
WWW.SLC.CO.UK

HOT COURSES FUNDING SEARCH
WWW.SCHOLARSHIP-SEARCH.ORG.UK

NCDT COURSE COSTS
WWW.NCDT.CO.UK/COST.ASP

NCDT FUNDRAISING FACTSHEET
WWW.NCDT.CO.UK/FACTS.ASP

STUDENTS AWARDS AGENCY FOR SCOTLAND
WWW.SAAS.GOV.UK

STUDENT FINANCE WALES
WWW.STUDENTFINANCEWALES.CO.UK

Further training

There will come a point in your professional career, perhaps when you're between roles, when you might think about refresher classes or further training. It can certainly be worthwhile, both professionally and in terms of your own self-belief, to flex those acting muscles and keep your skills sharp. It's all too easy to sit back and wait for the work to come your way. While practicing techniques such as breathing and

KEEP ON GROWING
James Beresford of The Actors Studio reflects on the importance of training, networking and self-development.

With the recent upsurge in interest in becoming a performer as a career, the number of graduates leaving drama schools and universities and seeking work in the industry grows each year. Added to the ready pool of actors already searching for work, this seems to make the chance of success an ever more distant possibility, leaving many despondent and unsure of what to do.

To combat this many people shun formal training or skill development, favouring rather to 'go it alone', attending a sea of open auditions or working for a pittance in shows that barely muster an audience. Those who have agent's representation lose sight of what they personally can do to promote or develop their careers, believing their agent to be a miracle worker who will, unaided, transport their career to new heights!

Somewhere in the middle of this downward spiral the discovery is made that those who are successful and fulfilled in their careers are the ones who have a firm grip on the reins and are in charge of what is going on around them. Attending regular courses and workshops, networking, expanding their portfolio of plays, speeches and songs and absorbing as much information as possible all assist the jobbing actor to navigate their way through the minefield of negativity that surrounds being unemployed, and open up a whole range of different possibilities both professionally and socially.

vocal exercises is useful, further training can also help you network, bring you face-to-face with other actors and professionals and keep you in the loop for auditions and castings.

There are many courses out there for specific training. You could choose to work on your skills such as singing, accents, stage combat, movement, or different acting techniques. When picking a course, find out as much information as possible about the course and school

It is important to research the courses and workshops that are available as fully as possible. Do not be afraid to ask for as much information as you need, and where possible try to attend courses run by people who are actively working within the industry. These people will not only give you valuable, up-to-date information, but they may have the potential to open doors to possible future employment.

As with many other aspects of the industry, information is passed through the grapevine! Ask what others have been doing: often the most positive feedback comes from first hand experience. There is something out there for everybody. Also bear in mind costing. Finances are always a sore point, and you may need to carefully juggle your situation in order to make things work.

The most important thing is keeping a sense of perspective on where you are. Collective learning and sharing of experiences assists everyone in any walk of life to view their situation with renewed clarity. Development whether personal or career based can only be positive, and with that, new possibilities will not be far away.

Previously an actor and then an agent, James Beresford is now manager of The Actors Studio at Pinewood Studios. Offering courses run by distinguished practitioners and expert teachers, including many directors and casting directors who are at the forefront of the film and television industries, an honest and frank appraisal of the individual's potential is always at the forefront of their philosophy. Information on The Actors Studio can be found at **www.actorsstudio.co.uk**.

to ensure their reputability. Endorsements from other actors and word-of-mouth feedback can help in deciding which course to choose before parting with your money. Don't be shy about learning new skills – the more strings to your bow, the more versatile you are, and the more opportunities you'll be suitable for.

In some cases you may be able to learn new skills one-to-one with private tuition or coaching. Look in The Stage for people advertising such services (where you will also find listings for one-off workshops).

Other ideas if funding is a problem

If you're concerned about the costs of further training you could choose to team up with other actors to read through plays or replay old drama school exercises. In addition, take time to read as many plays and scripts as possible, and catch innovative shows performed by professionals and your peers. Watching others perform will keep your ideas fresh which may be useful at your next audition. The crucial thing is to view acting as a career that requires ongoing support and development.

Further training: Useful links & organisations

THE ACTOR'S CENTRE

With a membership of 2,500 actors, The Actor's Centre is well known in the industry and has a very good reputation as one of the few institutions to cater to the ongoing needs of professional actors. In the words of The Actor's Centre, their mission is "to provide actors with professional development of the highest quality and the opportunity to enhance every aspect of their craft". Workshops and classes explore the total range of acting from classical theatre to mainstream TV. The ethos of The Actor's Centre is very much to help actors by plugging them into what's happening and what's about to happen in theatre, television, radio and film. Classes range from £17-£34 per day, with class sizes limited to a dozen.

WWW.ACTORSCENTRE.CO.UK
{T} 020 7240 3940
ADMIN@ACTORSCENTRE.CO.UK

THE ACTOR'S TEMPLE

Teaching the Meisner technique, The Actor's Temple holds regular classes, many of which are walk-in classes, though for the more popular ones you should pre-book. It's free to become a member – you then pay per class attended. Along with The Actor's Centre, The Actor's Temple enjoys a very good reputation and is, according to its founders, "committed to training profes-sional actors to achieve more direct, intense and truthful performances".

WWW.ACTORSTEMPLE.COM
{T} 020 7383 3535
INFO@ACTORSTEMPLE.COM

THE CITY LIT

The City Lit offers a wide range of classes including preparing for auditions, the Alexander technique, the Meisner technique, accents, sightreading, speaking Shakespeare, Acting in Chekhov, Acting in Shakespeare, acting for radio, clowning & performance, stage-fighting and more.

WWW.CITYLIT.AC.UK
{T} 020 7430 0544
{F} 020 7405 3347
ADVICE@CITYLIT.AC.UK

THEATRE ROYAL HAYMARKET, MASTERCLASSES

Each year the Theatre Royal Haymarket puts on a series of masterclasses from some of the UK's most renowned actors. Past masters have included Gillian Anderson, Anita Dobson, Simon Callow, Jeremy Irons, Kwame Kwei-Armah, Alan Rickman, Timothy West...Classes are free for 17-30 year olds and mature students, or if you're a Masterclass Friend (to become a Friend there's an annual donation of £45).

WWW.TRH.CO.UK
{T} 020 7930 8890
BOXOFFICE@TRH.CO.UK

A-Z of drama schools & colleges

ARTS EDUCATIONAL SCHOOL LONDON
14 BATH ROAD
CHISWICK
LONDON W4 1LY
{T} 020 8987 6655
DRAMA@ARTSED.CO.UK
WWW.ARTSED.CO.UK
COURSES:
B.A.(Hons) Acting, 3 years
M.A. Acting, 1 year
B.A. (Hons) Musical Theatre, 3 years
DETAILS:
The School of Acting offers contemporary, industry-relevant vocational training for actors. It equips the student to a high level for a career as a professional actor in a range of performance contexts including live performance, film, television and radio. The School of Acting works to create an environment for training, which is based on trust, mutual respect and passion. The school believes that it is from within this environment that students will be secure enough to take huge creative risks. In addition, the school believes that the individual performer learns best from within the group, and that the theatre ensemble grows from the constructive input of every individual.

ALRA (ACADEMY OF LIVE
AND RECORDED ARTS)
STUDIO 1, THE ROYAL PATRIOTIC BUILDING
FITZHUGH GROVE
LONDON SW18 3SX
{T} 020 8870 6475
INFO@ALRA.CO.UK
WWW.ALRA.CO.UK
COURSES:
B.A.(Hons) Acting, 3 years
National Diploma in Professional Acting, 1 year
DETAILS:
The courses are designed to give you the adaptability, flexibility and openness needed to sustain a career in the stage and screen industry, you will explore fully and progressively your creative, vocal and physical potential. We will instil in you the self-discipline the industry expects of you. You will be shown current working methods and practices to enable you to work effectively and professionally. You will be in continual contact with professional practitioners from all areas of the industry and you will receive lectures and workshops on the practical business of being an actor.

BIRMINGHAM SCHOOL OF ACTING (BSSD)

G2 - MILLENNIUM POINT
CURZON STREET
BIRMINGHAM B4 7XG
{T} 0121 331 7220
INFO@BSA.UCE.AC.UK
WWW.BSA.UCE.AC.UK
COURSES:
B.A.(Hons) Acting, 3 years
Graduate Diploma in Acting (over 21s)
DETAILS:
Birmingham School of Acting is a small specialist institution with 134 full time students on its two undergraduate acting courses and a staff of more than 60 working professionals. Birmingham School of Acting is a faculty of UCE Birmingham (University of Central England) and is accredited by the National Council for Drama Training (NCDT).

BRISTOL OLD VIC THEATRE SCHOOL

2 DOWNSIDE ROAD
BRISTOL BS8 2XF
{T} 0117 9733535
ENQUIRIES@OLDVIC.AC.UK
WWW.OLDVIC.AC.UK
COURSES:
B.A.(Hons) Acting, 3 years
2yr Diploma in Professional Acting
1yr Cert HE Professional Acting
1yr Professional Acting Course for Overseas Students
DETAILS:
Opened by Laurence Olivier in 1946, the school is an industry-led vocational training establishment preparing students for careers in acting, stage management, costume, design, scenic art, directing, theatre arts management, production management, lighting, electrics, sound, studio management, propmaking, VT editing and scenic construction. Work encompasses the breadth of theatre, television, radio, film, recording, events and trade presentations and the ever-increasing areas of employment open to a trained workforce in arts and entertainment.

CENTRAL SCHOOL OF SPEECH AND DRAMA

EMBASSY THEATRE
ETON AVENUE
LONDON NW3 3HY
{T} 020 7722 8183
ENQUIRIES@CSSD.AC.UK
WWW.CSSD.AC.UK
COURSES:
B.A.(Hons) Acting, 3 years
DETAILS:
Founded in 1906 by Elsie Fogerty to offer an entirely new form of training in speech and drama for young actors and other students. The choice of name – the Central School – highlighted the school's commitment to a broad range of training systems for vocal and dramatic performance. It espoused principles that were firmly held yet responsive to change. That sense of continuing critical openness to new developments is a lasting hallmark of the school.

25

Drama Centre London

Central Saint Martins College
Southampton Row
London WC1B 4AP
{t} 020 7514 7022
INFO@CSM.ARTS.AC.UK
WWW.CSM.ARTS.AC.UK/DRAMA/
Courses:
B.A.(Hons) Acting, 3 years
Details:
Founded in 1963 by a visionary group of tutors and students, Drama Centre London offers an inspirational, passionate environment for those who are resolutely serious about acting and their careers. An Advisory Council which includes Sir Anthony Hopkins and leading directors Declan Donnellan, Adrian Noble and Max Stafford-Clark guides the school's distinctive approach. Since 1999 Drama Centre has been part of Central Saint Martins College of Art and Design, a constituent college of the University of the Arts London and an internationally renowned institution which offers the most diverse and comprehensive range of undergraduate and postgraduate courses in art, design and performance in the country. Central Saint Martins is situated at the very heart of London, close to the theatres and opera houses of Covent Garden, the British Museum and the BBC. As University of the Arts London students, Drama Centre students have access to a range of services, including: advice on accommodation and careers; special support for international students; specialist libraries; internet and intranet facilities; a language centre; professional counselling; and support for students with disabilities.

Drama Studio London

Grange Court
1 Grange Road, Ealing
London W5 5QN
{t} 020 8579 3897
ADMIN@DRAMASTUDIOLONDON.CO.UK
WWW.DRAMASTUDIOLONDON.CO.UK
Courses:
1 & 2 Year Diplomas (over 21s)
Details:
Drama Studio London was born, in 1966, out of the need for a new, more realistic approach to actor training that took account of the professional requirements and demands of the theatre for which the students were being prepared. Over the years the goal has always remained the same: to graduate well-trained actors, technically and personally equipped to face the constantly changing demands of the professional theatre of today.

East 15 Acting School
Hatfields, Rectory Lane
Loughton
Essex IG10 3RY
{t} 020 8508 5983
east15@essex.ac.uk
www.east15.ac.uk
Courses:
B.A.(Hons) Acting, 3 years
B.A.(Hons) Physical Theatre, 3 years
1 Year Diploma (over 21s)
Details:
East 15 grew from the work of Joan Littlewood's famed Theatre Workshop. Much of the Littlewood approach was based upon the theories of Stanislavski, and the company inherited the socially committed spirit of the Unity Theatre movement, which brought many new voices into British Theatre for the first time. Theatre Workshop broke new ground, re-interpreting the classics for a modern age, commissioning new plays from socially committed writers, and creating an ensemble capable of inventing new work, such as the now legendary Oh What a Lovely War. Littlewood created a wonderful ensemble, who combined inspired, improvisational brilliance with method, technique, research, text analysis, and the expression of real emotions. Over the years, new training methods were evolved to strip actors of affectations, attitudes, ego trips. The quest was always to search for truth: of oneself, the character, the text.

Guildford School of Acting
Millmead Terrace
Guildford
Surrey GU2 4YT
{t} 01483 560701
enquiries@conservatoire.org
www.conservatoire.org
Courses:
National Diploma in Professional Acting, 3 years
B.A.(Hons) in Musical Theatre, 3 years
M.A. in Acting, 1 year (Over 21s)
Details:
From the moment you start at the Conservatoire to the moment you graduate will the most challenging time in your life. Training for the profession is as tough as training to compete in the Olympics. We have to prepare you for the competition you will meet once you have graduated. The course is designed to get the best out of you and to encourage you to be versatile in your skills. We concentrate on training the whole person. Our job is to improve your strengths and tackle your weaknesses with you and our overall aim is to help you become versatile as an actor who, can sing and dance and who can work on musicals or straight plays or even in television and radio; all your classes connect to that aim. Acting is the core to all that we do and the idea behind your training is that the techniques you learn mean that you can act through singing and dancing as well as through scripts for the stage, television, film or radio.

27

GUILDHALL SCHOOL OF MUSIC
AND DRAMA
SILK STREET
BARBICAN
LONDON EC2Y 8DT
{T} 020 7628 2571
DRAMA@GSMD.AC.UK
WWW.GSMD.AC.UK
COURSES:
B.A.(Hons) Acting, 3 years
MA in Training Actors (Voice) or
(Movement), 2 years part-time
DETAILS:
The modern Guildhall School is
distinctive in being the only major
European conservatoire which is both a
music school and a drama school, and
one which is pre-eminent in technical
theatre, professional development and
music therapy. The acting programme is
highly regarded in the profession for the
thoroughness of its audition processes,
the passion, quality and rigour of its
teaching, its emphasis on the integration
of craft training, the care and attention
for the individual development of each
student and the strong ensemble ethic
shared by staff and students.

ITALIA CONTI ACADEMY OF
THEATRE ARTS LTD
AVONDALE
72 LANDOR ROAD
LONDON SW9 9PH
{T} 020 7733 3210
ACTING@LSBU.AC.UK
WWW.ITALIACONTI-ACTING.CO.UK

COURSES:
B.A.(Hons) Acting, 3 years
DETAILS:
Founded in 1911 by the actress Italia
Conti, the Itali Conti Academy of Theatre
Arts trains actors for the professional
stage and screen. The Academy is
committed to providing an environment
in which its students can be trained and
educated to develop and broaden their
skills to their individual highest possible
standards. Italia Conti students receive
the unique benefits of training based on
nearly 100 years of knowledge and
experience geared to the needs of the
present day.

LONDON ACADEMY OF MUSIC
AND DRAMATIC ART
155 TALGARTH ROAD
LONDON W14 9DA
{T} 020 8834 0500
ENQUIRIES@LAMDA.ORG.UK
WWW.LAMDA.ORG.UK
COURSES:
B.A.(Hons) Acting, 3 years
Classical Acting Course, 1 year
Two Year Acting Course BA (Foundation
Degree)
DETAILS:
LAMDA is an independent drama school,
dedicated to the vocational training of
actors, stage managers and technicians
in the skills and levels of creativity
necessary to meet the highest demands
and best opportunities in theatre, film
and TV. The group work ethic is central

to LAMDA's teaching. The training does not deconstruct the student in order to rebuild a LAMDA product but encourages and develops innate skills. The courses are practical not academic. Class times are Monday - Friday 9am - 5.30pm with some evening and weekend classes. All classes are compulsory.

MANCHESTER METROPOLITAN UNIVERSITY SCHOOL OF THEATRE
MABEL TYLECOTE BUILDING
CAVENDISH STREET
MANCHESTER M15 6BG
{T} 0161 247 1305
ENQUIRIES@MMU.AC.UK
WWW.ARTDES.MMU.AC.UK
COURSES:
B.A.(Hons) Acting, 3 years
DETAILS:
The course offers students the opportunity to develop and match new and existing skills to a professional acting career. Workshops, seminars, and public performances are designed to synthesize component skills that include voice, movement, acting, textual analysis, and research. The course aims to nurture instinctive ability in an environment that allows for the development of new skills whilst simultaneously enabling individuals to recognise particular strengths and abilities. The final year of the course is entirely performance based with students working with both staff and guest directors from across Europe in

the preparation of a series of public performances. Former students include Sir Anthony Sher, Julie Walters, David Threlfall, Richard Griffiths, Bernard Hill, Steve Coogan, John Thomson, Noreen Kershaw, Amanda Burton and Adam Kotz.

MOUNTVIEW ACADEMY OF THEATRE ARTS
1 KINGFISHER PLACE
CLARENDON ROAD
LONDON N22 6XF
{T} 020 8881 2201
ENQUIRIES@MOUNTVIEW.ORG.UK
WWW.MOUNTVIEW.ORG.UK
COURSES:
B.A.(Hons) Acting, 3 years
Acting (1 Year Postgraduate Diploma)
DETAILS:
Founded in 1945, Mountview is now recognised as one of the country's leading Academies of Theatre Arts, offering an extensive and stimulating training for those interested in pursuing a performance, directing or technical theatre career. Mountview's courses are structured to give students a thorough grounding in all aspects of their chosen field. Our students are trained to a high level to develop a range of skills which will enable them to bring thought, energy and commitment to their professional work, giving them the tools to succeed in a competitive industry.

29

OXFORD SCHOOL OF DRAMA
SANSOMES FARM STUDIOS
WOODSTOCK OX20 1ER
{T} 01993 812883
INFO@OXFORDDRAMA.AC.UK
WWW.OXFORDDRAMA.AC.UK
COURSES:
Three Year Diploma in Acting
One Year Acting Course
DETAILS:
We offer practical, hands-on training to
talented students who are committed to
forging careers as actors. In order that
we are able to provide the best possible
training we have decided not to run
degree courses. This means that we
don't have pressures put upon us to
increase our number of students as is so
often the case in drama schools which
enter into partnership with a university.
It also means that our courses can
remain truly vocational, with no element
of essay-writing. However, we do
understand that our students want
recognition of their achievements in the
form of a national qualification, so both
our three-year and one-year courses
offer vocational qualifications accredited
by Trinity College London which are
equivalent to degrees (level 6 and level
5 on the National Qualifications
Framework respectively).

QUEEN MARGARET
UNIVERSITY COLLEGE
QUEEN MARGARET UNIVERSITY
EDINBURGH EH21 6UU
{T} 0131 317 3247
DRAMAADMIN@QMU.AC.UK
WWW.QMUC.AC.UK
COURSES:
BA (Hons) Drama and Performance,
3 to 4 years
DETAILS:
The School offers a dynamic programme of
training geared towards professional work
in the arts and entertainment industries
and a lively and inquisitive practical study
of contemporary theatre and links with the
industry are strong. In both undergraduate
and postgraduate education, the aim is to
develop graduates who are critical and
reflective independent practitioners and
are immediately employable within the
theatre and performance sectors.
Furthermore, as a school we believe that it
is vital that our work reflects contemporary working practice and therefore, where
appropriate, students collaborate across
programmes on a variety of projects.

ROSE BRUFORD COLLEGE
LAMORBEY PARK
BURNT OAK LANE
SIDCUP DA15 9DF
{T} 020 8308 2600
ENQUIRIES@BRUFORD.AC.UK
WWW.BRUFORD.AC.UK
COURSES:
B.A.(Hons) Acting, 3 years
DETAILS:
The programme is designed to produce an artist who is flexible and articulate, able to work in a variety of genres and repertoires with the ability to apply skills as demanded by a text and its performance conditions.

ROYAL ACADEMY OF DRAMATIC ART
62-64 GOWER STREET
LONDON WC1E 6ED
{T} 020 7636 7076
ENQUIRIES@RADA.AC.UK
WWW.RADA.ORG
COURSES:
B.A.(Hons) Acting, 3 years
DETAILS:
The three year course is a training for students who wish to earn a living working not only in the more traditional outlets but in the many alternative areas of theatre, film, television and radio. It is an arduous course with a minimum working day of 10 am to 6.30 pm with individual classes in the evening. The objective is to encourage development of individual skills at the highest level and to utilise those skills in contributing

unreservedly to the development of the group by actively participating in the content and conditions of its working life. The course divides itself roughly into two parts; intensive work on individual skills and the application of those skills to work on group projects and productions for public performance.

ROYAL SCOTTISH ACADEMY OF MUSIC AND DRAMA
100 RENFREW STREET
GLASGOW G2 3DB
{T} 0141 332 4101
DRAMAADMISSIONS@RSAMD.AC.UK
WWW.RSAMD.AC.UK
COURSES:
3 year undergraduate acting course
DETAILS:
The School of Drama is a dynamic, leading edge place of training and development for emergent artists. It is one of the UK's premiere schools and has a rapidly evolving international profile. It aims to nurture and promote the development of artists of excellence, enabling them to pursue fruitful and meaningful careers in a national and international context, thereby making a contribution to the cultural landscapes.

THE ROYAL WELSH COLLEGE
OF MUSIC AND DRAMA
CATHAYS PARK
CARDIFF CF10 3ER
{T} 029 2039 1327
DRAMA.ADMISSIONS@RWCMD.AC.UK
WWW.RWCMD.AC.UK
COURSES:
B.A.(Hons) Acting, 3 years
Postgraduate Diploma in Acting for
Stage, Screen and Radio, 1 year
DETAILS:
Established in 1949 at Cardiff Castle, the
college is the National Conservatoire of
Wales. We provide specialist practical and
performance-based training that enables
students to enter and influence the music,
theatre and related professions. We offer
an exceptional environment in which to
pursue a professional acting course. Our
established teaching team is made up of
highly-experienced professional practitioners, who will help you develop the
physical and emotional resources that will
enable you to respond to the wide-
ranging demands of the contemporary
acting professions. We have designed this
course to equip you with the full range of
knowledge and skills you will need to
succeed in theatre, film, TV and radio.

Section 2
Agents

The agent's role

Good agents are industry veterans who will put you forward for suitable upcoming auditions (often not publicly advertised) and protect your interests from unscrupulous producers. A good agent will work alongside you to help you develop a financially stable and fulfilling career. While it is not obligatory to get an agent, it is advisable. If casting directors (see the next chapter for more about them) are the doorways to the acting world then casting agents are the keys.

What does an agent do?

Their primary role is to put you forward for castings and help get you work. They will use their contacts and keep their ears to the ground to raise your profile and maximise the number of auditions and interviews you are considered for. Privy to opportunities that are generally kept out of the public realm, they have close relationships with the all-important casting directors.

The other important role of an agent is to negotiate fees on your behalf. Your agent should know the market rate for a particular production and the business of reaching an agreed fee should be their area of expertise. They will also be responsible for the contract itself. Not only will they be working on your behalf to get you the best deal (and their own, because of course they are dependent on the commission they make from you for their own living), they will be saving you from having to go through the often tricky nitty-gritty of fees and contracts, freeing you to concentrate on the main job in hand – the actual acting.

There should be no joining fee for signing-up with an agency, so be wary of those who try to get you to part with any money up front. The actors' union Equity advises against signing up with anyone who asks for money at this stage. (For more information about Equity see p222.) Most agents work on a sole representation basis – ie you're represented only by that one agent. Any work you get (whether

34

through the agent or your own networking and contacts) will be subject to commission, which varies from agency to agency. The rate of commission is generally between 10% and 20% – but remember that larger agencies, and indeed the more successful smaller ones, will also charge VAT on top of that.

No matter how much you resent seeing a slice of your earnings being given over to the Inland Revenue and a further slice to your agent, especially if it's acting work you've got through your own efforts rather than via the agent, don't try to hoodwink them by withholding details of acting work to avoid commission. This is a rocky road that's likely to lead to the break-up of the partnership.

Some agencies will give you a contract to sign. Make sure you read it through properly and, if you're happy, sign two copies, keeping one for yourself. An important part of the contract to look out for is the notice period for leaving an agency – there may be a period where you have left but are still obliged to pay commission, so check the details carefully.

Personal managers

Some agents are members of the Personal Managers' Association (PMA), offering a wider range of services to their clients – but remember that personal managers are not necessarily the same as agents. Personal managers will work with an actor one-to-one to field contact with the press, arrange tours and so on, as in the music industry, but may not have the same relationship with possible sources of work as an agent does.

Getting an agent

Ask fellow actors (and teachers if you have attended a drama course) for recommendations and tips; check websites; view agency websites (see if they are open to new clients or if their lists are closed) and utilise all the resources at your disposal (see Section 7 of this book; you can also search for agents at the Casting Call Pro website – **www.uk.castingcallpro.com** – and that of The Agents' Association, **www.agents-uk.com**). Agencies vary from the very large such as ICM with hundreds of (often prestigious) clients, to much smaller ones with a staff of only one or two and a client list of perhaps a few dozen.

Think about whether the size of the agency matters to you: larger ones are likely to have a greater reach, but may not be able to spare time for prolonged personal contact with clients. Conversely, a smaller agency can make you feel more cared for – but have fewer contacts. Either way, always be friendly in your dealings and get to know the staff.

Once you've drawn up your target shortlist, write to the agencies with a covering letter, your CV and a professional black and white photograph. Write your name and contact details on the back of the photograph, too. Don't email the agency unless they specifically invite it, and avoid phoning unless to check whether they are currently taking on new clients.

It's helpful, though more time-consuming, to tailor your approach to individual agents (see the advice writing a covering letter in Section 3). Address your letter to a specific person – contact names are listed in the directory of agents after this chapter. Be straight-to-the-point (without being rude) in your letter. Ensure you check the postage required before sending your package as a CV, headshot and cover letter will require more than just a standard 1st class stamp. No agency will thank you for obliging them to pay a shortfall in the postage!
In your covering letter explain why you feel this agency is right for you and highlight any showcase or productions you'll be performing in in the near future, should the agent wish to see you on stage. Be

aware that due to the sheer volume of interest they receive, and because their main responsibility is to their existing clients, agents can't see every production, so be patient and don't be put off by a standard 'our lists are full' reply.

There is a limit on the number of actors an agent can represent. For this reason they are careful about whom they represent and will be looking for actors whom they believe show potential and will be successful. Depending on their existing client list, they may feel they have reached capacity in certain areas (eg age, look etc.), though most agents would be willing to take on an extra client if they feel they have exceptional talent. In your letter, mention that you can supply a showreel on request.

An agent may respond by saying that you look interesting but are not suitable at that particular time (for a variety of reasons), but to keep in touch. This is sound advice: you can send an updated CV and headshot every now and then to keep you on their radar (but make sure you don't badger them to the point of irritation!).

Keep sending out letters and working your contacts. It can be dispiriting but if you're deterred by this initial rejection you have a long road ahead of you when it comes to casting auditions. Representation and roles may not come immediately, but that's not to say it won't happen. Your watchwords should be self-belief and perseverance.

Some agencies may expect you to come for an interview before they take you on – as always, dress smartly and be confident without being pushy, and turn up on time!

The actor/agent relationship

The relationship between an agent and an actor is vital to the ongoing success of the partnership. Dialogue is the key to a good working relationship with your agent. A good agent will let you know what they're putting you forward for and may also be able to offer you advice and give you post-audition feedback from the casting director. Equally, you should let an agent know how a casting went. The more feedback you give them, the better you can plan ahead and prepare for future castings.

There will be, unless you're very lucky, periods of unemployment during which you may be tearing your hair out. It's natural to wonder if your agent is doing all they can for you and to question your representation. Remember, though, that this is the nature of the industry you've chosen. Agents can sing your praises and get you a foot in the door but after that it's up to you. The truth is that many, many actors may be put forward and considered for a role, but the part will be given to only one. That you don't get a part is not the fault of your agent.

If you feel you're simply not being put forward for things and are effectively lying dormant on your agent's books then it's a good idea to raise this with them. In many cases your concerns will be addressed and allayed. (It's not in an agent's interest to ignore you – an out of work actor brings no revenue!) In some cases there may be a parting of the ways, mutual or otherwise, and you choose to seek new representation. Try to part on good terms and leave the door open. The acting profession is swift-moving and you'll run into the same people time and time again, so it makes good sense to try to keep people on your good side and maintain amicable relations.

The relationship between an agent and their actors is a two-way street. The agent's reputation depends not just on their negotiating skills and rapport with casting directors, but also their clients. You are representing them and so should be professional and avoid behaviour and situations that may reflect badly on the agent.

The PMA (**www.thepma.com**) has a code of conduct which member agencies adhere to, making the responsibilities of each party clear. The most important part of your relationship with any agent is to stay in touch (without making a nuisance of yourself) – communication will usually clear things up. If you're a member of Equity, you can download the organisation's helpful 'You and Your Agent' booklet from the members' section of the website **www.equity.org.uk**.

Self-marketing

Your agent is a vital part of your ongoing efforts to get work. This doesn't mean you should cease marketing yourself: keep sending out letters, networking and checking websites and publications for castings. It's to your advantage to market yourself as best you can and to keep plugging away. The agent isn't your sole route to work, so don't be tempted to sign up and assume you can relax and let them do all the work. Agents are likely to respond well to proactive clients, as long as you don't try to interfere with their way of doing things.

A-Z of agents

2020
2020 PRODUCTIONS LTD.
2020 HOPGOOD STREET
SHEPHERDS BUSH W12 7JU
{T} 020 8746 2020
INFO@2020CASTING.COM
WWW.2020CASTING.COM
FOUNDED: 1996

10 TWENTY TWO CASTING
PO BOX 1022
LIVERPOOL
L69 5WZ
{T} 0870 850 1022
NICK@10TWENTYTWO.COM
WWW.10TWENTYTWO.COM
FOUNDED: 2002
NO. OF CLIENTS: 2000

101 TALENT
25 BICKERTON WAY
CHESHIRE CW9 8FZ
{T} 0151 3245401
INFO@101TALENT.CO.UK
WWW.101TALENT.CO.UK
FOUNDED: 2007
NO. OF CLIENTS: 10

20 STORIES HIGH
6 CLARE TERRACE
MARMADUKE STREET
LIVERPOOL L7 1PB
{T} 0151 260 5185

NICKI@20STORIESHIGH.ORG.UK
WWW.20STORIESHIGH.ORG.UK
FOUNDED: 2006
NO. OF CLIENTS: 3

21ST CENTURY ACTORS MANAGEMENT
206 PANTHER HOUSE
38 MOUNT PLEASANT
LONDON WC1X 0AN
{T} 020 7278 3438
MAIL@21STCENTURYACTORS.CO.UK
WWW.21STCENTURYACTORS.CO.UK
FOUNDED: 1994
NO. OF CLIENTS: 20

247 TALENT
36 COOMBE RISE
BRIGHTON
BN2 8QN
{T} 0203 0518 247
LEE@247TALENT.CO.UK
WWW.247TALENT.CO.UK
FOUNDED: 2007
NO. OF CLIENTS: 700

360 CASTING
PO BOX 231
WALLASEY CH4 52PW
{T} 8456520360
INFO@360CASTING.CO.UK
WWW.360CASTING.CO.UK
FOUNDED: 2006
NO. OF CLIENTS: 75

A & B PERSONAL MANAGEMENT
PAURELLE HOUSE,
91 REGENT STREET,
LONDON W1B 4EL
{T} 020 7734 6047
BILLELLIS@AANDB.CO.UK
FOUNDED: 1982

A & J MANAGEMENT
242A THE RIDGEWAY
BOTANY BAY
ENFIELD
{T} 020 8367 7139
INFO@AJMANAGEMENT.CO.UK
WWW.AJMANAGEMENT.CO.UK
FOUNDED: 1985
NO. OF CLIENTS: 600

A STEP AHEAD ENTERTAINMENT
SINCLAIRSTON DRIVE
AYRSHIRE KA6 7DE
{T} 01292 590280
LAURAJ88@HOTMAIL.CO.UK
FOUNDED: 2006
NO. OF CLIENTS: 12

ACADEMY CASTINGS
BLUE SQUARE
272 BATH STREET
GLASGOW G2 4JR
{T} 0141 354 8873
ROBERT@ACADEMYCASTINGS.CO.UK
FOUNDED: 2003
NO. OF CLIENTS: 50

ACCENT BANK
420 FALCON WHARF
34 LOMBARD ROAD
LONDON W11 3RF
{T} 020 7223 5160
INFO@ACCENTBANK.CO.UK
WWW.ACCENTBANK.CO.UK
FOUNDED: 2005
NO. OF CLIENTS: 150

ACCESS ARTISTE MANAGEMENT LTD
PO BOX 39925
LONDON
EC1V 0WN
{T} 020 8505 1094
MAIL@ACCESS-UK.COM
WWW.ACCESS-UK.COM
FOUNDED: 1999
NO. OF CLIENTS: 80

ACT OUT AGENCY
22 GREEK STREET
STOCKPORT
CHESHIRE SK3 8AB
{T} 0161 429 7413
AB22@SUPANET.COM
FOUNDED: 1995
NO. OF CLIENTS: 40

ACTING ASSOCIATES
71 HARTHAM ROAD
N7 9JJ
{T} 2076073562
FIONA@ACTINGASSOCIATES.CO.UK
WWW.ACTINGASSOCIATES.CO.UK
FOUNDED: 1998
NO. OF CLIENTS: 49

ACTIVE ARTISTES
ACTIVE ARTISTES
MADDISON HOUSE
226 HIGH ST , CROYDON CR6 9DG
{T} 0871 874 0377
GEORGEEGRAHAM@AOL.COM
FOUNDED: 1980
NO. OF CLIENTS: 50

ACTNATURAL
PO BOX 25
ST AGNES
TR5 0ZN
{T} 01872 552 552
INFO@ACTNATURAL.CO.UK
WWW.ACTNATURAL.CO.UK

ACTORS DIRECT
GAINSBOROUGH HOUSE
109 PORTLAND STREET
MANCHESTER M1 6DN
{T} 0161 237 1904
INFO@ACTORSDIRECT.ORG.UK
WWW.ACTORSDIRECT.ORG.UK
FOUNDED: 1990
NO. OF CLIENTS: 22

ACTORS INTERNATIONAL
CONWAY HALL,
25 RED LION SQUARE,
LONDON
{T} 020 7242 9300
ACTORS-INTERNATIONAL@TALK21.COM
FOUNDED: 2000

ACTORS IRELAND
2-4 UNIVERSITY ROAD
BELFAST
BT7 1NH
GERALDINE@ACTORSIRELAND.COM
FOUNDED: 2000
NO. OF CLIENTS: 60

ACTORS MIND
ACTORS MIND LTD
SE12 9EL
{T} 020 8761 2539
ADMIN@ACTORSMIND.CO.UK
WWW.ACTORSMIND.CO.UK
FOUNDED: 2008
NO. OF CLIENTS: 7

ACTORS WORLD CASTING
W13 0HH
{T} 020 8 998 2579
KATHERINE@ACTORS-WORLD-PRODUCTION.COM
FOUNDED: 2005
NO. OF CLIENTS: 80

ACTORS' CREATIVE TEAM
PANTHER HOUSE
38 MOUNT PLEASANT
LONDON WC1X 0AN
{T} 020 72783388
OFFICE@ACTORSCREATIVETEAM.CO.UK
WWW.ACTORSCREATIVETEAM.CO.UK
FOUNDED: 2001
NO. OF CLIENTS: 17

Agents A

AFFINITY MANAGEMENT
THE COACH HOUSE, DOWN PARK
TURNERS HILL RD
CRAWLEY DOWN, SUSSEX RH10 4HQ
{T} 01342 715275
JSTEPHENS@AFFINITYMANAGEMENT.CO.UK
FOUNDED: 2000
NO. OF CLIENTS: 20

ALAN SHARMAN AGENCY
P2 WEXLER LOFTS
100 CARVER STREET
BIRMINGHAM B1 3AQ
{T} 1212120090
INFO@ALANSHARMANAGENCY.COM
WWW.ALANSHARMANAGENCY.COM
FOUNDED: 2007
NO. OF CLIENTS: 500

ALLEGRO TALENT
4 TRENT GARDENS
KIRK SANDALL
DONCASTER DN3 1SR
{T} 01302 884370
LUCYBARSBY@YAHOO.CO.UK
FOUNDED: 2008
NO. OF CLIENTS: 10

ALLSORTS AGENCY
SUITE 1 & 2 MARLOBOROUGH BUSINESS CENTRE
96 GEORGE LANE
LONDON E18 1AD
{T} 020 8989 0500
BOOKINGS@ALLSORTSAGENCY.COM
WWW.ALLSORTSAGENCY.COM
FOUNDED: 1996
NO. OF CLIENTS: 3

ALVAREZ MANAGEMENT
33,LUDLOW WAY
EAST FINCHLEY
LONDON N2 0JZ
{T} 020 8883 2206
SGA@ALVAREZMANAGEMENT.FSNET.CO.UK
FOUNDED: 1990
NO. OF CLIENTS: 53

ALW ASSOCIATES
1 GRAFTON CHAMBERS
GRAFTON PLACE
LONDON NW1 1LN
{T} 020 7388 7018
ALW_CAROLPAUL@TALKTALK.NET
FOUNDED: 1995
NO. OF CLIENTS: 50

AM:PM THE ACTORS' AGENCY
SOUTH 2 CENTRAL PARK
33 ALFRED STREET
BELFAST BT1 2BE
{T} 028 90235568
MARK@AMPMACTORS.COM
FOUNDED: 2004
NO. OF CLIENTS: 65

AMANDA ANDREWS AGENCY
30 CAVERSWALL ROAD
BLYTHE BRIDGE
STAFFORDSHIRE ST11 9BG
{T} 01782 393889
AMANDA.ANDREWS.AGENCY@TESCO.NET
WWW.AMANDAANDREWSAGENCY.CO.UK
FOUNDED: 2000
NO. OF CLIENTS: 30

43

AMANDA SAROSI ASSOCIATES
1 HOMBURY VIEW
E5 9EG
{T} 020 7993 6008
AMANDA@ASASSOCIATES.BIZ
FOUNDED: 2007
NO. OF CLIENTS: 25

AMC MANAGEMENT
31 PARKSIDE
WELWYN
HERTS. AL6 9DQ
{T} 01438 714652
ANNA@AMCMANAGEMENT.CO.UK
WWW.AMCMANAGEMENT.CO.UK

AMERICAN AGENCY
14 BONNY STREET
LONDON
NW1 9PG
{T} 020 7485 8883
AMERICANAGENCY@BTCONNECT.COM
WWW.AMERICANAGENCY.TV
FOUNDED: 2000
NO. OF CLIENTS: 60

ANA ACTORS
55 LAMBETH WALK
LONDON
SE11 6DX
{T} 020 7735 0999
INFO@ANA-ACTORS.CO.UK
WWW.ANA-ACTORS.CO.UK
FOUNDED: 1985
NO. OF CLIENTS: 35

ANDREW MANSON PERSONAL MANAGEMENT
288 MUNSTER ROAD
LONDON
SW6 6BQ
{T} 020 7386 9158
POST@ANDREWMANSON.COM
WWW.ANDREWMANSON.COM
FOUNDED: 1984
NO. OF CLIENTS: 80

ANGELA BARROW
UNIT 1 WATERLOO GARDENS
LONDON
N1 1TY
{T} 020 7700 4994
ACTORS@ANGELABARROW.CO.UK
WWW.ANGELABARROWACTORS.CO.UK
FOUNDED: 1998
NO. OF CLIENTS: 25

ANNA LEE GARRETT PERSONAL MANAGEMENT
24/26 ARCADIA AVENUE
FINCHLEY CENTRAL
LONDON N3 2JU
{T} 020 8349 7184
CONTACT@ANNALEEGARRETT.NET
WWW.ANNALEEGARRETT.NET
FOUNDED: 20065
NO. OF CLIENTS: 20

APM ASSOCIATES
PINEWOOD STUDIOS
IVER HEATH
BUCKS. SL0 0NH
{T} 01753 639204
APM@APMASSOCIATES.NET
WWW.APMASSOCIATES.NET

AQUITAINE PERSONAL MANAGEMENT
PO BOX 1896
STANFORD-LE-HOPE
ESSEX SS17 0WR
{T} 01375 488009
APM@AQUITAINE.ORG.UK
WWW.APM.AQUITAINE.ORG.UK
FOUNDED: 2000
NO. OF CLIENTS: 15

ARCHANGEL VOICES LIMITED
22 PORTSMOUTH AVENUE
THAMES DITTON
SURREY KT7 0RT
{T} 020 8873 7095
OFFICE@ARCHANGELVOICES.CO.UK
WWW.ARCHANGELVOICES.CO.UK
FOUNDED: 2008
NO. OF CLIENTS: 25

ARENA PERSONAL MANAGEMENT
PANTHER HOUSE,
38 MOUNT PLEASANT
LONDON WC1X 0AP
{T} 020 7278 1661
ARENAPMLTD@AOL.COM
WWW.ARENAPMLTD.CO.UK
FOUNDED: 1985
NO. OF CLIENTS: 18

ARTEMIS STUDIOS AGENCY
ARTEMIS STUDIOS
30 CHARLES SQUARE
BRACKNELL RG12 1AY
{T} 01344 429403
AGENCY@ARTEMIS-STUDIOS.CO.UK
WWW.AGENCY.ARTEMIS-STUDIOS.CO.UK
FOUNDED: 2007
NO. OF CLIENTS: 60

ASPIRE AGENCY @ STAGEABILITY
VESTRY HALL, ST. MICHAEL'S LANE
BRAINTREE
ESSEX CM7 1EY
{T} 01376 567677
ANN@STAGEABILITY.CO.UK
WWW.STAGEABILITY.CO.UK
FOUNDED: 2006
NO. OF CLIENTS: 43

ASTRAL ACTORS MANAGEMENT
7 GREENWAY CLOSE
LONDON NW9 5AZ
{T} 020 8728 2782
LIZ@ASTRALACTORS.COM
WWW.ASTRALACTORS.COM
FOUNDED: 2004
NO. OF CLIENTS: 40

ATSLI CASTING LTD
31 NINIAN ROAD
ROATH, CARDIFF CF23 5EG
{T} 029 2049 3950
SUSAN@ATSLI.TV
WWW.ATSLI.CO.UK
FOUNDED: 1997
NO. OF CLIENTS: 60

AUDREY BENJAMIN AGENCY
278A ELGIN AVENUE
MAIDA VALE, LONDON
{T} 020 7289 7180
A.BENJAMIN@BTCONNECT.COM
FOUNDED: 1985
NO. OF CLIENTS: 40

BACKGROUND TALENT
157 BROOKE ROAD
CLAPTON
LONDON, E5 2AG
{T} 020 8806 9267
INFO@BACKGROUNDTALENT.CO.UK
WWW.BACKGROUNDTALENT.CO.UK
FOUNDED: 1998
NO. OF CLIENTS: 300

BAM ASSOCIATES
BENETS COTTAGE
DOLBERROW
CHURCHILL BS25 5NT
{T} 01934 852 942
CASTING@EBAM.TV
WWW.EBAM.TV
FOUNDED: 1999
NO. OF CLIENTS: 50

BCM PROMOTIONS LTD
21 HOPE STREET
ILKESTON
DERBY DE7 5NF
{T} 0115 932 8615
BOOKWORM122@GMAIL.COM
WWW.BCMPROMOTIONS.COM
FOUNDED: 1997
NO. OF CLIENTS: 200

BEDAZZLE ARTS LTD.
GARDEN COTTAGE
SHORTGROVE
SAFFRON WALDEN CB11 3TX
{T} 07841 990 611
D.BEDAZZLE@MAC.COM
WWW.BEDAZZLEARTS.COM
FOUNDED: 2006
NO. OF CLIENTS: 20

BILLBOARD PERSONAL MANAGEMENT LTD
UNIT 5 UPPER
11 MOWLL STREET
LONDON SW9 6BG
{T} 020 7735 9956
INFO@BILLBOARDPM.COM
WWW.BILLBOARDPM.COM
FOUNDED: 1985
NO. OF CLIENTS: 50

BIZ MANAGEMENT
{T} 01483-765548
ERIKA@BIZMANAGEMENT.CO.UK
WWW.BIZMANAGEMENT.CO.UK
FOUNDED: 1999
NO. OF CLIENTS: 45

BLOOMFIELDS MANAGEMENT
77 OXFORD STREET
LONDON
W1D 2ES
{T} 020 7659 2001
EMMA@BLOOMFIELDSMANAGEMENT.COM
WWW.BLOOMFIELDSMANAGEMENT.COM
FOUNDED: 2004
NO. OF CLIENTS: 40

BLUE STAR ASSOCIATES
APT.8 SHALDON MANSIONS;
132 CHARING CROSS ROAD;
LONDON WC2H OLA
{T} 0207 836 6220 / 4128
HOPKINSTACEY@AOL.COM
WWW.BARRIESTACEY.COM
FOUNDED: 1977

BODENS
NEW BARNET
HERTS EN4 8RF
{T} 020 8447 0909
INFO@BODENSAGENCY.COM
WWW.BODENSAGENCY.COM
FOUNDED: 1979
NO. OF CLIENTS: 70

BOOM TALENT
218 PENARTH ROAD
CARDIFF
CF11 8NN
{T} 02920 550 565
SIONED.JAMES@BOOMERANG.CO.UK
WWW.BOOMTALENT.CO.UK
FOUNDED: 2007
NO. OF CLIENTS: 15

BOOST PERFORMERS AGENCY
83 WASHINGTON AVE
HEMEL HEMPSTEAD
HERTS HP2 6AW
{T} 0845 226 0809
AGENT@BOOSTPA.CO.UK
WWW.BOOSTPA.CO.UK
FOUNDED: 2006
NO. OF CLIENTS: 40

BRIAN TAYLOR ASSOCIATES
50 PEMBROKE ROAD
KENSINGTON
LONDON W8 6NX
{T} 020 7602 6141
BRIANTAYLOR@NQASSOC.FREESERVE.CO.UK
FOUNDED: 1970
NO. OF CLIENTS: 80

BRIDGES: THE ACTORS' AGENCY
ST GEORGES WEST
58 SHANDWICK PLACE
EDINBURGH EH2 4RT
{T} 0131 2266433
ADMIN@BRIDGESACTORSAGENCY.COM
WWW.BRIDGESACTORSAGENCY.COM
FOUNDED: 2008
NO. OF CLIENTS: 11

BROOD
HIGH STREET BUILDINGS
134 KIRKDALE
LONDON SE26 4BB
{T} 020 8699 1757
BROODMANAGEMENT@AOL.COM
WWW.BROODMANAGEMENT.COM
FOUNDED: 2003
NO. OF CLIENTS: 40

BRUNSKILL MANAGEMENT LTD
THE COURTYARD
EDENHALL
PENRITH CA118ST
{T} 01768 881430
ADMIN@BRUNSKILL.COM
FOUNDED: 1958
NO. OF CLIENTS: 150

BSA MANAGEMENT
FIRST FLOOR
75 BROWNLOW ROAD
LONDON N11 2BN
{T} 020 3240 1064
INFO@BSA-MANAGEMENT.CO.UK
WWW.BSA-MANAGEMENT.CO.UK
FOUNDED: 2008
NO. OF CLIENTS: 30

BURNETT GRANGER CROWTHER LTD
3 CLIFFORD STREET
LONDON
W1S 2LF
{T} 020 7437 8008
ASSOCIATES@BGCLTD.ORG
WWW.BURNETTGRANGERCROWTHER.CO.UK

THE BWH AGENCY
BARLEY MOW CENTRE
10 BARLEY MOW PASSAGE
LONDON
{T} 020 8996 1661
INFO@THEBWHAGENCY.
WWW.THEBWHAGENCY.CO.UK

BYRON'S MANAGEMENT
76 ST JAMES LANE
LONDON
N10 3DF
{T} 020 8444 4445
BYRONSMANAGEMENT@AOL.COM
WWW.BYRONSMANAGEMENT.CO.UK
FOUNDED: 1995
NO. OF CLIENTS: 140

C. A. ARTISTES MANAGEMENT
26-28 HAMMERSMITH GROVE
LONDON
W6 7BA
{T} 020 8834 1608
CASTING@CAARTISTES.COM
FOUNDED: 1962
NO. OF CLIENTS: 30

CANDYFLOSS ARTIST MANAGEMENT
97 NEWFORD CRESCENT
STOKE ON TRENT
STAFFORDSHIRE ST2 7EB
{T} 01782 545134
ENQUIRES@CANDYFLOSSENTERTAINMENTS.CO.UK
WWW.CANDYFLOSSENTERTAINMENTS.CO.UK
FOUNDED: 2004
NO. OF CLIENTS: 3500

**CANONGATE ACTOR AND
MODEL MANAGEMENT**
9 WATERS CLOSE
LEITH
EDINBURGH EH6 6RB
{T} 0131 555 4455
AL@CANONGATE.COM
WWW.CANONGATE.COM
FOUNDED: 2004
NO. OF CLIENTS: 100

CARAVANSERAI ASSOCIATES
334B LADBROKE GROVE
LONDON W10 5AS
{T} 5601534892
INFO@CSERAI.CO.UK
FOUNDED: 32008
NO. OF CLIENTS: 20

CASTING FACES UK
GLOBAL HOUSE
1 ASHLEY AVENUE
EPSOM, SURREY TF2 9UW
{T} 08707 709 330
RHIANNON@CASTINGFACES.COM
FOUNDED: 2001
NO. OF CLIENTS: 30

CBL MANAGEMENT
20 HOLLINGBURY RISE
BRIGHTON
BN1 7HJ
{T} 01273 321245
ENQUIRIES@CBLMANAGEMENT.CO.UK
WWW.CBLMANAGEMENT.CO.UK
FOUNDED: 2008
NO. OF CLIENTS: 20

CCM ACTORS
WC1 0AP
{T} 020 7278 0507
CASTING@CCMACTORS.COM
WWW.CCMACTORS.COM
FOUNDED: 1993
NO. OF CLIENTS: 19

CELEX CASTING
CELEX CASTING LTD
PO BOX 7317
DERBY DE1 0GS
{T} 01332 232445
ANNE@CELEX.CO.UK
FOUNDED: 1999
NO. OF CLIENTS: 4

CENTRE STAGE ACADEMY
THE STUDIO
GREENACRE COMMUNITY HALL
RAWDON, LEEDS LS19 6AS
{T} 0113 20 290 20
THESTUDIO@CENTRE-STAGE-ACADEMY.CO.UK
FOUNDED: 2000
NO. OF CLIENTS: 200

CENTRE STAGE MANAGEMENT
113 SANDFIELD LANE
GAINSBROUGH
LINCS DN21 1DB
{T} 0870 4430 115
INFO@CENTRESTAGEMANAGEMENT.CO.UK
WWW.CENTRESTAGEMANAGEMENT.CO.UK
FOUNDED: 1991
NO. OF CLIENTS: 300

CHALICE PERSONAL MANAGEMENT LTD
TEMPLE COURT
CATHEDRAL ROAD
CARDIFF CF11 9HA
{T} 02920 786537 / 07794051019
AGENT@CHALICEPERSONALMANAGEMENT.CO.UK
WWW.CHALICEPERSONALMANAGEMENT.CO.UK
FOUNDED: 2008
NO. OF CLIENTS: 70

CHAMELEON TALENT MANAGEMENT
PO BOX 1888
CROYDON
CR0 7DF
{T} 020 8656 7550
OFFICE@CHAMELEONTALENT.CO.UK
FOUNDED: 2008
NO. OF CLIENTS: 5

49

CHRIS DAVIS MANAGEMENT
TENBURY HOUSE
36 TEME STREET
TENBURY WELLS WR15 8AA
{T} 01584 819005
KFOLEY@CDM-LTD.COM
WWW.CDM-LTD.COM
FOUNDED: 1993
NO. OF CLIENTS: 90

CHRISTOPHER ANTONY ASSOCIATES
THE OLD DAIRY
164 THAMES ROAD
LONDON W4 3QS
{T} 2089949952
INFO@CHRISTOPHERANTONY.CO.UK
FOUNDED: 2005
NO. OF CLIENTS: 20

CHRYSTEL ARTS AGENCY & THEATRE
SCHOOL
OFFICE - 6 EUNICE GROVE
CHESHAM
BUCKS HP5 1RL
{T} 01494 773336
CHRYSTELARTS@WAITROSE.COM
FOUNDED: 2000
NO. OF CLIENTS: 33

CINEL GABRAN MANAGEMENT
P.O. BOX 5163
CARDIFF CF5 9BJ
{T} 0845 0 666605
INFO@CINELGABRAN.CO.UK
WWW.CINELGABRAN.CO.UK
FOUNDED: 1988
NO. OF CLIENTS: 60

CIRCUIT PERSONAL MANAGEMENT LTD
SUITE 71, SEC
BEDFORD STREET
STOKE ON TRENT ST1 4PZ
{T} 01782 285388
MAIL@CIRCUITPM.CO.UK
WWW.CIRCUITPM.CO.UK
FOUNDED: 1988
NO. OF CLIENTS: 24

CLARKE AND JONES LIMITED
28 FORDWYCH COURT
LONDON NW2 3PH
{T} 020 8438 0185
MAIL@CLARKEANDJONES.PLUS.COM
FOUNDED: 2003
NO. OF CLIENTS: 10

CLAYPOLE MANAGEMENT
PO BOX 123
DARLINGTON
DL3 7WA
{T} 0845 650 1777
CLAYPOLE_1@HOTMAIL.COM
WWW.CLAYPOLEMANAGEMENT.CO.UK
FOUNDED: 1999
NO. OF CLIENTS: 50+

CLIC AGENCY
RHOSLWYN
RHOS ISAF
GWYNEDD LL54 7NF
{T} 01286 831001
CLIC@BTINTERNET.COM
WWW.CLICAGENCY.CO.UK
FOUNDED: 2006
NO. OF CLIENTS: 50

CLIVE CORNER ASSOCIATES
3 BAINBRIDGE CLOSE
HAM TW12 5JJ
{T} 020 8332 1910
CORNERASSOCIATES@AOL.COM
FOUNDED: 1987
NO. OF CLIENTS: 80

CLOUD NINE AGENCY
96 TIBER GARDENS
TREATY STREET
LONDON N1 0XE
{T} 020 7278 0029
INFO@CLOUDNINEAGENCY.CO.UK
WWW.CLOUDNINEAGENCY.CO.UK
FOUNDED: 1995
NO. OF CLIENTS: 40

CMP MANAGEMENT
8/30 GALENA ROAD
HAMMERSMITH
LONDON W6 0LT
{T} 020 8741 0707
INFO@RAVENSCOURT.NET
WWW.RAVENSCOURT.NET
FOUNDED: 1999
NO. OF CLIENTS: 100

COLLIS MANAGEMENT
182 TREVELYAN ROAD
LONDON
SW17 9LW
{T} 020 8767 0196
MARILYN@COLLISMANAGEMENT.CO.UK
FOUNDED: 1992
NO. OF CLIENTS: 60

COLOURING BOOK CASTING LTD
CARLISLE BUSINESS CENTRE
60 CARLISLE ROAD
BRADFORD BD8 8BD
{T} 01274 729700
CBCMQ@MSN.COM
FOUNDED: 2000
NO. OF CLIENTS: 1000

COLOURS AGENCY
158 QUEENS DRIVE
GLASGOW
G42 8QN
{T} 0141 422 2288
ROSALYND@COLOURSAGENCY.COM
WWW.COLOURSAGENCY.COM
FOUNDED: 1998
NO. OF CLIENTS: 3000

COMPLETE ARTISTES
NORTHERN & SHELL TOWER
4 SELSDON WAY
LONDON E14 9GL
{T} 020 7308 6003
SABRINA.RAHMAN@NASNET.CO.UK

COPS ON THE BOX
BM BOX 7301
LONDON
WC1N 3XX
{T} 020 8650 9828
INFO@TVCOPS.CO.UK
WWW.COTB.CO.UK
FOUNDED: 1993
NO. OF CLIENTS: 200

CORINNE CALLUM ASSOCIATES
46 BRIGHTWELL CRESCENT
SW17 9AE
{T} 07504 987 402
CORINNECALLUM@LIVE.CO.UK
WWW.CORINNECALLUMASSOCIATES.CO.UK
FOUNDED: 2008
NO. OF CLIENTS: 10

COULTER MANAGEMENT AGENCY LTD
333 WOODLANDS RD.
GLASGOW
G3 6NG
{T} 0141 357 6666
CMAGLASGOW@BTCONNECT.COM
FOUNDED: 1995
NO. OF CLIENTS: 80

CPA MANAGEMENT
'THE STUDIOS' 219B NORTH STREET
ROMFORD
ESSEX RM1 4QA
{T} 01708 766444
JULIE@CPAMANAGEMENT.CO.UK
WWW.CPAMANAGEMENT.CO.UK
FOUNDED: 1995
NO. OF CLIENTS: 30

CRAIG REECE MANAGEMENT
BUILDING 231
VICTORIA ROAD
NORTH WEST CH45 2JF
{T} +44 (0) 845 56 20 874
REECEMGNT@YAHOO.COM
FOUNDED: 1999
NO. OF CLIENTS: 18

CREATIVE ARTISTS GROUP
88 SULIVAN COURT
PETERBOROUGH ROAD
LONDON SW6 3DB
{T} 020 7348 7906
CASTING@CREATIVEARTISTSGROUP.CO.UK
FOUNDED: 2007
NO. OF CLIENTS: 16

CRESCENT MANAGEMENT
10 BARLEY MOW PASSAGE
LONDON
W4 4PH
{T} 020 8987 0191
MAIL@CRESCENTMANAGEMENT.CO.UK
WWW.CRESCENTMANAGEMENT.CO.UK
FOUNDED: 1991
NO. OF CLIENTS: 19

CS MANAGEMENT
7 CANNON ROAD
LONDON N147HE
{T} 020 8886 4264
CAROLE@CSMANAGEMENTUK.COM
WWW.CSMANAGEMENTUK.COM
FOUNDED: 2001
NO. OF CLIENTS: 150

D STAR PROFESSIONAL AGENCY LTD
42 MACDONALD AVE
HORNCHURCH
ESSEX RM11 2NE
{T} 01708 442578
DEE@DSTAR.CO.UK
FOUNDED: 1998
NO. OF CLIENTS: 600

DALZELL AND BERESFORD
26 ASTWOOD MEWS
LONDON
SW7 4DE
{T} 020 7341 9411
MAIL@DBLTD.CO.UK
NO. OF CLIENTS: 20

DAVID PADBURY ASSOCIATES
44 SUMMERLEE AVENUE
FINCHLEY
LONDON N2 9QP
{T} 020 8883 1277
INFO@DAVIDPADBURYASSOCIATES.COM
WWW.DAVIDPADBURYASSOCIATES.COM
FOUNDED: 2003
NO. OF CLIENTS: 60

DAWN SEDGWICK MANAGEMENT
3 GOODWINS COURT
COVENT GARDEN
LONDON WC2N 4LL
FOUNDED: 2002
NO. OF CLIENTS: 15

DDA
3 BALLIOL CHAMBERS
HOLLOW LANE
HITCHIN SG4 9SB
{T} 020 7193 7833
INFO@DANIELDANCEYASSOCIATES.COM
WWW.DANIELDANCEYASSOCIATES.COM
FOUNDED: 2007
NO. OF CLIENTS: 20

DEBBIE EDLER MANAGEMENT LIMITED
LITTLE FRIARS COTTAGE
LOMBARD STREET
EYNSHAM, OXFORDSHIRE OX29 4HT
{T} 01865 884203
INFO@DEMAGENCY.CO.UK
WWW.DEMAGENCY.CO.UK
FOUNDED: 1995
NO. OF CLIENTS: 150

DENMARK STREET MANAGEMENT
SUITE 4 CLARENDON BUILDINGS
25 HORSELL ROAD
LONDON N5 1XL
{T} 020 7700 5200
MAIL@DENMARKSTREET.NET
WWW.DENMARKSTREET.NET
FOUNDED: 1985
NO. OF CLIENTS: 20

DEVINE ARTIST MANAGEMENT
SUITE 90, GREAT NORTHERN HOUSE
DEANSGATE, MANCHESTER M3 4EL
{T} 0844 8844578
DEVINEARTISTMANAGEMENT@YAHOO.CO.UK
WWW.DEVINEMANAGEMENT.CO.UK
FOUNDED: 2006
NO. OF CLIENTS: 20

DGPM
THE STUDIO
107A MIDDLETON ROAD
LONDON E8 4LN
{T} 020 7241 6752
INFODGPM@AOL.COM
FOUNDED: 2006
NO. OF CLIENTS: 26

53

DICK HORSEY MANAGEMENT LIMITED
COTTINGHAM HOUSE
CHORLEYWOOD ROAD
RICKMANSWORTH WD3 4EP
{T} 01923 710 614
ROGER@DHMLIMITED.CO.UK
FOUNDED: 1993
NO. OF CLIENTS: 30

DIRECT PERSONAL MANAGEMENT
PARK HOUSE
62 LIDGETT LANE
LEEDS LS8 1PL
{T} 0113 266 4036
DAPHNE.FRANKS@DIRECTPM.CO.UK
WWW.DIRECTPM.CO.UK
FOUNDED: 1985
NO. OF CLIENTS: 30

DP MANAGEMENT
1 EUSTON ROAD
LONDON
NW1 2SA
{T} 020 7059 0257
DANNY@DPMANAGEMENT.ORG
FOUNDED: 2005
NO. OF CLIENTS: 60

DQ MANAGEMENT
27 RAVENSWOOD PARK
NORTHWOOD
MIDDLESEX HA6 3PR
{T} 01273 721221
DQ.MANAGEMENT1@GOOGLEMAIL.COM
WWW.DQMANAGEMENT.COM
FOUNDED: 2003
NO. OF CLIENTS: 50

DRAGON PERSONAL MANAGEMENT
96 DIANA STREET
ROATH
CARDIFF CF24 4TU
{T} 02920-193974
CASTING@DRAGON-PM.COM
FOUNDED: 2008
NO. OF CLIENTS: 8

EDWARD HILL MANAGEMENT
{T} 01273 906781
INFO@EDAGENT.COM
FOUNDED: 1999
NO. OF CLIENTS: 36

EDWARD WYMAN AGENCY
67 LLANON ROAD
LLANISHEN
CARDIFF CF14 5AH
{T} 02920- 752351
EDWARD.WYMAN@BTCONNECT.COM
FOUNDED: 1969
NO. OF CLIENTS: 500

EKA MANAGEMENT
THE WAREHOUSE STUDIOS
GLAZIERS LANE
CULCHETH WA3 4AQ
{T} 0871 222 7470
BECKY@EKA-AGENCY.COM
WWW.EKA-AGENCY.COM
FOUNDED: 1997
NO. OF CLIENTS: 50

ELEVATION ARTISTES MANAGEMENT LTD
788-790 FINCHLEY ROAD
LONDON
NW11 7TJ
{T} 020 8203 9099
INFO@ELEVATIONARTISTES.CO.UK
WWW.ELEVATIONARTISTES.CO.UK
FOUNDED: 2007
NO. OF CLIENTS: 30

ELINOR HILTON ASSOCIATES
2ND FLOOR
28 CHARING CROSS ROAD
LONDON WC2H 0DB
{T} 020 7240 2555
INFO@ELINORHILTON.COM
WWW.ELINORHILTON.COM
FOUNDED: 2003
NO. OF CLIENTS: 50

ELITE-TALENT LTD
9 GLOUCESTER AVENUE
HEYWOOD
LANCASHIRE OL10 2PU
{T} 07912 642946
JACKIE@ELITE-TALENT.COM
WWW.ELITE-TALENT.COM
FOUNDED: 2007
NO. OF CLIENTS: 24

ELIZABETH DAVIES MANAGEMENT
170 LONG LANE
LONDON N3 2RA
{T} 07961 272 104
EDAVIESASSOCIATES@YAHOO.COM
FOUNDED: 1997
NO. OF CLIENTS: 15

ELLIOTT AGENCY
10, HIGH STREET
SHOREHAM BY SEA
WEST SUSSEX BN43 5DA
{T} 01273 454111
ELLIOTTAGENCY@BTCONNECT.COM
WWW.ELLIOTTAGENCY.CO.UK
FOUNDED: 1980
NO. OF CLIENTS: 500

ELSPETH COCHRANE PERSONAL MANAGEMENT
16 TRINITY CLOSE, THE PAVEMENT
LONDON SW4 0JD
{T} 020 7622 3566
ELSPETHCOCHRANE@TALKTALK.NET
WWW.ELSPETHCOCHRANE.COM
FOUNDED: 1970
NO. OF CLIENTS: 30

EMMA SHARNOCK ASSOCIATES
YORK HOUSE, 29 YORK ROAD
TUNBRIDGE WELLS
KENT TN1 1JX
{T} 01892 539007
ESA-AGENCY@BTCONNECT.COM
WWW.ESA-AGENCY.CO.UK
FOUNDED: 2005
NO. OF CLIENTS: 70

Actors' Handbook 2009-10

EMPTAGE HALLETT
14 RATHBONE PLACE
LONDON
W1T 1HT
{T} 020 7436 0425
MAIL@EMPTAGEHALLETTT.CO.UK
WWW.EMPTAGEHALLETT.CO.UK
FOUNDED: 1996
No. OF CLIENTS: 90

ENTERTAINMENT PEOPLE MANAGEMENT
BASEMENT STUDIOS
142 BUCKINGHAM PALACE ROAD
LONDON SW1W 9TR
{T} 020 7100 6070
RUSSELL.HAWKINS@EP-SITE.COM
WWW.EP-SITE.COM
FOUNDED: 1980
No. OF CLIENTS: 25

ESTA CHARKHAM ASSOCIATES
16 BRITISH GROVE
LONDON W4 2NL
{T} 020 8741 2843
ESTA@CLARA.CO.UK
FOUNDED: 2001
No. OF CLIENTS: 10

ET-NIK-A PRIME MANAGEMENT
& CASTINGS LIMITED
30 GREAT PORTLAND STREET
LONDON W1W 8QU
{T} 020 7299 3555
INFO@ETNIKAPMC.COM
WWW.ETNIKAPMC.COM
FOUNDED: 2000
No. OF CLIENTS: 60

EVOLUTION TALENT & MODEL AGENCY
THE TRUMAN BUILDING
91 BRICK LANE
LONDON E1 6QL
{T} 020 7770 6128
LOFTY@EVOLUTIONMNGT.COM
WWW.EVOLUTIONMNGT.COM
FOUNDED: 1999
No. OF CLIENTS: 3560

EXPLOSION ENTERTAINMENTS
111 WOODLAND WAY
ONGAR CM5 9ET
{T} 01992 610958
EXPLOSIONOFTALENT@MSN.COM
FOUNDED: 1999
No. OF CLIENTS: 12

EXPRESSIONS CASTING AGENCY
3 NEWGATE LANE
MANSFIELD
NOTTS NG18 2LB
{T} 01623 424334
EXPRESSIONS-UK@BTCONNECT.COM
WWW.EXPRESSIONSPERFORMINGARTS.CO.UK
FOUNDED: 1989
No. OF CLIENTS: 50

FIRST ACT PERSONAL MANAGEMENT
2 SAINT MICHAELS
NEW ARLEY, COVENTRY
WARWICKSHIRE CV7 8PY
{T} 01676 540285
FIRSTACTPM@AOL.COM
WWW.SPOTLIGHTAGENT.INFO/FIRSTACT
FOUNDED: 2004
No. OF CLIENTS: 27

FLAIR TALENT
46 BARRY ROAD
LONDON SE22 0HU
{T} 020 8693 8649
MODELS@FLAIRTALENT.COM
WWW.FLAIRTALENT.COM
FOUNDED: 2004
NO. OF CLIENTS: 300

FOOTLIGHTS MANAGEMENT
184 KATRINA GROVE
PONTEFRACT
WEST YORKSHIRE WF7 5NT
AGENT@FOOTLIGHTSAGENCY.CO.UK
WWW.FOOTLIGHTSAGENCY.CO.UK
FOUNDED: 2007
NO. OF CLIENTS: 55

FRANCES PHILLIPS
89 ROBESON WAY
BOREHAMWOOD
HERTFORDSHIRE WD6 5RY
{T} 020 8953 0303
DEREKPHILLIPS@TALK21.COM
WWW.FRANCESPHILLIPS.CO.UK
FOUNDED: 1983
NO. OF CLIENTS: 40

FRANCES ROSS MANAGEMENT
HIGHER LEYONNE
GOLANT
FOWEY,CORNWALL PL23 1LA
{T} 01726 833004
FRANCESROSS@BTCONNECT.COM
WWW.FRANCESROSSMANAGEMENT.CO.UK
FOUNDED: 2001
NO. OF CLIENTS: 10

FRESH AGENTS LTD
SUITE 5. SAKS HOUSE 19 SHIP STREET
BRIGHTON.
BN1 1AD
{T} 01273 711777
LAUREN@FRESHAGENTS.CO.UK
WWW.FRESHAGENTS.CO.UK
FOUNDED: 2000

G1 MANAGEMENT
3RD FLOOR
34 ALBION STREET
GLASGOW G1 1LH
G1.MANAGEMENT@YAHOO.CO.UK
FOUNDED: 2008

GADBURY CASTING
18 GADBURY FOLD
MANCHESTER
M46 0GX
{T} 01942 893 480
KATIE@GADBURY-CASTING.CO.UK
FOUNDED: 2007
NO. OF CLIENTS: 400

GAG REFLEX MANAGEMENT
102 OLDHAM STREET
MANCHESTER
M4 1LJ
{T} 0161 2286368
LEE@GAGREFLEX.CO.UK
WWW.GAGREFLEX.CO.UK
NO. OF CLIENTS: 11

GDM
26 Rasper Road
London N20 0LZ
{T} 020 8445 2927
GRANTDAVIDMANAGEMENT@GOOGLEMAIL.CO.UK
Founded: 2004
No. of clients: 8

George Heathcote Management
58 Northdown Street,
London
N1 9BS
{T} 020 7713 5232
GHEATHCOTE@FREEUK.COM

Geraldine Gillman Associates
Malcolm Primary School
Malcolm Road
Penge SE20 8RH
{T} 0844 800 5328
GERALDI.GILLMA@BTCONNECT.COM
Founded: 1987
No. of clients: 80

Global Artists
23 Haymarket,
London SW1Y 4DG
{T} 020 7839 4888
INFO@GLOBALARTISTS.CO.UK
WWW.GLOBALARTISTS.CO.UK
Founded: 1996

Global7
PO Box 56232
London N4 4XP
{T} 020 7281 7679
GLOBAL7CASTINGS@GMAIL.COM
WWW.SPOTLIGHTAGENT.INFO/GLOBAL7
Founded: 2007
No. of clients: 45

Gold Agency Ltd
Britannia House
Lower Road
Northfleet, Kent DA11 9BL
{T} 01474 561200
ANN@GOLDAGENCY.CO.UK
WWW.GOLDAGENCY.CO.UK
Founded: 2006
No. of clients: 45

Grays Management
Panther House
38 Mount Pleasant
London
{T} 020 7278 1054
E-MAIL@GRAYSMANAGEMENT.IDPS.CO.UK

Groundlings Management
Fratton Community Centre
Trafalgar Place
Portsmouth PO1 5JJ
{T} 023 9273 7370
RICHARD@GROUNDLINGS.CO.UK
WWW.GROUNDLINGS.CO.UK
Founded: 2005
No. of clients: 34

H2OH! ENTERTAINMENT
39, VINE STREET
BRIGHTON
BN1 4AG
{T} 07515 064149
HELEN@H2OHENTERTAINMENT.COM
FOUNDED: 2003
NO. OF CLIENTS: 400

HALL JAMES PERSONAL MANAGEMENT
PO BOX 604
PINNER MIDDLESEX
HA5 9GH
{T} 020 8429 8111
INFO@HALLJAMES.CO.UK
WWW.HALLJAMES.CO.UK
FOUNDED: 2006
NO. OF CLIENTS: 25

HAMILTON HODELL
66-68 MARGARET STREET
LONDON
W1W 8SR
{T} 020 7636 1221
INFO@HAMILTONHODELL.CO.UK
WWW.HAMILTONHODELL.CO.UK

HAND MODELS 1
GARDEN STUDIOS
11-15 BETTERTON STREET
COVENT GARDEN WC2H 9BP
{T} 020 7470 8739
CONTACT@HANDMODELS1.COM
WWW.HANDMODELS1.COM
FOUNDED: 2006
NO. OF CLIENTS: 110

HARVEY VOICES
54-55 MARGARET STREET
LONDON
W1W 8SH
{T} 020 7952 4361
EMMA@HARVEYVOICES.CO.UK
WWW.HARVEYVOICES.CO.UK
FOUNDED: 2006
NO. OF CLIENTS: 200

HAT MANAGEMENT
24, THORNLEY RISE
AUDENSHAW
MANCHESTER M34 5JX
{T} 0161 3708648
HAT.MGMT@HOTMAIL.CO.UK
FOUNDED: 2005
NO. OF CLIENTS: 34

HELEN STAFFORD MANAGEMENT
14 PARK AVENUE
ENFIELD
MIDDLESEX EN1 2HP
{T} 020 8360 6329
HELEN.STAFFORD@BLUEYONDER.CO.UK
FOUNDED: 1991
NO. OF CLIENTS: 30

HILARY GAGAN ASSOCIATES
187 DRURY LANE
LONDON
WC2B 5QD
{T} 020 7404 8794
HILARY@HGASSOC.FREESERVE.CO.UK

HOBSON'S INTERNATIONAL
62. CHISWICK HIGH ROAD
CHISWICK
LONDON W4 1SY
{T} 020 8995 3628
ACTORS@HOBSONS-INTERNATIONAL.COM
WWW.HOBSONS-INTERNATIONAL.COM
FOUNDED: 1986
NO. OF CLIENTS: 600

HUNKY DORY ACTORS MANAGEMENT
DOCKS COTTAGE
LLANTRITHYD
COWBRIDGE, VALE OF GLAMORGAN CF71 7UB
{T} 01446 781365
ENQUIRIES@HUNKYDORYAGENCY.CO.UK
WWW.HUNKYDORYAGENCY.CO.UK
FOUNDED: 2008

ICON ACTORS MANAGEMENT
TANZARO HOUSE
ARDWICK GREEN NORTH
MANCHESTER M12 6FZ
{T} 0161 273 3344
INFO@ICONACTORS.NET
WWW.ICONACTORS.NET
FOUNDED: 2000
NO. OF CLIENTS: 60

IDLE HANDS
TY BACH, ALBION ROAD
WEST YORKSHIRE BD10 9PY
{T} 01274 412487
IDLEHANDSTHEATRECOMPANY@YAHOO.CO.UK
FOUNDED: 2006
NO. OF CLIENTS: 11

IMPACT INTERNATIONAL MANAGEMENT
1ST FLOOR DANCEWORKS
16-18 BALDERTON STREET
LONDON W1K 6TN
{T} 020 7495 6655
INFO@IMPACT-LONDON.CO.UK
WWW.IMPACT-LONDON.CO.UK
FOUNDED: 2000
NO. OF CLIENTS: 200

IMPERIAL PERSONAL MANAGEMENT LTD
102 KIRKSTALL ROAD
LEEDS LS3 1JS
{T} 0113 244 3222
KATIE_ROSS@BTINTERNET.COM
WWW.IPMCASTING.COM
FOUNDED: 2007
NO. OF CLIENTS: 40

INDEPENDENT TALENT GROUP
76 OXFORD STREET
LONDON W1D 1BS
{T} 020 7636 6565
COLLEENHOWE@INDEPENDENTTALENT.COM
WWW.INDEPENDENTTALENT.COM
FOUNDED: 1975
NO. OF CLIENTS: 100

INDUSTRY ARTISTS
332 ROYAL EXCHANGE
MANCHESTER
M2 7BR
{T} 0161 839 1551
MARK@INDUSTRYACTORS.CO.UK
WWW.INDUSTRYACTORS.CO.UK
FOUNDED: 2002
NO. OF CLIENTS: 30

INSPIRATION MANAGEMENT
ROOM 227, THE ABERDEEN CENTRE
22-24 HIGHBURY GROVE
LONDON N5 2EA
{T} 020 7704 0440
MAIL@INSPIRATIONMANAGEMENT.ECLIPSE.CO.UK
WWW.INSPIRATIONMANAGEMENT.ORG.UK
FOUNDED: 1986
NO. OF CLIENTS: 21

INTERCITY CASTING
PORTLAND TOWER, PORTLAND ST, MANCHESTER
M1 3LF
{T} 0161 238 4950
INTERCITY@BTCONNECT.CO.UK
FOUNDED: 1982
NO. OF CLIENTS: 80

INTERNATIONAL ARTISTES
4TH FLOOR
HOLBORN HALL
193-197 HIGH HOLBORN WC1V 7BD
{T} 020 7025 0600
MMILBURN@INTERNATIONALARTISTES.COM
WWW.INTERNATOINALARTISTES.COM
FOUNDED: 1945

IT&M MANAGEMENT
GARDEN STUDIOS
11-15 BETTERTON STREET
LONDON WC2H 9BP
{T} 020 7470 8786
INFO@IT-M.CO.UK
FOUNDED: 1981
NO. OF CLIENTS: 75

JACLYN AGENCY
52 BESSEMER ROAD
NORWICH
NORFOLK NR4 6DQ
{T} 01603 622027
INFO@JACLYNAGENCY.CO.UK
WWW.JACLYNAGENCY.CO.UK
FOUNDED: 1956
NO. OF CLIENTS: 500

JACOB DRAMATICS MANAGEMENT
4 RABY DRIVE
EAST HERRINGTON
SUNDERLAND SR3 3QE
{T} 0191 5203450
JACOBJKY@AOL.COM
FOUNDED: 2006
NO. OF CLIENTS: 5

JAMES BYRNE ASSOCIATES
3 MANSELL CLOSE
WIDNES
CHESHIRE WA8 9WL
{T} 0151 4206200
THEACTORSAGENCY@YAHOO.CO.UK

JANET HOWE CASTING
58 HIGH STREET
NEWCASTLE UNDER LYME
STAFFS ST5 1QE
{T} 01782 661777
INFO@JANETHOWE.COM
FOUNDED: 1997
NO. OF CLIENTS: 50

JANET PLATER MANAGEMENT LTD
D FLOOR MILBURN HOUSE, DEAN STREET
NEWCASTLE UPON TYNE NE1 1LF
{T} 0191 221 2490
INFO@JANETPLATERMANAGEMENT.CO.UK
WWW.JANETPLATERMANAGEMENT.CO.UK
FOUNDED: 1997
NO. OF CLIENTS: 65

JANICE TILDSLEY ASSOCIATES
47 ORFORD ROAD
LONDON E17 9NJ
{T} 020 8521 1888
INFO@JANICETILDSLEYASSOCIATES.CO.UK
WWW.JANICETILDSLEYASSOCIATES.CO.UK
FOUNDED: 2003
NO. OF CLIENTS: 60

JB ASSOCIATES
MANCHESTER HOUSE
84 - 86 PRINCESS STREET
MANCHESTER M1 6NG
{T} 0161 237 1808
INFO@J-B-A.NET
WWW.J-B-A.NET
FOUNDED: 1997
NO. OF CLIENTS: 70

JB PERSONAL MANAGEMENT
STUDIO 106, WESTBOURNE STUDIOS
242 ACKLAM ROAD
LONDON W10 5JJ
{T} 020 7575 3012
JENNY@JBPERSONALMANAGEMENT.COM
WWW.JBPERSONALMANAGEMENT.COM
FOUNDED: 2007
NO. OF CLIENTS: 30

JD MURPHY CASTING LTD
CASITA, BLYTHE ROAD
COLESHILL B46 1AF
{T} 01675 430062
INFO@JDMURPHYCASTING.COM
WWW.JDMURPHYCASTING.COM
FOUNDED: 2007
NO. OF CLIENTS: 12

JIGSAW ARTS MANAGEMENT
64-66 HIGH STREET
BARNET
HERTFORDSHIRE EN5 5SJ
{T} 020 8447 4534
ADMIN@JIGSAW-ARTS.CO.UK
WWW.JIGSAW-ARTS.CO.UK/AGENCY
FOUNDED: 2005
NO. OF CLIENTS: 35

JLM PERSONAL MANAGEMENT
4TH FLOOR
HOLBORN HALL
193-197 HIGH HOLBORN, LONDON WC1V 7BD
{T} 020 7025 0630
INFO@JLMPM.CO.UK
WWW.JLMPM.CO.UK
FOUNDED: 1978

JOHN DOE ASSOCIATES
W10 4AR
{T} 020 8960 2848
INFO@JOHNDOEMGT.COM
WWWJOHNDOEMGT.COM
FOUNDED: 2004
NO. OF CLIENTS: 150

JOHN PETERS MANAGEMENT
11 ST HELIERS AVENUE
HOUNSLOW
MIDDLESEX TW3 3SL
JOHNPETERSMANAGEMENT@YAHOO.CO.UK
FOUNDED: 2003
NO. OF CLIENTS: 10

JOHN STRANGE MANAGEMENT
FILM CITY
401 GAVIN ROAD
GLASGOW G51 2QJ
{T} 0141 4450444
INFO@STRANGEMANAGEMENT.CO.UK
WWW.STRANGEMANANGEMENT.CO.UK
FOUNDED: 2003
NO. OF CLIENTS: 31

JOHNSTON & MATHERS ASSOCIATES
PO BOX 3167
BARNET
EN5 2WA
{T} 020 8449 4968
JOHNSTONMATHERS@AOL.COM
FOUNDED: 2000
NO. OF CLIENTS: 47

JONATHAN LIPMAN
7 POLAND STREET
LONDON
W1F 8PU
{T} 08712 210011
CARLY@JONATHANLIPMAN.COM
WWW.JONATHANLIPMAN.COM
FOUNDED: 2007
NO. OF CLIENTS: 20

JPA MANAGEMENT
30 DAWS HILL LANE
HIGH WYCOMBE HP11 1PW
{T} 01494 520 978
JACKIE.PALMER@BTINTERNET.COM
WWW.JPAMANAGEMENT.CO.UK
FOUNDED: 1995
NO. OF CLIENTS: 54

JULIE FOX ASSOCIATES LTD
47 FURZE PLATT ROAD
MAIDENHEAD
BERKS SL6 7NH
{T} 01628 777583
JULIE@JULIEFOX.NET
FOUNDED: 2002
NO. OF CLIENTS: 20

K D ASSOCIATES
12 THE DRIVE
NORTHAMPTON
NORTHANTS NN1 4SH
{T} 01604 715598
KD.ASSOCIATES@VIRGIN.NET
WWW.KDASSOCIATES.BIZ
FOUNDED: 2006
NO. OF CLIENTS: 20

K TALENT
K TALENT ARTIST MANAGEMENT
1ST FLOOR, 28 GRAYS INN ROAD
LONDON WC1X 8HR
{T} 0844 5672470
MEL@KTALENT.CO.UK
WWW.KTALENT.CO.UK
FOUNDED: 2003
NO. OF CLIENTS: 50

KAL MANAGEMENT
95 GLOUCESTER ROAD
HAMPTON
TW12 2UW
{T} 020 8783 0039
KAPLAN222@AOL.COM
FOUNDED: 1980

KAY GANNON
CENTRAL CHAMBERS
93 HOPE STREET
GLASGOW G2 6LD
{T} 0141 221 8622
KAY@REVOLUTIONTALENTMANAGEMENT.COM
WWW.KAYGANNON.COM
FOUNDED: 2005
NO. OF CLIENTS: 30

KD ENTERTAINMENTS
80 AXIOM AVENUE
WESTWOOD
PETERBOROUGH PE3 7EJ
{T} 01733 269 397
KEITHDANIELS221279@HOTMAIL.COM
WWW.KDENTERTAINMENTS.CO.UK
FOUNDED: 2006
NO. OF CLIENTS: 15

KELLY MANAGEMENT
3RD FLOOR
50 SOUTH MOLTON STREET, MAYFAIR
LONDON W1K 5SB
{T} 020 7495 5211
ASSISTANT@KELLY-MANAGEMENT.COM
WWW.KELLY-MANAGEMENT.COM
FOUNDED: 2006
NO. OF CLIENTS: 25

KEW PERSONAL MANAGEMENT
KEW PERSONAL MANAGEMENT
PO BOX 56584
LONDON SW18 9GE
{T} 020 8871 3697
INFO@KEWPERSONALMANAGEMENT.COM
WWW.KEWPERSONALMANAGEMENT.COM
FOUNDED: 2005
NO. OF CLIENTS: 25

KEYLOCK MANAGEMENT
16 BULBECKS WALK
SOUTH WOODHAM FERRERS
ESSEX CM3 5ZN
{T} 01245 321638
AGENCY@KEYLOCKMANAGEMENT.COM
FOUNDED: 2008
NO. OF CLIENTS: 80

KMC AGENCIES LTD
HEAD OFFICE: PO BOX 122
48 GREAT ANCOATS STREET
MANCHESTER M4 5AB
{T} 0161 237 3009
CASTING@KMCAGENCIES.CO.UK
FOUNDED: 1996

LAINE MANAGEMENT
LAINE HOUSE
131 VICTORIA ROAD
SALFORD M6 8LF
{T} 0161 7897775
SAM@LAINEMANAGEMENT.CO.UK
WWW.LAINEMANAGEMENT.CO.UK
FOUNDED: 1980
NO. OF CLIENTS: 1500

LAKESIDE CASTING AGENCY
TOF FLOOR
63 SCOTLAND ROAD
CARLISLE CA3 9HT
INFO@LAKESIDECASTINGS.COM

LANGLAND
THE QUADRANT
55-57 HIGH STREET
WINDSOR SL4 1LP
{T} 01753 833348
ANDREW.SPURGEON@LANGLAND.CO.IUK
WWW.LANGLAND.CO.UK
FOUNDED: 1991
NO. OF CLIENTS: 20

LAURA WOODHOUSE MANAGEMENT
8 FLORA GROVE
ST ALBANS
HERTS AL1 5ET
{T} 01234 249710
LOLLY.WOODHOUSE@BTINTERNET.COM
FOUNDED: 2003
NO. OF CLIENTS: 10

LEADING ROLE AGENCY LTD
37A ALEXANDRA ROAD
PENN
WOLVERHAMPTON WV4 5UA
{T} 01902 565866
LEADINGROLEAGENCY@TISCALI.CO.UK
FOUNDED: 2008
NO. OF CLIENTS: 7

LEEDS LIMELIGHT AGENCY
18 KING EDWARD C RESCENT
HORSFORTH
LEEDS LS18 4BE
{T} 0113 2253187
ROBERT@LEEDSLIMELIGHT.COM
FOUNDED: 1998
NO. OF CLIENTS: 9

LEIGH MANAGEMENT
14 ST DAVIDS DRIVE
EDGWARE
ENGLAND HA7 3NY
{T} 020 8951 4449
LEIGHMANAGEMENT@AOL.COM

LIBERTY MANAGEMENT
4 OXCLOSE DRIVE
DRONFIELD
DERBYSHIRE S18 8XP
{T} 0114 2899151
OFFICE@LIBERTYMANAGEMENT.CO.UK
WWW.LIBERTYMANAGEMENT.CO.UK
FOUNDED: 2005
NO. OF CLIENTS: 70

LIGHT CAMERA ACTION
27 ASPEN GREEN
HUNTINGDON
CAMBRIDGESHIRE PE29 1GN
{T} 01480 411790
JOHN@LIGHTCAMERAACTION.CO.UK
WWW.LIGHTCAMERAACTION.CO.UK
FOUNDED: 2008
NO. OF CLIENTS: 34

LILLIAN MAY ASSOCIATES
59 HENSHAW STREET
LONDON
SE17 1PE
{T} 020 7703 8442
LILLIAN.MAY.ASSOCIATES@HOTMAIL.CO.UK
FOUNDED: 2006
NO. OF CLIENTS: 10

LIME ACTORS AGENCY & MANAGEMENT
NEMESIS HOUSE
MANCHESTER M2 3WQ
{T} 0161 236 0827
GEORGINA@LIMEMANAGEMENT.CO.UK
FOUNDED: 1999
NO. OF CLIENTS: 70

LINKS MANAGEMENT
34-68 COLOMBO STREET
LONDON
SE1 8DP
{T} 020 7928 0806
AGENT@LINKS-MANAGEMENT.CO.UK
WWW.LINKS-MANAGEMENT.CO.UK
FOUNDED: 1984
NO. OF CLIENTS: 20

LINKSIDE AGENCY
21 POPLAR ROAD,
LEATHERHEAD
SURREY KT22 8SF
{T} 01372 802374
LINKSIDE_AGENCY@YAHOO.CO.UK
FOUNDED: 1988
NO. OF CLIENTS: 40

LINTON MANAGEMENT
CAROL@LINTON.TV
WWW.LINTONMANAGEMENT.CO.UK
FOUNDED: 1991
NO. OF CLIENTS: 15

LISA D MANAGEMENT
SUMMIT HOUSE
LONDON ROAD
BRACKNELL RG12 2AQ
{T} 01344 707 342
AGENTS@LISAD.CO.UK
FOUNDED: 2000
NO. OF CLIENTS: 40

LIZ BISSET MANAGEMENT
272 BATH STREET
GLASGOW
G2 4JR
{T} 0844 800 6662
LEE@LIZBISSETMANAGEMENT.CO.UK
FOUNDED: 1980
NO. OF CLIENTS: 350

LIZ HOBBS MANAGEMENT LTD
65 LONDON ROAD
NEWARK
NOTTS NG24 1RZ
{T} 08700 702 702
CASTING@LIZHOBBSGROUP.COM
WWW.LIZHOBBSGROUP.COM
FOUNDED: 1990
NO. OF CLIENTS: 50

LOUISE GUBBAY ASSOCIATES
26 WESTMORE ROAD
TATSFIELD
KENT TN162AX
{T} 01959 573080
LOUISE@LOUISEGUBBAY.COM
WWW.LOUISEGUBBAY.COM
FOUNDED: 2006
NO. OF CLIENTS: 50

M.E.P MANAGEMENT
1 MALVERN AVENUE
HIGHAMS PARK
LONDON E4 9NP
{T} 020 8523 3540
MEP@BTCLICK.COM
WWW.MEPMANAGEMENT.COM
FOUNDED: 2001
NO. OF CLIENTS: 24

MAC-10 MANAGEMENT
OFFICE 69
2 HELLIDON CLOSE
MANCHESTER M12 4AH
{T} 0161 275 9510
INFO@MAC-10.CO.UK
WWW.MAC-10.CO.UK
FOUNDED: 2001
NO. OF CLIENTS: 455

MAD DOG CASTING LTD
THIRD FLOOR
15 LEIGHTON PLACE
LONDON NW5 2QL
{T} 020 7482 4703
INFO@MADDOGCASTING.COM
WWW.MADDOGCASTING.COM
FOUNDED: 1999
NO. OF CLIENTS: 2500

MAIN ARTISTS
34 SOUTH MOLTON STREET
LONDON
W1K 5BP
{T} 020 7495 4955
ANDREW@MAINARTISTS.COM
FOUNDED: 2006
NO. OF CLIENTS: 43

MANAGEMENT 2000
11, WELL STREET
TREUDDYN
FLINTSHIRE CH7 4NH
{T} 01352 771231
JACKEY@MANAGEMENT-2000.CO.UK
FOUNDED: 2000
NO. OF CLIENTS: 40

MARCUS & MCCRIMMON MANAGEMENT
1 HEATHGATE PLACE
75 AGINCOURT ROAD
LONDON NW3 2NU
{T} 020 7485 4040
INFO@MARCUSANDMCCRIMMON.COM
WWW.MARCUSANDMCCRIMMON.COM
FOUNDED: 1998
NO. OF CLIENTS: 50

MARGARET HOWARD AGENCY
HIGH STREET
BUSHEY
HERTS WD23 1TT
MHAGENCY@AOL.COM
FOUNDED: 2007
NO. OF CLIENTS: 60

MARK JERMIN MANAGEMENT
8 HEATHFIELD
SWANSEA
SA1 6EJ
{T} 01792 458855
INFO@MARKJERMIN.CO.UK
WWW.MARKJERMIN.CO.UK
FOUNDED: 2007
NO. OF CLIENTS: 500

MARKHAM & MARSDEN LTD
405 STRAND
LONDON
WC2R 0NE
{T} 020 7836 4111
INFO@MARKHAM-MARSDEN.COM
WWW.MARKHAM-MARSDEN.COM
FOUNDED: 1990
NO. OF CLIENTS: 60

MARLOWES
52B OAKBURY ROAD
HAMMERSMITH
LONDON SW6 2NW
{T} 020 7193 7227
MAIL@MARLOWES-AGENCY.COM
WWW.MARLOWES-AGENCY.COM
FOUNDED: 2008
NO. OF CLIENTS: 40

MAXIMILIAN MANAGEMENT AGENCY
37 PORTLAND MEWS
SANDYFORD
NEWCASTLE UPON TYNE NE2 1RW
{T} 0191 2611683
CONTACT@MAXIMILIANLTD.CO.UK
WWW.MAXIMILIANLTD.CO.UK
FOUNDED: 2007
NO. OF CLIENTS: 10

MBA
CONCORDE HOUSE
18 MARGARET STREET
BRIGHTON BN21TS
{T} 01273 685970
MBA.CONCORDE@VIRGIN.NET
WWW.MBAGENCY.O.UK
FOUNDED: 1960
NO. OF CLIENTS: 70

MCAMANAGEMENT
49 ST LEONARDS ROAD
EAST SHEEN SW14 7NQ
{T} 020 8241 4372
MCA.MANAGEMENT@YAHOO.CO.UK
FOUNDED: 2004
NO. OF CLIENTS: 20

McLAREN MANAGEMENT LTD
McLAREN HOUSE, TAY AVENUE
COMRIE, CRIEFF
PERTHSHIRE PH6 2FF
{T} 01764 671137
ENQUIRES@MCLARENMANAGEMENT.CO.UK
WWW.MCLARENMANAGEMENT.CO.UK
FOUNDED: 2000
NO. OF CLIENTS: 30

McLean-Williams Management
14 Rathbone Place
London W1T 1HT
{T} 020 7631 5385
ALEX@MCLEAN-WILLIAMS.COM
WWW.MCLEAN-WILLIAMS.COM
Founded: 2002
No. of clients: 60

MCS Agency Limited
47 Dean Street
Soho
London W1D 5BE
{T} 020 7734 9995
INFO@MCSAGENCY.CO.UK
WWW.MCSAGENCY.CO.UK
Founded: 1990
No. of clients: 200

MEMA Ltd
P O Box 259
Coventry
CV5 8YU
{T} 02476 715544
CHRISSY@MIDLAND-ENTERTAINMENT.COM
WWW.MIDLAND-ENTERTAINMENT.COM
Founded: 1994

MFL Agency Ltd
Windsor House
21 Richmond Place
Ilkley LS29 8TW
{T} 01943 430740
MFL.AGENCY@BLUEYONDER.CO.UK
Founded: 2003
No. of clients: 60

MGA Management
11/4 Abbdey Street
Edinburgh EH7 5XN
{T} 0131 466 9392
MURRAY@THEMGACOMPANY.COM
WWW.MGA-MANAGEMENT.COM
Founded: 2006
No. of clients: 10

MHM
Heather barn
Crerys Hill Lane
High Wycombe HP15 6AA
{T} 01494 711400
MHMAGENTS@GMAIL.COM
WWW.MHMAGENTS.COM
Founded: 2005
No. of clients: 35

Mia Thomson Associates
35 Central Avenue
Polegate
East Sussex BN26 6HA
{T} 01323 486 143
MIA@MIATHOMSONASSOCIATES.CO.UK
WWW.MIATHOMSONASSOCIATES.CO.UK
Founded: 2007
No. of clients: 20

Mitchell Maas McLennan
The Offices of Millennium Dance 2000
29 Thomas street
Woolwich, London SE18 6HU
{T} 020 8301 8745
AGENCY@MMM2000.CO.UK
Founded: 2005
No. of clients: 40

MODELSANDARTISTS.COM
2 CRANLEY GARDENS
SOUTH KENSINGTON
LONDON SW7 3DA
{T} 020 7373 6840
CASSY@MODELSANDARTISTS.COM

MORELLO CHERRY ACTORS AGENCY
25 PARK STREET
2ND FLOOR
MANCHESTER M3 1EU
{T} 0161 839 1454
APPLICATIONS@MCAA.CO.UK
HTTP://WWW.MCAA.CO.UK/
FOUNDED: 2006
NO. OF CLIENTS: 50

MORWENNA PRESTON MANAGEMENT
22 STREATHAM CLOSE
LONDON SW16 2NQ
{T} 020 8835 8147
INFO@MORWENNAPRESTON.COM
WWW.MORWENNAPRESTON.COM
FOUNDED: 2003
NO. OF CLIENTS: 40

MOUTHPIECE MANAGEMENT
PO BOX 145
INKBERROW
WORCESTERSHIRE WR7 4ZG
{T} 01527 850 149
KARIN@MOUTHPIECEMANAGEMENT.CO.UK
WWW.MOUTHPIECEMANAGEMENT.CO.UK
FOUNDED: 2007
NO. OF CLIENTS: 44

MV MANAGEMENT
RALPH RICHARDSON MEMORIAL STUDIOS
KINGFISHER PLACE, CLARENDON ROAD
WOOD GREEN, LONDON N22 6XF
{T} 020 8889 8231
THEAGENCY@MOUNTVIEW.AC.UK
FOUNDED: 2001
NO. OF CLIENTS: 21

MWM UK LTD
UNIT 1 RUSHTON FARM
WARREN HOUSE ROAD
WOKINGHAM, BERKS RG40 5RE
{T} 01189 788884
KAREN@MWM-UK.COM
WWW.MWM-UK.COM
FOUNDED: 2004
NO. OF CLIENTS: 88

NADOBRA MANAGEMENT
270A MITCHAM ROAD
SW17 9NT
{T} 07870 901362
CASTING@NADOBRA.COM
HTTP://WWW.NADOBRA.COM/MGMT
FOUNDED: 2008
NO. OF CLIENTS: 5

NANCY HUDSON ASSOCIATES LTD
P O BOX 1344, HIGH WYCOMBE NORTH
BUCKS HP11 9ER
{T} 020 7499 5548
AGENTS@NANCYHUDSONASSOCIATES.COM
WWW.NANCYHUDSONASSOCIATES.COM
FOUNDED: 1999
NO. OF CLIENTS: 70

NATASHA STEVENSON MANAGEMENT
STUDIO 7C, CLAPHAM NORTH ARTS CENTRE
VOLTAIRE ROAD
LONDON SW4 6DH
{T} 020 7720 3355
INBOX@NATASHASTEVENSON.CO.UK
NATASHA.STEVENSON@NATASHASTEVENSON.CO.UK
FOUNDED: 1998
NO. OF CLIENTS: 90

NE REPRESENTATION
3 - 5 BAKEHOUSE HILL
DARLINGTON
COUNTY DURHAM DL1 5QA
{T} 01325 488385
ALLISON@NEREPRESENTATION.CO.UK
HTTP://WWW.NEREPRESENTATION.CO.UK
FOUNDED: 2006
NO. OF CLIENTS: 50

NELSON BROWNE MANAGEMENT LTD.
40 BOWLING GREEN LANE
LONDON EC1R 0NE
{T} 020 7970 6010
ENQUIRIES@NELSONBROWNE.COM
WWW.NELSONBROWNE.COM
FOUNDED: 2007
NO. OF CLIENTS: 90

NEW FACES LTD
2ND FLOOR, THE LINEN HALL
162-168 REGENT STREET
LONDON W1B 5TB
{T} 020 7439 6900
VAL@NEWFACESTALENT.CO.UK
FOUNDED: 2000
NO. OF CLIENTS: 35

NEXT DIRECTION LTD
180 BARRIER POINT ROAD
LONDON
E16 2SE
{T} 020 7476 0401
NEXTDIRECTION@AOL.COM
FOUNDED: 2000
NO. OF CLIENTS: 4

NFD THE FILM AND TV AGENCY
PO BOX 76
LEEDS LS25 9AG
{T} 01977 681949
ALYSON@NFDPRODUCTIONS.COM
WWW.FILM-TV-AGENCY.COM
FOUNDED: 1987
NO. OF CLIENTS: 300

NIC KNIGHT MANAGEMENT
23 BUCKLER COURT
EDEN GROVE
LONDON N7 8EF
{T} 0203 093 5422
ENQUIRIES@NICKNIGHTMANAGEMENT.COM
FOUNDED: 2007
NO. OF CLIENTS: 25

NIGEL CLARE MANAGEMENT
PO BOX 1000
LINCOLN LN5 5GZ
{T} 01522 537893/575600
NIGEL@NIGELCLAREENTS.CO.UK
WWW.NIGELCLAREENTS.CO.UK
FOUNDED: 2000
NO. OF CLIENTS: 14

NJR MANAGEMENT
PO BOX 147
MALVERN
WORCS WR13 6YP
{T} 01684-541887
NIKKI@NJRMANAGEMENT.COM
WWW.NJRMANAGEMENT.COM
FOUNDED: 2004
NO. OF CLIENTS: 40

NORRIE CARR AGENCY
HOLBORN STUDIOS
49 EAGLE WHARF RD
N1 7ED
{T} 020 7253 1771
INFO@NORRIECARR.COM
WWW.NORRIECARR.COM
FOUNDED: 1963
NO. OF CLIENTS: 800

NORTH OF WATFORD
BRIDGE MILLS
HEBDEN BRIDGE
WEST YORKSHIRE HX7 8EX
{T} 01422 845361
INFO@NORTHOFWATFORD.COM
FOUNDED: 1984
NO. OF CLIENTS: 24

NORTH WEST ACTORS
36 LORD STREET, RADCLIFFE
MANCHESTER M26 3BA
{T} 0161 724 6625
INFO@NORTHWESTACTORS.CO.UK
WWW.NORTHWESTACTORS.CO.UK
FOUNDED: 2007
NO. OF CLIENTS: 26

NORTHONE MANAGEMENT
HG08 ABERDEEN CENTRE
HIGHBURY GROVE
LONDON N5 2EA
{T} 020 7359 9666
ACTORS@NORTHONE.CO.UK
WWW.NORTHONE.CO.UK
FOUNDED: 1986
NO. OF CLIENTS: 24

NS ARTISTES' MANAGEMENT
10 CLAVERDON HOUSE
HOLLY BANK ROAD, BILLESLEY
BIRMINGHAM B13 0QY
{T} 0121 684 5607
NSMANAGEMENT@FSMAIL.NET
WWW.NSARTISTESMANAGEMENT.CO.UK
FOUNDED: 2005
NO. OF CLIENTS: 50

NYLAND MANAGEMENT
20 SCHOOL LANE
HEATON CHAPEL
STOCKPORT SK4 5DG
{T} 0161 442 2224
NYLANDMGMT@FREENET.CO.UK
WWW.NYLANDMANAGEMENT.COM
FOUNDED: 1986
NO. OF CLIENTS: 60

O9 MANAGEMENT LTD
2ND FLOOR ST ANNES BUSINESS CENTRE
RICHMOND ROW
LIVERPOOL L3 3BL
{T} 0871 789 2009
PAUL@O9MANAGEMENT.TV
WWW.O9MANAGEMENT.TV
FOUNDED: 2008
NO. OF CLIENTS: 6

OBJECTIVE TALENT MANAGEMENT
3RD FLOOR, RIVERSIDE BUILDING
COUNTY HALL, WESTMINSTER BRIDGE ROAD
LONDON SE1 7PB
{T} 020 7202 2300
CORRIE@OBJECTIVETALENTMANAGEMENT.COM
FOUNDED: 2007
NO. OF CLIENTS: 5

OCEANA TELEVISION & MEDIA LTD
TECHNOLOGY HOUSE
AMPTHILL ROAD
BEDFORD MK42 9QQ
{T} 01234 327957
LESA.BROWN@OCEANATVLTD.COM
FOUNDED: 2005
NO. OF CLIENTS: 15

OI OI AGENCY
THE COACH HOUSE
PINEWOOD FILM STUDIOS
PINEWOOD ROAD, IVER, BUCKS SL6 6DA
{T} 01753 655514
HELEN@OIOI.ORG.UK
WWW.OIOI.ORG.UK
FOUNDED: 2004
NO. OF CLIENTS: 400

ONSCREEN-AGENCY.COM
NO.199
LANSDOWNE ROW, MAYFAIR
LONDON W1J 6HL
{T} 020 7193 7547
INFO@ONSCREENAGENCY.COM
WWW.ONSCREENAGENCY.COM
FOUNDED: 2004
NO. OF CLIENTS: 15

OREN
CHAPTER ARTS CENTRE
MARKET PLACE
CARDIFF CF5 1QE
{T} 0845 459 1420
ADMIN@OREN20.COM
WWW.OREN20.COM
FOUNDED: 1984
NO. OF CLIENTS: 20

ORR MANAGEMENT AGENCY
1ST FLOOR 147/149 MARKET ST
FARNWORTH BOLTON
BL4 8EX
{T} 01204 579842
BARBARA@ORRMANAGEMENT.CO.UK

OTTO PERSONAL MANAGEMENT LTD
OFFICE 2, SHEFFIELD INDEPENDENT FILM
5 BROWN STREET
SHEFFIELD S1 2BS
{T} 0114 2752592
ADMIN@OTTOPM.CO.UK
WWW.OTTOPM.CO.UK
FOUNDED: 1985
NO. OF CLIENTS: 35

OUR COMPANY
ROOM 205, CHANNELSEA HOUSE
CANNING ROAD
STRATFORD, LONDON E15 3ND
{T} 020 8221 1151
INFO@OUR-COMPANY.CO.UK
WWW.OUR-COMPANY.CO.UK
FOUNDED: 2006
NO. OF CLIENTS: 16

PAOLA FARINO
109 ST GEORGES ROAD
LONDON
SE1 6HY
{T} 020 7207 0858
INFO@PAOLAFARINO.CO.UK
WWW.PAOLAFARINO.CO.UK
FOUNDED: 2007
NO. OF CLIENTS: 18

PARK MANAGEMENT
UNIT C3
62 BEECHWOOD ROAD
LONDON
{T} 020 7923 1498
ACTORS@PARK-MANAGEMENT.CO.UK

PAT LOVETT ASSOCIATES
40 MARGARET STREET
LONDON W1G 0JH
{T} 020 7495 6400
INFO@PLA-UK.COM
FOUNDED: 1981
NO. OF CLIENTS: 150

PATRICK HAMBLETON MANAGEMENT
TOP FLOOR
136 ENGLEFIELD ROAD
LONDON N1 3LQ
{T} 020 7226 0947
CAROLYN@PHM.UK.COM
FOUNDED: 2006
NO. OF CLIENTS: 73

PAUL SPYKER MANAGEMENT
PO BOX 48848
COVENT GARDEN
LONDON WC1B 3WZ
{T} 020 7462 0046
BELINDA@PSMLOPNDON.COM
FOUNDED: 2008
NO. OF CLIENTS: 100

PAUL TELFORD MANAGEMENT
3 GREEK STREET
SOHO
LONDON W1D 4DA
{T} 020 7434 1100
INFO@TELFORD-MGT.COM
FOUNDED: 1993
NO. OF CLIENTS: 50

PELHAM ASSOCIATES
THE MEDIA CENTRE
9-12 MIDDLE STREET
BRIGHTON BN1 1AL
{T} 01273 323010
AGENT@PELHAMASSOCIATES.CO.UK
WWW.PELHAMASSOCIATES.CO.UK
FOUNDED: 1993
NO. OF CLIENTS: 55

PERFORMANCE ACTORS AGENCY
137 GOSWELL ROAD
LONDON
EC1V 7ET
{T} 020 7251 5716
PERFORMANCE@P-A-A.CO.UK
WWW.PERFORMANCEACTORS.CO.UK
FOUNDED: 1984
NO. OF CLIENTS: 35

PERFORMERS DIRECTORY AND AGENCY
PO BOX 29942
LONDON SW6 1FL
{T} 020 7610 6699
ADMIN@PERFORMERSDIRECTORY.CO.UK
FOUNDED: 1995
NO. OF CLIENTS: 1000

PH MANAGEMENT
1 CAMP ROAD
BRISTOL
BS8 3LW
{T} 020 8144 6369
MANAGEMENT@PHPRODUCTIONS.CO.UK
FOUNDED: 2007
NO. OF CLIENTS: 16

PHA CASTING
MANCHESTER M12 6FZ
{T} 0161 273 4444
CASTING@PHA-AGENCY.CO.UK
WWW.PHA-AGENCY.CO.UK
FOUNDED: 1969
NO. OF CLIENTS: 200

PHPM
184 BRADWAY ROAD
SHEFFIELD
SOUTH YORKSHIRE S17 4QX
{T} 0114 235 3663
PHILIPPA@PHPM.CO.UK
WWW.SPOTLIGHTAGENT.INFO/PHILIPPA-HOWELL
FOUNDED: 1996
NO. OF CLIENTS: 77

PICCADILLY MANAGEMENT
23 NEW MOUNT STREET
MANCHESTER M4 4DE
{T} 0161 953 4057
INFO@PICCADILLYMANAGEMENT.COM
WWW.PICCADILLYMANAGEMENT.COM
NO. OF CLIENTS: 50

PLATINUM ARTISTES
THE LODGE
66, ST LEONARDS ROAD
WINDSOR SL4 3BY
{T} 07860 573476
PLATINUMARTISTES@YAHOO.CO.UK
WWW.PLATINUMARTISTES.CO.UK
FOUNDED: 2008
NO. OF CLIENTS: 30

POSITIVE MEDIA AND MANAGEMENT
6 MEADENVALE
PETERBOROUGH
PE1 5PX
{T} 0871 2109757
INFO@POSITIVEMEDIAANDMANAGEMENT.COM
FOUNDED: 2004
NO. OF CLIENTS: 10

PRICE GARDNER MGT
PO Box 59908
LONDON
SW16 5QH
{T} 020 7610 2111
INFO@PRICEGARDNER.CO.UK
WWW.PRICEGARDNER.CO.UK
FOUNDED: 2000
NO. OF CLIENTS: 40

PURE MANAGEMENT LTD
44 SALISBURY ROAD
MANCHESTER M41 0RB
{T} 0161 747 2377
DEBBIE@PURE-MANAGEMENT.CO.UK
WWW.PURE-MANAGEMENT.CO.UK
FOUNDED: 2005
NO. OF CLIENTS: 40

RAMA GLOBAL LIMITED
HUNTINGDON HOUSE,
278-290 HUNTINGDON STREET,
NOTTINGHAM NG1 3LY
{T} 0115 952 4333
ADMIN@RAMA-MANAGEMENT.CO.UK
WWW.RAMA-MANAGEMENT.CO.UK
FOUNDED: 2005
NO. OF CLIENTS: 10

RANDALL RICHARDSON ACTORS
2ND FLOOR
145-157 ST JOHN STREET
LONDON EC1V 4PY
{T} 020 7060 1645
MAIL@RANDALLRICHARDSON.CO.UK

RAPID CASTING
16 ROCKLODGE GARDENS
ROKER
SR6 9NU
{T} 0191 5494678
RAPID@DBOX.CO.UK
WWW.RAPIDCASTING.CO.UK
FOUNDED: 2007
NO. OF CLIENTS: 44

RAPID TALENT
5 VANCOUVER ROAD
EASTBOURNE
EAST SUSSEX BN23 5BF
{T} 020 7734 5775
ENQUIRIES@RAPIDTALENT.CO.UK
WWW.RAPIDTALENT.CO.UK
FOUNDED: 2006
NO. OF CLIENTS: 750

RAW AGENCY
BIZZY HOUSE, 73A MAYPLACE ROAD WEST
BEXLEYHEATH
KENT DA7 4JL
{T} 020 8303 2627
CLIENTS@RAW-AGENCY.COM
WWW.RAW-AGENCY.COM
FOUNDED: 2001
NO. OF CLIENTS: 150

RAY KNIGHT CASTING
21A LAMBOLLE PLACE
LONDON
NW3 4PG
{T} 020 7449 2478
CASTING@RAYKNIGHT.CO.UK
FOUNDED: 1988

Agents P-R

RBA MANAGEMENT LTD
37-45 WINDSOR STREET
LIVERPOOL
L8 1XE
{T} 0151 708 72 73
INFO@RBAMANAGEMENT.CO.UK
WWW.RBAMANAGEMENT.CO.UK
FOUNDED: 1995
NO. OF CLIENTS: 23

RBM
RBM
3RD FLOOR
168 VICTORIA STREET, LONDON SW1E 5LB
{T} 020 7630 7733
INFO@RBMACTORS.COM
WWW.RBMACTORS.COM
FOUNDED: 1987
NO. OF CLIENTS: 16

REALITY CHECK MANAGEMENT LTD
PARAMOUNT BUILDING
206-212 ST JOHN STREET
LONDON EC1V 4JY
{T} 020 7324 1450
INFO@REALITYCHECK-M.COM
WWW.REALITYCHECKMANAGEMENT.COM
NO. OF CLIENTS: 200

REGAN RIMMER MANAGEMENT
SUITE 4, LITTLE RUSSELL HOUSE
22 LITTLE RUSSELL STREET
LONDON WC1A 2HS
{T} 020 7404 9957
THEGIRLS@REGAN-RIMMER.CO.UK
FOUNDED: 2001
NO. OF CLIENTS: 100

RHINO MANAGEMENT
STUDIO HOUSE
DELAMARE ROAD
CHESHUNT, HERTS EN8 9SH
{T} 0845 362 5456
RHINO-RPM2@HOTMAIL.COM
FOUNDED: 2003
NO. OF CLIENTS: 25

RICH VOICES
14 PRINCE REGENT MEWS
LONDON NW1 3EW
{T} 020 7387 4782 EXT 2
FRANCESCA@RICHVOICES.BIZ
FOUNDED: 2003
NO. OF CLIENTS: 90

RICHARD KORT MANAGAMENT
THEATRE HOUSE
2-4 CLASKETGATE
LINCOLN LN2 1JS
{T} 01522 526888
RICHARDKORT@DIAL.PIPEX.COM
WWW.RICHARDKORTASSOCIATES.COM
FOUNDED: 2005
NO. OF CLIENTS: 50

RITA WALKER MANAGEMENT
34 DOVERS GREEN ROAD
REIGATE
SURREY RH2 8BT
{T} 01737 248313
RITAWALKER@NTLWORLD.COM
FOUNDED: 2008
NO. OF CLIENTS: 2

ROB GROVES PERSONAL MANAGEMENT
3 MELBOURNE HOUSE
SALENTO CLOSE
LONDON N3 1BX
{T} 020 8349 0111
ROB@ROBGROVES.CO.UK
WWW.ROBGROVES.CO.UK
FOUNDED: 2008
NO. OF CLIENTS: 42

ROBERTA KANAL AGENCY
82 CONSTANCE ROAD
TWICKENHAM
TW2 7JA
{T} 020 8894 2277
ROBERTA@KANAL.FSNET.CO.UK
FOUNDED: 1970

ROSEBERY MANAGEMENT
HOXTON HALL
130 HOXTON STREET
LONDON N1 6SH
{T} 020 7684 0187
ADMIN@ROSEBERYMANAGEMENT.COM
WWW.ROSEBERYMANAGEMENT.COM
FOUNDED: 1984
NO. OF CLIENTS: 30

ROSSMORE MANAGEMENT
70-76 BELL STREET
LONDON
NW1 6SP
{T} 020 7258 1953
AGENTS@ROSSMOREMANAGEMENT.COM
WWW.ROSSMOREMANAGEMENT.COM
FOUNDED: 1993

ROUGH HANDS AGENCY
29 JAMES STREET
EPPING
ESSEX CM16 6RR
{T} 01992 578835
ROUGHHANDSAGENCY@YAHOO.CO.UK
FOUNDED: 2003
NO. OF CLIENTS: 12

ROWE ASSOCIATES
33 PERCY ST
LONDON
W1T 2DF
{T} 01992 308519
AGENTS@GROWE.CO.UK
WWW.GROWE.CO.UK
FOUNDED: 2003
NO. OF CLIENTS: 30

ROYCE MANAGEMENT
29 TRENHOLME ROAD
LONDON SE20 8PP
{T} 020 8778 6861
OFFICE@ROYCEMANAGEMENT.CO.UK
WWW.ROYCEMANAGEMENT.CO.UK
FOUNDED: 1980
NO. OF CLIENTS: 40

RSM (CHERRY PARKER MANAGEMENT)
15 THE FAIRWAY
LEIGH ON SEA
SS9 4QN
{T} 01702 522647
INFO@RSM.UK.NET
WWW.RSM.UK.NET
FOUNDED: 1996
NO. OF CLIENTS: 26

RUBICON MANAGEMENT
27 INDERWICK RD
CROUCH END
LONDON N8 9LB
{T} 020 8374 1836
JACK@RUBICONMGT.FSNET.CO.UK
FOUNDED: 1997
NO. OF CLIENTS: 40

RWM MANAGEMENT
THE ABERDEEN CENTRE
22-24 HIGHBURY GROVE
LONDON N1 2EA
{T} 020 7226 3311
RWM.MARIO-KATE@VIRGIN.NET
NO. OF CLIENTS: 60

SANDRA GRIFFIN MANAGEMENT
6 RYDE PLACE
RICHMOND ROAD
SURREY TW1 2EH
{T} 020 8891 5676
OFFICE@SANDRAGRIFFIN.COM
WWW.SANDRAGRIFFIN.COM

SANDRA HARRIS ASSOCIATES
171 CRANLEY GARDENS
N10 3AG
{T} 020 8444 6562
SANDRA@HIGHLYACCLAIMED.CO.UK
FOUNDED: 2005
NO. OF CLIENTS: 6

SANDRA REYNOLDS AGENCY
SHAKESPEARE HOUSE
168 LAVENDER HILL
LONDON SW11 5TF
{T} 020 7387 5858
INFO@SANDRAREYNOLDS.CO.UK
WWW.SANDRAREYNOLDS.CO.UK
FOUNDED: 1975
NO. OF CLIENTS: 150

SANDRA SINGER ASSOCIATES
21 COTSWOLD ROAD
WESTCLIFF-ON-SEA
ESSEX SS0 8AA
{T} 01702 331616
SANDRASINGERUK@AOL.COM
WWW.SANDRASINGER.COM
NO. OF CLIENTS: 90

SANGWIN ASSOCIATES
8-30 GALENA ROAD
HAMMERSMITH W6 0LT
{T} 020 8748 8698
INFO@SANGWINASSOC.COM
FOUNDED: 2000

SARA CROUCH MANAGEMENT
1 DUCHESS ST
LONDON
W1N 3DE
{T} 020 7436 4626
SARACROUCH@BTINTERNET.COM
FOUNDED: 1995

SASHA LESLIE MANAGEMENT
34 PEMBER ROAD
NW10 5LS
{T} 020 8969 3249
SASHA@ALLSORTSDRAMA.COM
FOUNDED: 1998

SAY TWO CASTING SOLUTIONS
UNIT 12, THE CARRINGTON CENTRE
THE GREEN, ECCLESTON, NR CHORLEY
LANCASHIRE PR7 5US
{T} 01257 453956
SAYTWOCASTINGSOLUTIONS@YAHOO.COM
FOUNDED: 1985
NO. OF CLIENTS: 40

SCOTT MARSHALL PARTNERS LTD
2ND FLOOR
15 LITTLE PORTLAND STREET
LONDON W1W 8BW
{T} 020 7637 4623
SMPM@SCOTTMARSHALL.CO.UK

SCOTT-NIVEN ASSOCIATES
43 FOXWARREN
ESHER
SURREY KT10 0JZ
THETEAM@SCOTT-NIVENASSOCIATES.COM
WWW.SCOTT-NIVENASSOCIATES.COM
FOUNDED: 2008
NO. OF CLIENTS: 5

SCOTT-PAUL YOUNG ENTERTAINMENTS LTD
NORTHERN LIGHTS HOUSE
110 BLANDFORD ROAD NORTH.
LANGLEY, BERKSHIRE. SL3 7TA
{T} 01753 693250
CASTINGDIRECT@SPY-ENTS.COM
WWW.SPY-ARTISTSWORLD.COM
FOUNDED: 1986
NO. OF CLIENTS: 122

SHANA GOLDMANS MANAGEMENT
PO BOX 23
SHIPBOURNE ROAD
TONBRIDGE TN11 9NY
{T} 01273 789252
CASTING@SHANA-GOLDMANS.CO.UK
WWW.SHANA-GOLDMANS.CO.UK
FOUNDED: 2004
NO. OF CLIENTS: 200

SHARON FOSTER MANAGEMENT
15A HOLLYBANK ROAD
BIRMINGHAM B13 0RF
{T} 0121 443 4865
MAIL@SHARONFOSTER.CO.UK
WWW.SHARONFOSTER.CO.UK
FOUNDED: 2006
NO. OF CLIENTS: 32

SHARRON ASHCROFT MANAGEMENT
SHARRON ASHCROFT MANAGEMENT
DEAN CLOUGH MILLS
HALIFAX HX3 5AX
{T} 01422 343949
INFO@SHARRONASHCROFT.COM
FOUNDED: 1996
NO. OF CLIENTS: 69

SHELLY EDEN ASSOCIATES
E10 5NQ
{T} 020 8558 3536
SHELLYEDEN@AOL.COM
FOUNDED: 2000
NO. OF CLIENTS: 15

SHINING MANAGEMENT LTD
12 D'ARBLAY STREET
LONDON
W1F 8DU
{T} 020 7734 1981
INFO@SHININGVOICES.COM
WWW.SHININGVOICES.COM
FOUNDED: 2002
NO. OF CLIENTS: 55

SIMON & HOW ASSOCIATES
90-92 LEY STREET
ILFORD
ESSEX IG1 4BX
{T} 0845 064 6666
SAM@SIMON-HOW.COM
WWW.SIMON-HOW.COM
FOUNDED: 2007
NO. OF CLIENTS: 20

SMILE TALENT
THE OFFICE
55 FITZWALTER PLACE
CHELMSFORD ROAD GREAT DUNMOW CB6 1HB
{T} 01371 876757 OR 879161
INFO@SMILETALENT.COM
WWW.SMILETALENT.BIZ
FOUNDED: 2001
NO. OF CLIENTS: 41

SOHO ARTISTES
THE LOFT, 204 VALLEY ROAD
LONDON SW16 2AE
{T} 020 7884 1295
INFO@SOHOARTISTES.COM
WWW.SOHOACTORS.CO.UK
FOUNDED: 2005
NO. OF CLIENTS: 2000

SOLOMON ARTISTES MANAGEMENT INTL
30 CLARENCE STREET
SOUTHEND ON SEA
ESSEX SS1 1BD
{T} 01702 437118
INFO@SOLOMON-ARTISTES.CO.UK
WWW.SOLOMON-ARTISTES.CO.UK
FOUNDED: 1995
NO. OF CLIENTS: 2000

SOUL MANAGEMENT
10 COPTIC STREET
LONDON WC1A 1NH
{T} 020 7580 1120
INFO@SOULMANAGEMENT.CO.UK
WWW.SOULMANAGEMENT.CO.UK
FOUNDED: 2004
NO. OF CLIENTS: 30

STAGE CENTRE LTD
41 NORTH RD
LONDON
N7 9DP
{T} 020 7607 0872
INFO@STAGECENTRE.ORG.UK
WWW.STAGECENTRE.ORG.UK
FOUNDED: 1982
NO. OF CLIENTS: 24

STAGEWORKS THE AGENCY
525 OCEAN BOULEVARD
BLACKPOOL
FY41EZ
{T} 01253 336429
SIMON.GEORGE@STAGEWORKSWWP.COM
WWW.STAGEWORKSWWP.COM
FOUNDED: 1975

STARSTRUCK MANAGEMENT
85 HEWSON RD
LINCOLN
LN1 1RZ
{T} 01522 887894
STARSTRUCKACADEMY@HOTMAIL.COM
FOUNDED: 2003
NO. OF CLIENTS: 30

STEPHANIE EVANS ASSOCIATES
RIVINGTON HOUSE
82 GREAT EASTERN STREET
LONDON EC2A 3JF
{T} 0870 609 2629
STEPH@STEPHANIE-EVANS.COM
WWW.STEPHANIE-EVANS.COM
FOUNDED: 2003
NO. OF CLIENTS: 50

STEVE DANIELS MANAGEMENT
OFFICE 9
284 HIGH ROAD
NORTH WEALD CM16 6EG
{T} 01992 522080
TALENT@STEVEDANIELSMANAGEMENT.CO.UK
WWW.STEVEDANIELSMANAGEMENT.CO.UK
FOUNDED: 2005
NO. OF CLIENTS: 8

STIRLING MANAGEMENT
37, OLDSTEAD GROVE
FERNCREST
BOLTON BL3 4XW
{T} 0845 017 6500
GLEN@STIRLINGMANAGEMENT.CO.UK
WWW.STIRLINGMANAGEMENT.CO.UK
FOUNDED: 2004
NO. OF CLIENTS: 20

SUSAN SHAPER MANAGEMENT
5 DOVEDALE GARDENS
465 BATTERSEA PARK ROAD
LONDON SW11 4LR
{T} 020 7585 1023
SHAPERMG@BTINTERNET.COM
FOUNDED: 1991
NO. OF CLIENTS: 50

SUSI EARNSHAW MANAGEMENT
68 HIGH STREET
BARNET
EN5 5SJ
{T} 020 8441 5010
CASTINGS@SUSIEARNSHAW.CO.UK
WWW.SUSIEARNSHAW.CO.UK

SUZANNA BROWN MANAGEMENT LTD.
LOWER GROUND
15-16 MARGARET STREET
LONDON W1W 8RW
{T} 020 7436 8506
SUZANNA@SUZANNABROWN.CO.UK
WWW.SUZANNABROWN.CO.UK
FOUNDED: 2006
NO. OF CLIENTS: 25

T*STA AGENCY
PO BOX 1013
HEMEL HEMPSTEAD
HERTS HP3 9YL
{T} 01442 250320
JOHN@T-STA.CO.UK
WWW.T-STA.CO.UK
FOUNDED: 2004
NO. OF CLIENTS: 100

TCG ARTIST MANAGEMENT
14A GOODWIN'S COURT
COVENT GARDEN
LONDON WC2N 4LL
{T} 020 7240 3600
INFO@TCGAM.CO.UK
FOUNDED: 1998
NO. OF CLIENTS: 70

THAMES VALLEY THEATRICAL AGENCY
DORCHESTER HOUSE, WIMBLESTRAW ROAD
BERINSFIELD
OXON OX10 7LZ
{T} 01865 340333
DONNA@THAMESVALLEYTHEATRICALAGENCY.CO.UK
NO. OF CLIENTS: 100

THE ACTORS GROUP
21-31 OLDHAM STREET
MANCHESTER
M1 1JG
{T} 0161 834 4466
AGENT@TAGACTORS.CO.UK
WWW.THEACTORSGROUP.CO.UK
FOUNDED: 1980
NO. OF CLIENTS: 21

THE BWH AGENCY LTD
BARLEY MOW CENTRE
10 BARLEY MOW PASSAGE
CHISWICK, LONDON W4 4PH
{T} 020 8996 1661
INFO@THEBWHAGENCY.CO.UK
FOUNDED: 2004

THE CASTINGS FACTORY
1 VICTORIA STREET
LIVERPOOL
L2 5QA
{T} 0151 2273866
MICHELLE@CASTINGSFACTORY.CO.UK
WWW.CASTINGSFACTORY.CO.UK
FOUNDED: 2006
NO. OF CLIENTS: 250

THE COMMERCIAL AGENCY
{T} 020 7233 8100
MAIL@THECOMMERCIALAGENCY.CO.UK
WWW.THECOMMERCIALAGENCY.CO.UK
FOUNDED: 2002
NO. OF CLIENTS: 150

THE HARRIS AGENCY LTD
71 THE AVENUE
WATFORD, HERTFORDSHIRE WD17 4NU
{T} 01923 211644
THEHARRISAGENCY@BTCONNECT.COM
FOUNDED: 1977
NO. OF CLIENTS: 50

THE IDENTITY AGENCY GROUP
112A CHOBHAM ROAD
LONDON E15 1LZ
{T} 020 8555 5171
CASTING@IDENTITYDRAMASCHOOL.COM
FOUNDED: 2003
NO. OF CLIENTS: 50

THE JACQUELINE CHADWICK AGENCY
OAKDENE STUDIOS, BREWERY LANE
LEIGH
LANCASHIRE WN7 2RJ
{T} 01942 67 57 47
CHADWICKACADEMY@BTCONNECT.COM
FOUNDED: 1998
NO. OF CLIENTS: 400

THE NARROW ROAD COMPANY
3RD FLOOR
76 NEIL STREET
LONDON WC2H 9PL
{T} 020 7379 9598/020 7379 9586
AGENTS@NARROWROAD.CO.UK
FOUNDED: 1986

THE VOICEOVER GALLERY
24 HAWGOOD STREET
LONDON E3 3RU
{T} 020 7987 0951
LONDON@THEVOICEOVERGALLERY.CO.UK
FOUNDED: 2004
NO. OF CLIENTS: 85

THE W-A-P-A AGENCY
6-8 ACKROYD PLACE
HALIFAX HX1 1YH
{T} 01422 351958
ENQUIRES@W-A-P-A.CO.UK
WWW.W-A-P-A.CO.UK
FOUNDED: 2006
NO. OF CLIENTS: 90

THE YOUNG ACTORS COMPANY LTD
Y.A.C. HOUSE
3 MARSHALL ROAD
CAMBRIDGE CB1 7TY
{T} 01223 416474
STEPHEN@THEYOUNGACTORSCOMPANY.COM
WWW.THEYOUNGACTORSCOMPANY.COM
FOUNDED: 1991

TIM SCOTT PERSONAL MANAGEMENT
284 GRAYS INN ROAD
LONDON
WC1X 8EB
{T} 020 7833 5733
TIMSCOTT@BTINTERNET.COM

TONICHA LAWRENCE AGENCY
SERENISSIMA
CHURCH HILL
THORNER LS14 3EG
{T} 0113 2893433
TONICHALAWRENCE@FASTMAIL.CO.UK
FOUNDED: 2007
NO. OF CLIENTS: 25

TOP TALENT AGENCY
P.O. BOX 860
ST. ALBANS AL4 9AZ
{T} 01727 812666
TOPTALENT@YMAIL.COM
FOUNDED: 2008
NO. OF CLIENTS: 67

TOTAL VANITY
35 WYVENHOE ROAD
HARROW
MIDDLESEX HA2 8LR
TERESA.HELLEN@TOTALVANITY.COM
FOUNDED: 2003
NO. OF CLIENTS: 55

TWO'S COMPANY
244 UPLAND ROAD
LONDON
SE22 0DN
{T} 020 8299 4593
2SCOMPANY@BRITISHLIBRARY.NET
FOUNDED: 2004
NO. OF CLIENTS: 6

UBIQUITOUS MANAGEMENT
CASTLEMEAD
LOWER CASTLE STREET
BRISTOL BS1 3AG
{T} 0117 917 5267
INFO@UBIQUITOUSMANAGEMENT.COM
WWW.UBIQUITOUSMANAGEMENT.COM
FOUNDED: 1990
NO. OF CLIENTS: 22

UNITED CASTING
FILM CITY
GLASGOW
G51 2LY
PAUL@UNITEDCASTING.CO.UK
WWW.UNITEDCASTING.CO.UK
FOUNDED: 1999
NO. OF CLIENTS: 700

URBAN TALENT
NEMESIS HOUSE
1 OXFORD COURT, BISHOPSGATE
MANCHESTER M2 3WQ
{T} 0161 228 6866
LIZ@NMSMANAGEMENT.CO.UK
WWW.URBANTALENT.TV
FOUNDED: 1996

VA MANAGEMENT
SAVANT HOUSE
63-65 CAMDEN HIGH STREET
LONDON NW1 7JL
{T} 020 7383 5050
INFO@VICIOUSMANAGEMENT.COM
WWW.VICIOUSMANAGEMENT.COM
FOUNDED: 2003
NO. OF CLIENTS: 45

VALERIE BROOK AGENCY
10 SANDRINGHAM ROAD
CHEADLE HULME
CHESHIRE SK8 5NH
{T} 0161 4861 631
COLINBROOK@FREENETNAME.CO.UK
FOUNDED: 1996
NO. OF CLIENTS: 120

VERTAS PERSONAL MANAGMENT
17 CHAPEL FIELD
GAMLINGAY
SG19 3QP
{T} 01767 650349
INFO@VERTASPM.COM
WWW.VERTASPM.COM
FOUNDED: 2008
NO. OF CLIENTS: 20

VSA
186 SHAFTESBURY AVENUE
LONDON
WC2H 8JB
INFO@VSALTD.COM
WWW.VSALTD.COM

W-A-P-A AGENCY
6-8 AKROYD PLACE
HALIFAX
WEST YORKSHIRE HX1 1YH
{T} 01422 351958
ENQUIRIES@W-A-P-A.CO.UK
WWW.W-A-P-A-.CO.UK
FOUNDED: 2006
NO. OF CLIENTS: 150

WARING & MCKENNA
11-12 DOVER STREET
LONDON
W1S 4LJ
{T} 020 7629 6444
DJ@WARINGANDMCKENNA.COM
WWW.WARINGANDMCKENNA.COM

WENDY LEE MANAGEMENT
2ND FLOOR
36 LANGHAM STREET
LONDON W1W 7AP
{T} 020 7703 5187
WENDY-LEE@BTCONNECT.COM
FOUNDED: 1999
NO. OF CLIENTS: 40

WEST CENTRAL MANAGEMENT
PANTHER HOUSE
38 MOUNT PLEASANT
LONDON WC1X 0AN
{T} 020 7833 8134
MAIL@WESTCENTRALMANAGEMENT.CO.UK
WWW.WESTCENTRALMANAGEMENT.CO.UK
FOUNDED: 1980
NO. OF CLIENTS: 20

WEST END MANAGEMENT
THE PENTHOUSE
42/17 SPERIS WHARF
GLASGOW G4 9TH
{T} 0141 331 1340
INFO@WEST-ENDMGT.COM
FOUNDED: 2000
NO. OF CLIENTS: 50

WILLIAMS BULLDOG MANAGEMENT LTD
38 HOPEWELL YARD
HOPEWELL STREET
LONDON SE5 7QS
{T} 020 7701 4326
DOM@WILLIAMSBULLDOG.CO.UK
FOUNDED: 1999
NO. OF CLIENTS: 16

WILLIAMSON & HOLMES
9 HOP GARDENS
ST MARTIN'S LANE
LONDON WC2N 4EH
{T} 020 7240 0407
JACKIE@WILLIAMSONANDHOLMES.CO.UK
FOUNDED: 1999
NO. OF CLIENTS: 30

WILLOW MANAGEMENT
151 MAIN STREET
YAXLEY
PETERBOROUGH PE7 3LD
{T} 01733 240392
PB@WILLOWMANAGEMENT.CO.UK

WINGS AGENCY
49, MIDHURST ROAD
FERNHURST
GU27 3EN
{T} 01428 658 900
ADMIN@WINGSAGENCY.CO.UK
FOUNDED: 1999
NO. OF CLIENTS: 50

Co-operative agencies

A co-operative agency is one run by actors themselves: a group of actors (usually 20 or so) working together to represent each other. Work such as answering the phone, administering the office and working contacts will be undertaken on a rota basis. Many co-operative agencies will charge commission at the lower end of the scale (closer to 10% than 20%), which can be attractive to an actor. While they can and do work, co-operative agencies may not always carry the same clout with casting directors as the more traditional agencies.

If the potential disadvantage of joining a co-operative agency is being less influential than mainstream agencies, there are advantages too: one is that members have more day-to-day involvement with their career management. Everyone in the co-op is invested in success and motivated by similar goals. Another advantage is that co-ops sometimes pursue a broader range of work, such as corporate and educational opportunities.

Think carefully about why you might want to join a co-op – that's sure to be one of the questions its existing members ask you in an interview. Don't be offended if you're asked to go through a probationary period – it's only reasonable that a group of people with a particular dynamic will want to make sure, for both parties' sake, that things will work out. Good communication between members of a co-op is vital to its success.

A-Z of co-operative agencies

1984 PERSONAL MANAGEMENT
BASED IN: LONDON
{T} 020 7251 8046
INFO@1984PM.COM
WWW.1984PM.COM
1984 is a co-operative personal management agency representing approximately 20 actors across film, theatre, television and commercials.

ACTORS ALLIANCE
BASED IN: LONDON
{T} 020 7407 6028
ACTORS@ACTORSALLIANCE.FSNET.CO.UK
WWW.ACTORSALLIANCE.CO.UK
Actors alliance is a co-operative agency providing representation to its members in the entertainment industry. Our aim is to provide helpful and accurate recommendations to casting professionals in the fields of film, television, theatre and corporate work.

ACTORS' CREATIVE TEAM
BASED IN: LONDON
{T} 020 7278 3388
OFFICE@ACTORSCREATIVETEAM.CO.UK
WWW.ACTORSCREATIVETEAM.CO.UK
Actors' Creative Team is a co-operative agency established in 2001 and is jointly owned and run by professional actors. Each member acts as an agent, representing colleagues and finding them work in every area of the profession.

ACTORS DIRECT
BASED IN: MANCHESTER, LEEDS, LONDON, SOUTH-WEST
{T} 0161 237 1904
INFO@ACTORSDIRECT.ORG.UK
WWW.ACTORSDIRECT.ORG.UK
Founded in 1994, Actors Direct has 25 members, with roughly equal numbers of men and women, mainly based around the north-west of England. Members are expected to have excellent office skills and a strong sense of team spirit. The group does not represent under 16s or walk on artists. Actors Direct is actively seeking submissions from mixed race, oriental, black and Asian actors.

ACTORS NETWORK AGENCY (ANA)
BASED IN: LONDON
{T} 020 7735 0999
INFO@ANA-ACTORS.CO.UK
WWW.ANA-ACTORS.CO.UK
ANA was established in 1985 and represents 20-30 actors in film, theatre, television and commercials.

89

Actors' Handbook 2009-10

ACTORUM
BASED IN: LONDON
{T} 020 7636 6978
INFO@ACTORUM.COM
WWW.ACTORUM.COM
Actorum was established in 1974 by
Danny Schiller and Vivienne Burgess. We
were the first actors' co-operative in the
United Kingdom. Over 30 years on,
Actorum remains the premiere co-
operative agency, constantly aiming to
provide a first class, personal,
knowledgeable and dynamic service
to the industry.

ALPHA PERSONAL MANAGEMENT
BASED IN: LONDON
{T} 020 7241 0077
ALPHA@ALPHAACTORS.COM
WWW.ALPHAACTORS.COM
Alpha Personal Management was
established in 1983, and is a co-operative
personal management agency repre-
senting approximately 20 actors across
film, theatre, television and commercials.

ARENA PERSONAL MANAGEMENT
BASED IN: LONDON
{T} 020 7278 1661
ARENAPMLTD@AOL.COM
WWW.ARENAPMLTD.CO.UK
arena is a professional, hard working,
actors' co-operative agency established
in the 1980s. We represent professionally trained or experienced performers.
We do not represent extras, models,
dancers or children.

AXM
BASED IN: LONDON
{T} 020 7837 3304
INFO@AXMGT.COM
WWW.AXMGT.COM
We are a non-profit organisation that
exists to represent its members' interests
in film, television, theatre, presentation,
roleplay, voiceover and all other areas of
performance arts. We are always
interested in hearing from actors from all
backgrounds who wish to join us.

CARDIFF CASTING
BASED IN: CARDIFF
{T} 02920 233321
ADMIN@CARDIFFCASTING.CO.UK
WWW.CARDIFFCASTING.CO.UK
Cardiff Casting, established in 1981,
represents approximately 20 actors
across film, theatre, television and
commercials.

CCM
BASED IN: LONDON
{T} 020 7278 0507
CASTING@CCMACTORS.COM
WWW.CCMACTORS.COM
Established in 1993, CCM represents
approximately 20 actors across film,
theatre, television and commercials.
When not working, we take turns in the
office – this is normally one day a week
fulfilling the following tasks; liaising with
casting directors; submitting clients for
current castings; and actively searching
for opportunities within the industry.

CIRCUIT PERSONAL MANAGEMENT
BASED IN: MIDLANDS/NORTH WEST
{T} 01782 285388
MAIL@CIRCUITPM.CO.UK
WWW.CIRCUITPM.CO.UK
Circuit is an Actors' Co-operative
established in 1988. Our client list is
primarily Midlands and North-West based,
working throughout the UK in theatre,
television, radio, voice-over, film and
corporates (both video and role-play).

CITY ACTORS MANAGEMENT
BASED IN: LONDON
{T} 020 7793 9888
INFO@CITYACTORS.CO.UK
WWW.CITYACTORS.CO.UK
London's premier co-operative agency
was established in 1982 and continues
to thrive.

CRESCENT MANAGEMENT
BASED IN: LONDON
{T} 020 8987 0191
MAIL@CRESCENTMANAGEMENT.CO.UK
WWW.CRESCENTMANAGEMENT.CO.UK
Crescent Management is a theatrical
agency dedicated to supplying profes-
sional, trained, talented actors for the
stage and screen. Established since 1991
and representing approximately 25 actors.

DENMARK STREET MANAGEMENT
BASED IN: LONDON
{T} 020 7700 5200
MAIL@DENMARKSTREET.NET
WWW.DENMARKSTREET.NET
Established in 1985, Denmark Street
Management has developed over the
years to become one of the UK's leading
co-operative agencies - specialising in
providing highly skilled professional
actors for theatre, film, television,
commercials and radio.

DIRECT LINE PERSONAL MANAGEMENT
{T} 020 8694 1788
DAPHNE.FRANKS@DIRECTPM.CO.UK
WWW.DIRECTPM.CO.UK
Founded in Leeds in 1985, Direct
Personal Management represents a
range of actors of varying ages and
types. All are experienced Equity
members. Our clients work in theatre,
film, television, radio, voice-over, video
and corporate projects. We do not
represent extras or walk-ons. Many of
our actors are from the North of
England and we also represent actors
from London and other areas including
Wales. Our actors work throughout the
United Kingdom and also internationally.

IML
BASED IN: LONDON
{T} 020 7587 1080
INFO@IML.ORG.UK
WWW.IML.ORG.UK
ML is a co-operative actors' agency, registered as a Friendly Society. It was founded in 1980, making it one of the oldest co-ops, as well as being one of the UK's most successful

INSPIRATION MANAGEMENT
BASED IN: LONDON
{T} 020 7704 0440
MAIL@INSPIRATIONMANAGEMENT.ORG.UK
WWW.INSPIRATIONMANAGEMENT.ORG.UK
We are an actors' co-operative agency, established in 1986, and have become one of the most respected and longest-running co-operatives in the country. Based in Islington (within easy reach of London's West End) we have over twenty members, representing a wide range of skills and experience.

LINKS MANAGEMENT
BASED IN: LONDON
{T} 020 7928 0806
AGENT@LINKS-MANAGEMENT.CO.UK
WWW.LINKS-MANAGEMENT.CO.UK
Established in 1984 and currently representing 17 actors, with work areas including film, television, theatre and commercials.

NORTH OF WATFORD
{T} 01422 845361
INFO@NORTHOFWATFORD.COM
WWW.NORTHOFWATFORD.COM
North Of Watford Actors' Agency is a co-operative agency representing actors living and working all over the United Kingdom.

NORTHONE MANAGEMENT
BASED IN: LONDON
{T} 020 7359 9666
ACTORS@NORTHONE.CO.UK
WWW.NORTHONE.CO.UK
NorthOne Management was founded as an actors agency in 1986. Since then its founding members have moved on, but bequeathed a wealth of accumulated experience, which the current members enjoy. It is only by the collective co-operation of the members that NorthOne flourishes, whether as an actor or an agent. This prerequisite of co-operation and involvement, we believe, also makes the actor a more professionally aware member of the industry.

OTTO PERSONAL MANAGEMENT
BASED IN: SHEFFIELD
{T} 0114 2752592
ADMIN@OTTOPM.CO.UK
WWW.OTTOPM.CO.UK
Otto Personal Management is an actors' co-operative management which was set up in Sheffield in 1985 and is now based in the heart of Sheffield's Cultural Quarter. Our actors have a wide and

varying history in all aspects of the
media industry. Theatre, Film, Television,
Radio, Voice over, Multimedia and
Corporate Videos etc.

PERFORMANCE ACTORS AGENCY
BASED IN: LONDON
{T} 020 7251 5716
PERFORMANCE@P-A-A.CO.UK
WWW.P-A-A.CO.UK
Founded in 1984, Performance Actors
Agency has built an outstanding
reputation of providing actors to the
industry. Run by actors, for actors,
Performance Actors Agency represents
talented, committed, and hard working
performers who have chosen to be part of
a team. Our members' work includes film
and television, the Royal Shakespeare
Company, repertory theatre and the West
End, corporate work, radio and voiceovers.

RbA MANAGEMENT
BASED IN: LIVERPOOL
{T} 0151 708 7273
INFO@RBAMANAGEMENT.CO.UK
WWW.RBAMANAGEMENT.CO.UK
RbA Management (formerly Rattlebag
Actors Agency) was launched in 1995
and has grown to become one of the
leading agencies in the north of
England, with credits in TV, film,
commercials, theatre and radio. RbA
Management is interested in hearing
from professional actors with a base in
the northwest of England. The agency
does not deal in extra or walk-on work.

STIVEN CHRISTIE MANAGEMENT
BASED IN: EDINBURGH
{T} 0131 228 4645
INFO@STIVENCHRISTIE.CO.UK
WWW.STIVENCHRISTIE.CO.UK
Formed in 1983, the business was
originally called The Actors Agency. It
was established by a group of young
Scottish based actors who wished to
learn more about the overall industry
within which they were working and to
aid them in this process the new agency
was set up as a co-operative
partnership. We promote our talent
across the entire spectrum of
performance media. Our clients can be
found in film, television, radio, theatre,
commercials, voice-over, presentation
and role-play projects. The Agency is run
as a commercial enterprise by the
partners Douglas Stiven and Simon
Christie who work from the offices
located in Dunfermline and associates in
Edinburgh and London

THE ACTORS FILE
BASED IN: LONDON
{T} 020 7278 0087
MAIL@THEACTORSFILE.CO.UK
WWW.THEACTORSFILE.CO.UK

The Actors File Co-operative Personal Management was created 21 years ago. As one of the first waves of co-operatives in Britain it was at the forefront of the changing face of representation. We do our utmost to stay there, remaining competitive and accessible. Started by five actors (three of whom are still with us) we now represent around 25 actors covering a wide range of types and skills.

THE ACTOR'S GROUP
BASED IN: MANCHESTER
{T} 0161 8344466
ENQUIRIES@THEACTORSGROUP.CO.UK
WWW.THEACTORSGROUP.CO.UK

The Actors' Group was formed in 1980 and was the first co-operative actors' agency outside of London. TAG (as the agency quickly became known) continues to work in all media nationally and internationally. Since its inception the agency has provided actors for work on the stages of the RSC, the RNT, The Old Vic, The Young Vic, The Royal Court and practically every regional Rep, as well as small/middle scale theatre, children's theatre and TIE, film and television. Our experienced membership ranges from young actors, to those middle-aged as well as established older actors. The age range spans 18 to 72.

THE CENTRAL LINE
BASED IN: NOTTINGHAM
{T} 0115 941 2937
CENTRALLINE@BTCONNECT.COM
WWW.THE-CENTRAL-LINE.CO.UK

The Central Line is a co-operative personal management agency formed in 1983 and based in Nottingham. We supply actors nationwide – most of them have London bases and are flexible and responsive

WEST CENTRAL MANAGEMENT
BASED IN: LONDON
{T} 020 7833 8134
MAIL@WESTCENTRALMANAGEMENT.CO.UK
WWW.WESTCENTRALMANAGEMENT.CO.UK

Established in 1984. Co-operative management representing 15-20 actors. Areas of work include theatre, musicals, television, film, commercials and corporate. Members are expected to work 4 days in the office per month. Will consider attending performances at venues within Greater London with 2 weeks' notice. Accepts submissions (with CVs and photographs) from actors previously unknown to the company sent by post or e mail. Will also accept invitations to view individual actors' websites.

Section 3
Applying for work

Casting directors

Casting directors are employed by directors and producers to sieve through the pool of acting talent and suggest the most appropriate actors for the part. Their job is to know the acting talent inside out and to facilitate meetings between potential candidates and the director. Armed with a character breakdown, they usually work with casting agents to shortlist suitable candidates who they think will match the role's requirements and the director's expectations.

By and large, casting directors will be brought in for specific projects (eg a film or theatre production) rather than employed on ongoing contracts. There are more than 250 casting directors in the UK, some working as individuals freelancing to production companies and others as part of larger collectives or companies. Many casting directors pride themselves on an encyclopaedic knowledge of actors and are renowned for keeping detailed notes on whoever crosses their path.

In the majority of cases the casting director does not choose or have final say over who gets a role. This is up to the director and the producer. It is in the casting director's interests to be on the side of the actor, as their reputation will be consolidated by a successful casting. The vision and choices displayed by a casting director will reflect well on them and enhance their standing in the industry, just as a poor pool of talent for casting sessions can damage their credibility.

In addition to sourcing actors, a casting director is also responsible for liaising with agents, directors and actors to schedule castings. They will often sit in on the castings and may give the actor tips beforehand on what the director will be looking for. It's important to listen to these – never forget that it's usually in the casting director's interest to get you the job just as much as it is yours, and they are likely to know more about what the director and producer will respond to.

Approaching casting directors

You can approach casting directors directly with a CV, photo and covering letter, but in many instances they will prefer to work through agents. Often they will request that your agent sends a showreel before deciding whether or not to bring you in for a casting.

They will, however, constantly be on the look out for promising new actors, and some may attend a production you are in or may occasionally be willing to meet with you if your CV is of a suitably promising calibre.

Rather than bombarding every casting director across the nation with your details unannounced, find out first whether they accept unsolicited contact from actors at all – some do, some don't. A brief, polite phone call or email should establish this, and remember to stick to what they say: some may want submissions by post only, others may accept them by email.

Details of many casting directors can be found at the Casting Directors' Guild website – **www.thecdg.co.uk** – though bear in mind the site is not directly aimed at actors. You could also keep an eye out in show and TV credits for casting directors' names.

CVs

To maximise your chances of being called in for an audition, it is vital you spend the time constructing a professional CV. While a headshot can give an employer some idea of your facial characteristics, the CV should show your versatility, experience, dependability and professionalism. Professionalism really is key here: no matter how suitable you may be for a role, a poorly spelt, structured or printed CV can quickly remove you from consideration.

The CV should start with your contact details and those of your agent if you have one. Where possible include your email address and mobile phone number, as casting directors often need to get in contact with potential cast at very short notice and a quick response time can be critical in securing an audition slot.

Next come your key physical characteristics, such as age, playing age, build, height, weight, hair color, eye color, ethnicity and native accent – though don't go overboard on the detail as your photograph will reveal some of it anyway. A simple statement such as 'tall with slim build' can sometimes convey more than a list of statistics. If you do decide to include your weight and height remember to include them in both metric (metres and kilos) and imperial (feet and pounds) format.

Whether you put your date of birth is debatable; some people think it can limit your options by precluding you for some roles in the mind of a casting director, whereas others think it should be included as a simple yardstick.

Finally you may wish to include your Spotlight number, your Equity status (whether or not you are a member) and whether or not you hold a valid UK driving licence in this section.

: : : ::

Playing age

Regardless of whether you include your actual age, you will need to include your playing age. Don't try to overstretch at this point and be honest: a playing age of 16 to 35 is simply unrealistic – do you really think you look both 16 and 35? A good rule of thumb is to limit the age range to a maximum of 10 years. Another test is to get independent advice. Send your photo to teachers, friends and colleagues and ask them to tell you honestly how old you look.

Credits and training

After these key contact details and physical characteristics you should include your credits and training. Again, some people prefer to put training first, others credits – it's up to you. As long as each section is clearly laid out and the CV isn't too long it shouldn't matter unduly, though we'd recommend that you lead with your credits – whatever your field, any employer or agent will look for your experience above all else. The ideal CV length is one page, so if you do need to cut back on credits, omit the oldest and least prestigious.

Credits should include the role you played (put this first), the production, the director, the venue, theatre company and the date (just the year will do). The norm is to list the most recent credits first as these are the most telling and the most relevant and there's no point keeping your big guns at the foot of the CV. If you have a number of credits across different genres you might want to list them under different sections (eg film, theatre, television, radio, corporate, commercials).

Above all, get the details right: historians may have identified more than 50 variations of the name Shaxper, but in the business 'Shakespeare' is what they expect! Avoid amateur productions if possible, or at least put these below professional experience.

Remember, first impressions are hard to reverse, so keep your CV clear, focused and honest. Don't exaggerate your role and certainly don't claim experience you've never had. Sure, a credit may slip through the net but most won't. Actors, agents, directors and casting directors are continually networking, working together professionally and meeting socially. There's every chance that lies will be found out and come back to haunt you.

Your training should include the institution, the course and the dates you attended and, if relevant, any awards or distinctions you received. It's not obligatory to include referees, though if you have a particularly prestigious referee (eg a respected actor, tutor or industry professional) it may help to include them.

Other skills

Additional skills and interests can be listed in a different section. These can be useful if you have genuine skills such as sporting abilities (horse riding is the classic), musical abilities or particular interests which may be valuable to a role. If you are confident in a range of regional or national accents, list these too, but you really need to be sure of your accuracy, or you'll soon get caught out. Don't list skills you don't have – at best you'll end up looking foolish, at worst you'll earn the reputation as a chancer or a liar. Applying for work is one part of acting where your ability to pretend should be suppressed!

Each of these sections should be clearly marked, with bold section titles so the reader can quickly establish where the key information can be found. However, don't go crazy with fancy layouts, big boxes and wacky typefaces – what people want to see is the information.

Check and check again

Before sending your CV to anyone, check the spelling and accuracy of all the information listed. Pass it to friends and family for a second opinion and further spell checking. Finally, ensure your name is clearly visible at the top of all pages. It should be clear from your layout that the document is a CV, so no need for the label "CV" anywhere – simply focus on the key information.

In general, remember the 15-second rule: that's probably how long your CV will be looked at in the first pass, and if you can get through to the second stage of a longer look, you're well on the way. Fifteen seconds might seem depressing – but think how quickly all of us form impressions of other people when we meet them.

Keep your CV simple and informative – this doesn't have to mean it's anonymous, and a good CV always reaches a balance between conveying the details of your experience and showing what sort of person you are.

Online CVs

A number of websites offer an online CV service. Professionally formatted, these CVs or online profiles generally allow you to enter then amend your credits, training, and at least one photo. Some of these websites include your CV in an online directory which is searchable by industry professionals and can offer a good level of exposure. Online CVs, to which you can direct people either with a link via email or a URL they can look up, can reduce the laborious task of faxing and mailing out your CV. Services of this kind specifically for actors include Spotlight and Casting Call Pro – see Section 7 for more details.

Bear in mind that this method of communication doesn't find favour with everyone. Some people won't want to receive CVs via email, preferring the more traditional paper copy. In general, any agent or casting director who specifies that they don't want submissions by email is perhaps less likely to be well disposed to going to a website for your details. If you're a young actor and used to doing everything online, remember that not everyone in the industry does things that way – acting is a field where personal contact counts a great deal.

Covering letters

Together with your headshot and your CV, the covering letter is your calling card. As such, it's important to set the right tone and create a good impression. While it's true that a good letter can really do you favours, it's also true that a bad, poorly presented letter can result in your application being dumped in the bin. Agents, directors and casting directors receive a mountain of unsolicited approaches and won't be able to devote more than a few moments to each, therefore it's essential that you don't give them any reason to dismiss your approach.

You might think that spelling and grammar are irrelevant and the real substance is in your acting ability, but before you get to show off your talents you need to be called to audition. You'll not get that far if you have been ruled out of the selection process by writing a poorly phrased, poorly presented letter riddled with mistakes. You'll be doing yourself a serious disservice if you send off a letter that's unprofessional in appearance and content.

BASIC DOS

- print rather than handwrite (unless you have exceptionally clear handwriting which would make you stand out)

- buy good quality paper (consider having a professional letterhead printed, too)

- personalise the letter with the name of the recipient

- check spelling and grammar

- check the factual content – eg names/addresses/contact nos

- read, read and read again before posting

- send it in a clean envelope and write the address neatly and legibly, with your return address on the back

- photocopy or keep an electronic copy for future reference and to keep tabs on who you've contacted.

Given that there will be dozens, hundreds or thousands of other letters you might wonder how you can distinguish yourself, and set your submission apart from the others. The tone of a letter is one of the most important elements and yet one of the hardest to get right. You don't want to sound sycophantic, arrogant, outlandish or zany. Including a keepsake or memento or some other such wacky device might raise a momentary smile in the office, but it's also likely to land you in the bin.

Instead, take an entirely professional approach. Start by finding out the name of the person to whom you're writing, and ensuring you know how to spell it correctly. Address your contact by their full name rather than by their first name or title.

Write in the first person singular (I) and adhere to the usual rules of grammar and letter writing. A standard letter will often start with your address at the top right, then the recipient's address (at the left-hand side of the paper) with the date opposite or beneath, followed by the greeting ("Dear Matt Barnes"), the body of the letter and concluded "Yours sincerely", with a space for your signature and

BASIC DON'TS

- don't address your letter to a generic title – eg Dear Sir/Madam
- don't be overly familiar/informal
- don't write a bog-standard, top and tailed letter which is clearly a generic mailing to all and sundry
- don't use meaningless or cliched phrases synonymous with dull covering letters – eg "for your perusal", "I implore/ beseech you", "you'll regret it if you don't give me the..."
- don't forget to sign the letter – an easy omission
- don't forget to include any other important materials – eg headshots/CV...
- ...but don't include anything else in the hope of getting attention
- don't forget to stamp the letter with the correct postage.

beneath that your name (printed). As you begin writing the body of your letter, be yourself but keep in mind that yours will be one of many and that the agent/director won't have the time or patience to read an essay. A letter should consist of a couple of clear, succinct paragraphs outlining why you are interested in the role/agency and why you think you're suitable and should be considered. Lay the text out neatly and clearly. Finally, consider inviting the recipient, if they're someone particularly influential, to an upcoming show you're in.

If you're sitting there thinking all this advice is obvious and you don't need it, remember that people overlook these watchwords time and time again – and they miss out on work because of it.

If your letter is accompanied by a headshot and CV, they'll have an idea of your look and your career to date, so don't simply parrot what the CV says. Writing a good letter is a fine line between being arid/uninformative and irritatingly verbose and/or self-aggrandising. When writing, try to think how it will come across to the reader, a person who doesn't know you. As with your CV, the letter is a balance between coming over as cold and clinical or being too gimmicky. Be to the point... but also be human. Once again, it's a good idea to run your draft by a friend or colleague for a second opinion before sending it.

Email letters

Email covering letters may lack the tactile and visual benefits of a good quality piece of letterheaded paper – but the rules of writing remain the same. Be brief and informative, explaining what you're applying for and why you'd be suitable, but don't make it sound like it's you that's the machine rather than the computer. It's worth putting your phone number in a signature at the bottom of the mail – some people like to put a voice to the applicant. Take extra care to read and spell-check an email letter, as you won't be able to beg the postman to stop it going out: pushing the button too quickly is all too easy.

If you're attaching a CV and photo, make sure you use standard file formats such as Word and JPG – never expect the recipient to be an IT expert. Most importantly, make sure they accept email submissions at all.

Headshots

The industry standard for photos is a black and white 10 x 8"
(25 x 20cm) headshot taken by a professional photographer. The
headshot will usually take in the top of your shoulders (but shouldn't
include the rest of your body) in a natural pose straight to camera,
clearly displaying your entire face. Most importantly the photo should
look like you. If you can't replicate the look on the photo when you're
called into audition at 6am on a Sunday then your headshot is not
doing you any justice. You need a headshot which shows the casting
director exactly what you look like. If you have a birthmark, mole or
wrinkle don't try and edit it out, embrace your individuality and let
your headshot provide the casting director with an honest representation of who you are.

Choosing a photographer
A good photographer may well cost in excess of £250 for a session
(and don't forget to check if they're VAT registered), so this is not
something to take lightly. It may sound expensive but it really does
need to be done properly. Before calling a photographer check their
website to see if they offer any discounts to students, recent
graduates, or Equity, Spotlight or Casting Call Pro members. Note also
that some casting websites offer their own photography service –
Casting Call Pro, for example, offers discounted professional
headshots to members.

Word-of-mouth recommendation counts for a lot – assuming there's
no commission involved, actors will only refer photographers whose
work they're happy with. Ask other actors where they've had their
headshots done, see which names crop up again and again and look
out for those who offer a professional, friendly service at competitive
rates. In addition, use online and offline directories to search for
examples of photographers' work, their prices and their location.
These days you'll find that most photographers and studios have a
website with examples of their work which you can browse before
parting with any cash. If you are considering going to a studio ask

which photographer you'll be working with and try to see examples of their work. Taking an actor's headshot is a pretty specific skill and something entirely different from modelling shots or wedding photography. Make sure your photographer knows what taking an actor's headshot involves and always ask to see examples of past work.

A great way to choose a photographer is to visit Casting Call Pro's resources section at **www.uk.castingcallpro.com/resources.php**.

What is included

When negotiating a fee – and it is worth an initial approach to see if there's room for negotiation – remember to factor in the number of shots the photographer will take, the number of prints included and the cost of extra copies: you don't want to be disappointed to receive five prints when you'd been expecting ten.

The photographer will own the rights to any of the photos they take of you, even though you pay for the initial session – another good reason to check how many prints you will get, as you are likely to have to pay for extra copies. Check at the start whether the photographer's charges for these are competitive. If you want to reproduce the picture in any form (eg online, in Spotlight, at Casting Call Pro or as publicity for a show) you will need to get permission from your photographer. They should also be credited whenever you display or print the picture: this is a legal obligation.

During the session

Make sure you get a good night's sleep before the session and arrive wearing clothes which make you feel comfortable, confident and relaxed. Ensure the clothes don't distract from your face (no loud shirts or patterned blouses). You may consider taking a collection of tops to ensure they capture the right 'you'. Don't wear too much make-up and don't get your hair cut the day before – give a new cut time to settle in. It is also sensible to avoid props, backgrounds and accessories – in fact, avoid anything which draws attention away from your face. Most good photographers will be able to advise you on such things, so do listen to them, as the good ones will have been doing this for many years.

A PHOTOGRAPHER'S TIPS

Professional headshot photographer Claire Grogan
(www. clairegrogan.co.uk) offers some useful pointers.

As an ex-actor myself I understand only too well the importance we all place on our headshots. We search for that elusive shot, the one that utterly captures our personality and uniqueness, the photo that covers every possible casting and makes us look absolutely fantastic! A lot to ask for, I know, but here are a few points to consider.

When choosing your photographer make sure you look at lots of different examples of their work and then choose one whose photos you really like with a style that you feel would suit you. Chat to them first on the phone and find out costs, location, how long the session times are and whether there's anywhere to change tops or adjust your hair/make up etc.

In terms of the film versus digital question, there's not a huge difference; both are great for Spotlight. I still prefer film but that's just a personal choice. Remember that final images from a film shoot can also be put on a CD as a digital scan – just ask your photographer if they can do this for you.

When deciding what to wear for your main shot choose a couple of fairly neutral/classic tops that you feel good in. Think carefully and honestly about your casting potential so you can wear a couple of other appropriate things to subtly suggest different looks such as professional/gritty/romantic etc. These work well for additional photos on your Spotlight portfolio. For females I recommend a fairly natural make-up to start with and then add more if you want a slightly more glam look later in the shoot. For males, just a bit of cover-up if you need it on the odd blemish or under-eye shadows.

Prepare yourself well for the shoot and try to get a good night's sleep – you won't get the best results if you turn up bleary eyed! Try as much as possible to relax and be yourself during the shoot; that way you should end up with some great shots to choose from.

Do make sure you look clearly at the camera, particularly so that your eyes can be seen fully – though don't stare or look vacant, of course! Your eyes are like the style in which you write your covering letter – they reveal a lot of your personality at a glance. Aim for a hint of a smile rather than something too full-on, otherwise it will come across as a bit 'too much' and perhaps mean your eyes are less noticeable.

Opinions differ on whether natural or artificial light works best, but many casting directors will prefer the former. Discuss it with your photographer – some will even take your picture out of doors.

Choosing a shot
When choosing a shot select one which looks most like you and which you think best reflects your look and talents. Ask the opinion of people you trust. While family and friends can be helpful and supportive, they may not be the best judges; better to ask fellow actors, your agent or the photographer.

If you've been given a digital image, check the size of the file: don't go emailing huge files of more than 1Mb to people as it can slow up their connection or go over their storage limit. If you're not confident with these technicalities, ask the photographer.

A-Z of photographers

10 OUT OF 10 PHOTOGRAPHY
14 FOREST HILL BUSINESS CENTRE
CLYDE VALE
LONDON SE23 3JF
{T} 0845 1235664
PAULJNEED@HOTMAIL.COM
WWW.PAULJNEED.CO.UK

AA TRUE PHOTOGRAPHY
FRESH FIELDS
WREKENTON
GATESHEAD NE9 7EL
{T} 0191 4910108
TRUE@BLUEYONDER.CO.UK
WWW.TRUESTILLS.COM

ACTOR SUCCESS
24A, BATHURST WALK
RICHINGS PARK
BUCKINGHAMSHIRE SL0 9AZ
{T} 01753 650939
INFO@ACTORSUCCESS.CO.UK
WWW.ACTORSUCCESS.CO.UK

ACTORHEADSHOTS.CO.UK
TOP FLOOR FLAT
66 WANSEY STREET
SE17 1JP
{T} 07740 507970
INFO@ACTORHEADSHOTS.CO.UK
WWW.ACTORHEADSHOTS.CO.UK

ACTORS PHOTOGRAPHY
PRESTWICH
MANCHESTER M25 9GL
{T} 0161 7737670
IAN-VERNON@FREEUK.COM
WWW.IAN-VERNON.FREEUK.COM/ACTORS.HTML

ACTORS WORLD PHOTOGRAPHIC
{T} 020 8998 2579
PHOTO@ACTORS-WORLD-PRODUCTION.COM
WWW.ACTORS-WORLD-PRODUCTION.COM

ADAM MATHESON PHOTOGRAPHY
13 EMPRESS DRIVE
HELENSBURGH
DUNBARTONSHIRE G84 8QL
{T} 07742 167229
ENQUIRY@MATHESONPHOTO.COM
WWW.MATHESONPHOTO.COM

ADAM PARKER
1 HOXTON HOUSE
34 HOXTON STREET
LONDON N1 6LR
{T} 020 7684 2005
CCP@ADAMPARKER.CO.UK
WWW.ADAMPARKER.CO.UK

ADE WARE PHOTOGRAPHIC
5, RECTORY COURT, BOTLEY
SOUTHAMPTON SO30 2SJ
{T} 07714 690736
ADRIAN_WARE@YAHOO.COM
WWW.MODELPHOTS.COM

ADRIAN QUESTER PHOTOGRAPHY
51A LOWER RICHMOND ROAD
PUTNEY
LONDON SW15 1ET
{T} 07786 448540
ADRIAN.QUESTER@GMAIL.COM
WWW.PBASE.COM/ADRIANQUESTER/PORTFOLIO

ALAN MCCREDIE PHOTOGRAPHY
STUDIO 4.08
ST MARGARET'S HOUSE
151 LONDON ROAD, EDINBURGH EH7 6AE
{T} 07720 330604
ALAN@ALANMC.CO.UK
WWW.ALANMC.CO.UK

ALAN STRUTT
ALANSTRUTT@YAHOO.COM
WWW.ALANSTRUTT.COM

ALASTAIR WIGHT PHOTOGRAPHY
15 ROTHESAY MEWS
EDINBURGH EH3 7SG
{T} 07985 558143
ALASTAIRWIGHT@GOOGLEMAIL.COM
WWW.ALASTAIRWIGHT.COM

ALISTAIR GUY PHOTOGRAPHY
MORTIMER CRESCENT
LONDON NW6 5NR
{T} 020 7419 6019
INFO@ALISTAIRGUY.COM
WWW.ALISTAIRGUY.COM

ALISTAIR HUGHES
23 VYNER STREET
LONDON
E2 9DG
{T} 020 8980 1224
ALISTAIR@ALISTAIRHUGHES.CO.UK
WWW.ALISTAIRHUGHES.CO.UK

ALVARO MARI-THOMPSON
STUDIO 49, STRATFORD WORKSHOPS
BURDFORD ROAD
LONDON E15 2SP
{T} 07968 928 640
ALVARO@HAUSHINKA.COM
WWW.ACTINGSHOTS.COM

AM-LONDON
3A GODOLPHIN ROAD
LONDON W128JE
{T} 020 8735 0540
CASEY@AM-LONDON.COM
WWW.AM-LONDON.COM

AMETHYST PHOTOGRAPHY
7 HAMBLETONIAN YARD
STOCKTON ON TEES
TS18 1DS
{T} 01642 887630
WAYNE@AMETHYST-PHOTOGRAPHY.ORG.UK

AMZI PHOTOGRAPHY
116 LEXINGTON BUILDING
FAIRFIELD ROAD
LONDON E3 2UE
{T} 020 8123 9988
CONTACT@AMZIPHOTOGRAPHY.COM
WWW.AMZIPHOTOGRAPHY.COM

ANDREW CHAPMAN PHOTOGRAPHY
198 WESTERN ROAD
CROOKES
SHEFFIELD S10 1LF
{T} 0114 2663579
ANDREW@CHAPMANPHOTOGRAPHER.ECLIPSE.CO.UK
WWW.ANDREWSPHOTOS.CO.UK

ANDY BRADSHAW
65 BRADBURN COURT
SE3 7TP
{T} 07734 323203
ANDY@ANDYBRADSHAW.COM
WWW.ANDYBRADSHAW.COM

ANGEL PARMAR PHOTOGRAPHY
21 WIGLEY RD
FELTHAM
MIDDLESEX TW13 5HD
{T} 07793 065248
INFO@ANGELPARMAR.COM
WWW.FLICKR.COM/PHOTOS/AJPHOTOGRAPHY

ANGUS DEUCHAR PHOTOGRAPHER
SW19 1EP
{T} 020 8286 3303
ANGUS@ACTORSPHOTOS.CO.UK
WWW.ACTORSPHOTOS.CO.UK

ANTHONY JONES
SE6 4UQ
{T} 07963 820021
MAIL@AJPHOTO.INFO
WWW.AJPHOTO.INFO/PAGES/PORTRAIT01.HTML

ANTHONY STRAEGER
14 GRANGECLIFFE GARDENS
LONDON
SE25 6SZ
ANTHONY@STRAEGERPHOTO.CO.UK
WWW.STRAEGERPHOTO.CO.UK

ANTHONY WILSON PHOTOGRAPHY
N6 5BN
{T} 07739 010615
ANTHONYWILSONPHOTOGRAPHY@GMAIL.COM

APPLE TREE PHOTOGRAPHY
58 ST PAUL'S AVENUE
BARRY
VALE OF GLAMORGAN CF62 8HT
{T} 07939 611157
APPLETREEPHOTOGRAPHY@GMAIL.COM

ARNETT-PHOTOGRAPHY
WEST KENSINGTON
LONDON
W14 9DX
{T} 07951 991530
ANETPHOTOGRAPHY@AIM.COM
WWW.ARNETT-PHOTOGRAPHY.COM

ARRANCORBETT.CO.UK
D/S/11
CREEK ROAD
DEPTFORD, LONDON SE8 3BU
{T} 020 8123 5609
ARRAN@ARRANCORBETT.CO.UK
WWW.ARRANCORBETT.CO.UK/PHOTOGRAPHY

ARTSHOT PHOTOGRAPHY
3 CONNAUGHT ROAD
WALTHAMSTOW
LONDON E17 8QB
ANGELA@ARTSHOT.CO.UK
WWW.ARTSHOT.CO.UK

AURELIE KOREN PHOTOGRAPHY
23 QUEENS ROAD
23 QUEENS ROAD N11 2QJ
{T} 07949 913759
AURELIEKOREN@BLUEYONDER.CO.UK
**WWW.AURELIEKORENPHOTOGRAPHY.WEBEDE
N.CO.UK**

AVOCADO PORTRAITS
25 HYNDLAND STREET
UNLIMITED STUDIOS LOWER LEVEL
GLASGOW G11 5QF
{T} 0141 416 2 416
INFO@AVOCADO-PORTRAITS.COM
WWW.AVOCADO-PORTRAITS.COM

BAKER ASHTON PHOTOGRAPHY
15 RECTORY RD
STOKE NEWINGTON
N16 7QL
{T} 07858 345775
BAKERASHTON89@HOTMAIL.COM
WWW.BAKERASHTONPHOTOGRAPHY.COM

BAND PHOTOGRAPHY
14 ATHA STREET
LS11 7BT
{T} 0113 276 5981
INFO@SIMONMURRAY.COM
WWW.SIMONMURRAY.COM

BECKY MAYNES PHOTOGRAPHY
LONDON
{T} 07958 548 403
BECKY@BECKYMAYNES.COM
WWW.BECKYMAYNES.COM

BEN BROOMFIELD PHOTOGRAPHY
{T} 07734 852620
BEN.BROOMFIELD@GMAIL.COM
WWW.BENBROOMFIELD.COM

BEN CARPENTER PHOTOGRAPHY
LONDON
SW15 3PB
{T} 07505 442829
MAIL@BENCARPENTERPHOTOGRAPHY.COM
WWW.BENCARPENTERPHOTOGRAPHY.COM

BEN JACKSON PHOTOGRAPHY
FLAT A
3 LARKHALL RISE
CLAPHAM NORTH SW4 6JB
{T} 07753 613320
BENJACKSON40@AOL.COM

BEN RECTOR PHOTOGRAPHY
{T} 07770 467791
BEN@BENRECTOR.COM
WWW.BENRECTOR.COM

BLOOMING PHOTOGRAPHY STUDIOS
28B HIGH STREET, CHARLTON KINGS,
CHELTENHAM
GLOUCESTERSHIRE GL52 3AS
{T} 07858 775922
BEN@BLOOMINGPHOTOGRAPHY.CO.UK
WWW.BLOOMINGPHOTOGRAPHY.CO.UK

BOUTIQUE STUDIO
119E CLEVELAND STREET
LONDON
W1T 6PY
{T} 020 7636 2625
INFO@THEBOUTIQUE.TV
WWW.THEBOUTIQUE.TV

BRANDON BISHOP PHOTOGRAPHY LTD
65-67 RIDLEY ROAD
DALSTON
LONDON E8 2NP
{T} 020 7275 7468
BRANDONBISHOPPHOTOGRAPHY@YAHOO.CO.UK
WWW.BRANDONBISHOPPHOTOGRAPHY.COM

BRENDAN HARRINGTON PHOTOGRAPHY
3 BRANNOCK HEIGHTS
NEWRY BT35 8DH
{T} 028 30266408
BRENDANHARRINGTON@BTINTERNET.COM
WWW.BRENDANHARRINGTONPHOTOGRAPHY.COM

BRENT HELSEL PHOTOGRAPHIE
80 THREE COLT STREET
LONDON E14 8AP
{T} 020 7987 6521
BRENT@BRENTHELSEL.COM
WWW.BRENTHELSEL.COM

BRIAN BAKER PHOTOGRAPHY
{T} 01708 701448
BRIANBAKERPHOTOGRAPHY@NTLWORLD.COM
WWW.BRIANBAKERPHOTOGRAPHY.CO.UK

BRIAN TARR PHOTOGRAPHY
6 BANGOR ST.
CARDIFF CF243LR
{T} 029 2049 8601
BRIAN.TARR@NTLWORLD.COM
WWW.BRIANTARR.CO.UK

BRIDGET JONES
COLNEY HATCH LANE
MUSWELL HILL, LONDON N10 1BA
{T} 020 8883 8775
BRIDGETJONES88@BTINTERNET.COM
WWW.BRIDGETJONESPHOTOGRAPHY.CO.UK

BRUCE SMITH PHOTOGRAPHER
FLAT 2, 5 BRAMHALL ROAD
WATERLOO
LIVERPOOL L22 3XA
{T} 07904 485253
B.S@MAC.COM
WWW.BRUCESMITHPHOTOGRAPHER.COM

BULL ON THE MOON STUDIOS
UNIT 4 36-42 NEW INN YARD
SHOREDITCH
LONDON EC2A 3EY
{T} 07748 414887
INFO@BULLONTHEMOON.COM
WWW.BULLONTHEMOON.COM

BUTLERIMAGE
NELSON CLOSE
ROMSEY
HAMPSHIRE SO51 7DA
{T} 07515 901954
STUDIO@BUTLERIMAGE.CO.UK
WWW.BUTLERIMAGE.CO.UK

C J Williams Photography
Ealing Studios
Ealing
London W5 5EP
{T} 020 8758 8413
TERRY@CJWILLIAMS.COM
WWW.CJWILLIAMS.COM

Carl Proctor Photography
3RD Floor. 76 Neal Street
Covent Garden
London WC2H 9PL
{T} 020 7379 6200
CARLPHOTOS@BTCONNECT.COM
WWW.CARLPROCTORPHOTOGRAPHY.COM

CarolinePhotos
10 Elm Drive
Chobham
Surrey GU24 8PP
{T} 01276 857633
INFO@CAROLINEPHOTOS.COM
WWW.CAROLINEPHOTOS.COM

CASTINGIMAGE
East London
E5 8JH
{T} 07905 311 408
PHOTO@CASTINGIMAGE.COM
WWW.CASTINGIMAGE.COM

Catherine Shakespeare Lane
43 Monsell Road
London N4 2EF
{T} 020 7226 7694
CAT@COL-ART.CO.UK
WWW.CSL-ART.CO.UK

CCPHOTOART.biz
5 Coastguard Cottages
Conyer
Kent ME9 9HH
{T} 07799 174199
CHIEF@CCPHOTOART.BIZ
WWW.CCPHOTOART.BIZ

CHARLIE CARTER
W6 9LT
{T} 020 8222 8742
CHARLIE@CHARLIECARTER.COM

Charlotte Steeples Photography
W5 5RP
{T} 07764 604 537
CHARLOTTE@CHARLOTTESTEEPLES.CO.UK
WWW.CHARLOTTESTEEPLES.CO.UK

CHASING HIPPOS
Suffolk
NR33 0DR
{T} 07786 801548
BENSONREED@HOTMAIL.COM

Chiron Miller Photography
London
{T} 07811 325881
CHIRON@CHIRONMILLER.COM
WWW.CHIRONMILLER.COM

Chris Baker
Barnet
CHRIS@CHRISBAKERPHOTOGRAPHER.COM
WWW.CHRISBAKERPHOTOGRAPHER.COM/

CHRIS BROWN
8 APOLLO WAY
SG2 7QU
{T} 01438 229090
CG.BROWN@NTLWORLD.COM
HTTP://CHRISB.PHOTIUM.COM/

CHRIS MOCK PHOTOGRAPHY
75 ELTHORNE PARK ROAD
HANWELL
LONDON W7 2JB
{T} 07811 174247
C.MOCK@NTLWORLD.COM
WWW.CHRISMOCKPHOTOS.CO.UK

CHRIS SAUNDERS
1, MURRAY RD
SHEFFIELD S11 7GF
{T} 0114 2631642
CHRISMSAUNDERS@HOTMAIL.COM
WWW.CHRISMSAUNDERS.COM

CHRISTOPHER HOLMES PHOTOGRAPHY
4 EXCHANGE COURT, FLEECE INN YARD
HIGHGATE
KENDAL LA9 4TA LA9 4TA
{T} 01539 730064
CHRISHOLMESPHOTO@BTINTERNET.COM
WWW.CHRISHOLMESPHOTO.CO.UK

CHRISTOPHER PERKINS PHOTOGRAPHY
26 LANDSEER DRIVE
MACCLESFIELD
CHESHIRE SK10 3RU
{T} 07803 507150
MAIL@CHRISTOPHER-PERKINS.COM
WWW.CHRISTOPHER-PERKINS.COM

CLAIRE GROGAN PHOTOGRAPHY
ARCHWAY
LONDON N19 N19 3LG
{T} 020 7272 1845
CLAIRE@CLAIREGROGAN.CO.UK
WWW.CLAIREGROGAN.CO.UK

CLIFTON PHOTOGRAPHIC COMPANY
74 ALMA RD
CLIFTON
BRISTOL BS8 2DJ
{T} 0117 9098985
ED@CLIFTONPHOTO.CO.UK
WWW.CLIFTONPHOTO.CO.UK

CLIVE MOORE PHOTOGRAPHY
LONDON
SW24DH
{T} 07788 815649
CLIVELYUK@YAHOO.CO.UK
WWW.CLIVEMOORE.COM

COLIN HOCKLEY PHOTOGRAPHY
12 STANMORE LODGE
STANMORE HILL
STANMORE, MIDDX HA7 3EX
{T} 020 8954 8415
COLIN@COLINHOCKLEYPHOTOGRAPHY.CO.UK
WWW.COLINHOCKLEYPHOTOGRAPHY.CO.UK

CORPHOTO
10 HAMPTON COURT
HAMPTON ROAD
BRISTOL BS6 6JN
{T} 07780 608382
RACHEL@CORPHOTO.CO.UK
WWW.CORPHOTO.CO.UK

CUCURRUCU
22 BRIDGEMAN HOUSE
FRAMPTON PARK ROAD
LONDON E9 7RB
{T} 020 8986 7759
RICO@HOTMAIL.COM

CURRAN MATTHEWS PHOTOGRAPHY
41 BERRYMEAD GARDENS
LONDON
W3 8AB
{T} 020 8992 3242
INFO@CURRANMATTHEWS.COM
WWW.CURRANMATTHEWS.COM

DAMIEN MAGUIRE PHOTOGRAPHY
UNIVERSAL SQUARE
DEVONSHIRE STREET NORTH
MANCHESTER M12 6JH
{T} 0161 273 6255
DAMIEN@CONTACTDIGITAL.CO.UK
WWW.DAMIENMAGUIRE.CO.UK

DAN BLUMENAU
{T} 020 7193 5978
DAN@DAN-BLUMENAU.COM

DAN HARWOOD-STAMPER
STUDIO 57
57 HIGH STREET
HP1 3AF
{T} 01442 242410
DAN_STAMPER@HOTMAIL.COM
WWW.DANHARWOODSTAMPER.CO.UK

DARREN BAKER PHOTOGRAPHY
17 EAST PARK FARM DRIVE
CHARVIL
READING RG10 9UG
{T} 0118 9321780
DARRENBAKERPHOTO@MAC.COM
WWW.DARRENBAKERPHOTOGRAPHY.COM

DAVID BROOKS PHOTOGRAPHER
96 MANSFIELD ROAD
NW3 2HX
{T} 020 7482 2465
DAVIBROOKS75@HOTMAIL.COM
MYSPACE.COM/DAVIDBROOKSPHOTO

DAVID CRAIK PHOTOGRAPHY
34 COPPED HALL DRIVE
CAMBERLEY
SURREY GU15 1NP
{T} 07855 018638
DAVID_CRAIK@HOTMAIL.COM

DAVID FISHER PHOTOGRAPHY
THE OXFORD FRAMING GALLERY
67 LONDON ROAD
OXFORD OX3 7RD
{T} 01865 764465
DAVID@DAVIDFISHER.CO.UK
WWW.DAVIDFISHER.CO.UK

DAVID JAMES PHOTOGRAPHY
MUSWELL HILL
LONDON N10 3DU
{T} 07808 597362
INFO@DAVIDJAMESPHOTOS.COM
WWW.DAVIDJAMESPHOTOS.COM

DAVID LAWRENCE PHOTO
STUDIO 7, NEW LYDENBURG COMM. ESTATE
WOOLWICH
LONDON SE7 8NF
{T} 020 8858 2820
DAVID@DAVIDLAWRENCEPHOTO.CO.UK
WWW.DAVIDLAWRENCEPHOTO.CO.UK

DAVID LOCKE
LONDON
{T} 07940 444641
DAVID@HEADSHOTLONDON.CO.UK
WWW.HEADSHOTLONDON.CO.UK

DAVID LOWDELL PHOTOGRAPHY
70A TOWNGATE
WYKE, BRADFORD
WEST YORKSHIRE BD12 9JB
{T} 01274 690301
DAVID@DLPBRADFORD.COM
WWW.DLPBRADFORD.COM

DAVID PETERS DIGITAL
UNIT 14, FORDHOUSE ROAD TRADING ESTATE
STEEL DRIVE
WOLVERHAMPTON WV10 9XB
{T} 01902 397739
DP@DAVIDPETERS.CO.UK
WWW.DAVIDPETERS.CO.UK

DAVID PRICE PHOTOGRAPHY
{T} 07950 542 494
INFO@DAVIDPRICEPHOTOGRAPHY.CO.UK
WWW.DAVIDPRICEPHOTOGRAPHY.CO.UK

DAVID WILLIAM EDWARDS
BETHNAL GREEN
LONDON E2 9PT
{T} 07905 384803
MAIL@DAVIDWILLIAMEDWARDS.CO.UK
WWW.DAVIDWILLIAMEDWARDS.CO.UK

DAVISON PICTURES
6 BYRON COURT
BOSTON ROAD, LONDON. W7 2AY
{T} 07917 758754
ADMIN@DAVISONPICTURES.CO.UK
WWW.DAVISONPICTURES.CO.UK

DEFENSIVE MEDIA
STUDIO 28, SHEPPERTON STUDIOS, STUDIOS ROAD
SHEPPERTON, MIDDLESEX
TW17 0QD TW19 7NU
{T} 07826 520 312
PHOTO@MIKEHOLDSWORTH.COM
WWW.MIKEHOLDSWORTH.COM

DEPARTMENT-F
21A CULLESDEN ROAD
KENLEY
SURREY CR8 5LRT
{T} 020 8668 0493
RUSS.BRENNAN@LIVE.CO.UK
WWW.MYSPACE.COM/DARKDUKEUK

DEREK BROWN PHOTOGRAPHY
ANNANDALE ROAD
GREENWICH
LONDON SE10 0DB
{T} 020 8488 6856
CASTCALLPRO@DEREKBROWN.CO.UK
WWW.DEREKBROWN.CO.UK

117

DEVELOPING PERCEPTIONS PHOTOGRAPHY
OAKSHAW STREET WEST
PAISLEY &
GLASGOW PA1 2DE
{T} 0141 8871948
ANDREW@DEVELOPINGPERCEPTIONS.CO.UK
HEADSHOTS.DEVELOPINGPERCEPTIONS.CO.UK

DGPHOTOGRAPHIC.COM
46 ASHBOURNE AVE
LONDON
Nw110DS
{T} 07855 907893
DGPHOTOGRAPHIC@GMAIL.COM
WWW.DGPHOTOGRAPHIC.COM

DIGITAL STUDIOS
CM1 2PW
{T} 07984 455050
INFO@DIGITALSTUDIOS.CO.UK

EAMON KENNEDY
27 WORLAND ROAD
STRATFORD
LONDON E154EY
{T} 07949 581069
EPKFOTO@GMAIL.COM
WWW.EAMON-KENNEDY.CO.UK

EAMONN MCGOLDRICK PHOTOGRAPHER
{T} 07810 482491
WWW.EAMONNMCGOLDRICK.COM

EARL PIGGOTT-SMITH PHOTOGRAPHY
58 ELLARDS DRIVE
WEDNESFIELD
WOLVERHAMPTON WV11 3ST

{T} 07921 716724
EPS_PHOTO@BTINTERNET.COM
WWW.EARLPIGGOTT-SMITHPHOTOGRAPHY.CO.UK

EDINBURGH HEAD SHOTS
96 BUCCLEUCH STREET
EDINBURGH
EH8 9NH
{T} 07756 178 947
PICS@JOHNNEED.CO.UK
WWW.JOHNNEED.CO.UK

EJ PHOTO'S
4 FORDHAM ROAD
SOHAM
CAMBS CB7 5AQ
{T} 07725 694298
LIZ@EJ-PHOTOS.CO.UK
WWW.EJ-PHOTOS.CO.UK

ELAINE TURNER
AXBRIDGE
SOMERSET
BS26 2BN
{T} 077147 62718
EAC@ELAINETURNER.CO.UK
WWW.ELAINETURNER.CO.UK

ELLIOTT FRANKS PHOTOGRAPHY
BOW
LONDON SW19 1WW
{T} 07802 537 220
ELLIOTT@ELLIOTTFRANKS.COM
WWW.ELLIOTTFRANKS.CO.UK

EMILY BENNETT-COLES PHOTOGRAPHY
12 GLOVERS LODGE
LEWIS ROAD
RICHMOND, SURREY TW10 6SB
{T} 020 8948 8143
EMILYBENNETT-COLES@HOTMAIL.CO.UK
WWW.EMILYBENNETTCOLES.COM

F8 GALLERY
17 HILDERTHORPE
ROAD
BRIDLINGTON YO15 3AY
{T} 0845 2570388
CLIFFORDNORTON@BTCONNECT.COM
WWW.CLIFFNORTONPHOTOGRAPHY.COM

FATIMAH NAMDAR
49 HOLMSDALE ROAD
LONDON N6 5TH
{T} 020 8341 1332
FNAMDAR@MAC.COM
WWW.FATIMAHNAMDAR.COM/

FAYE THOMAS
TW9 4DT
{T} 07752 358106
FAYE@FAYETHOMAS.COM
WWW.FAYETHOMAS.COM

FFOTOGRAFFIAETH KEITH MORRIS PHOTOGRAPHY
34 CAMBRIAN ST
ABERYSTWYTH
CEREDIGION SY23 1NZ
{T} 01970 611106
KEITH@ARTSWEBWALES.COM
WWW.ARTSWEBWALES.COM

FLAME-INC.COM
CHELTENHAM
GL52 2HF
{T} 07748 795228
ROBBIE@FLAME-INC.COM

FRASER PHOTOGRAPHY
NORTH WEST
CH2 3BP
{T} 07737 066537
FRASERPHOTOS@YAHOO.CO.UK

GALE PHOTOGRAPHY
7 EAGLE LANE
WATCHFIELD
SN6 8TF
{T} 01793 783859
INFO@LIFESTYLEPHOTOS.CO.UK
WWW.LIFESTYLEPHOTOS.CO.UK

GAP PHOTOGRAPHY
NW6 5JS
{T} 07956 521334
GIOVANNI@GAPPHOTOGRAPHY.COM
WWW.GAPPHOTOGRAPHY.COM

GARNHAM PHOTOGRAPHY
52A WARLOCK ROAD
LONDON W9 3LW
{T} 07711 941208
MARTINGARNHAM@AOL.COM
WWW.GARNHAMPHOTOGRAPHY.CO.UK

GARY BRASHIER PHOTOGRAPHY
{T} 020 8943 0875
INFO@GARYBRASHIER.COM
WWW.GARYBRASHIER.COM

GARY TREADWELL
MOORINGS
FALMOUTH
CORNWALL TR11 2AJ
{T} 01326 212098
GTREADWELL@BTINTERNET.COM
WWW.GARYTREADWELL.COM

GDPHOTOGRAPHY
138 LEAHURST ROAD
HITHER GREEN
138 LEAHURST ROAD, HITHER GREEN SE13
5NN
{T} 07866 590 820
GARETHRICHARDSON27@GMAIL.COM
WWW.GDPHOTOGRAPHY.CO.UK

GEMMA MOUNT PHOTOGRAPHY
3RD FLOOR, 5 TORRENS STREET
ISLINGTON
LONDON EC1V 1NQ
{T} 07976 824923
GEMMA@GEMMAMOUNTPHOTOGRAPHY.COM
WWW.GEMMAMOUNTPHOTOGRAPHY.COM

GEORGIA APSION
11 BUCKINGHAM STREET
BRIGHTON
EAST SUSSEX BN1 3LT
{T} 07973 269155
GEORGIA.APSION@GOOGLEMAIL.COM

GORM SHACKELFORD
SE5 7RB
{T} 07963 948915
GS@GORMSHACKELFORD.COM
WWW.GORMSHACKELFORD.COM/HEADSHOTS.HTML

GRAHAM BENNETT PHOTOGRAPHY
19 GROVE AVENUE
MUSWELL HILL
LONDON N10 2AS
{T} 020 8374 1697
GRAHAMDB@GMAIL.COM
WWW.GRAHAMBENNETT.BIZ

GRAND DESIGNER STUDIO
1 LANSDOWNE ROAD
CROYDON CR9 2BN
{T} 07921 866299
DAVID@GRANDDESIGNERSTUDIO.COM
WWW.GRANDDESIGNERSTUDIO.COM

HARALD HAUGAN PHOTOGRAPHY
151A HIGH STREET
RUISLIP HA4 8JY
{T} 0189 5677135
HARALD@PHOTOH2.COM
WWW.H2P.CO.UK

HARRY RAFIQUE PHOTOGRAPHY
18 GROVE END GARDENS
GROVE END ROAD
LONDON NW8 9LL
{T} 020 7266 5398
HARRY@HR-PHOTOGRAPHER.CO.UK
WWW.HR-PHOTOGRAPHER.CO.UK

HARRY SEWELL PHOTOGRAPHY
77 ROUNDWOOD COURT
3 MEATH CRESCENT
LONDON E2 0QL
{T} 07882 475873
MAIL@HARRYSEWELL.CO.UK
WWW.HARRYSEWELL.CO.UK

HEADSHOT LONDON PHOTOGRAPHY
3 THE HANGAR, PERSEVERANCE WORKS
KINGSLAND ROAD, SHOREDITCH
SHOREDITCH E2 8DD
{T} 07940 444 641
DAVID@HEADSHOTLONDON.CO.UK
WWW.HEADSHOTLONDON.CO.UK

HEADSHOTS BY KRIS
114 CAMDALE ROAD
SE18 2DR
{T} 07722 332355
KRIS@KRISWEBB.CO.UK
WWW.KRISWEBB.CO.UK/HEADSHOTS.ASPX

HEADSHOTS STUDIOS
NATURAL DAYLIGHT STUDIO, BALHAM
6 LEXTON GARDENS
LONDON SW12 0AY
{T} 07770 694 686
INFO@HEADSHOTSTUDIOS.CO.UK
WWW.HEADSHOTSTUDIOS.CO.UK

HEADSHOTZ STUDIO
32 WITTERING CLOSE
KT2 5GA
{T} 020 8547 2927
FRAZERCBROWN@HOTMAIL.COM

HEADSTRONG PHOTOGRAPHY
4 HEADLEY COURT
STATION APPROACH
TN8 5LS
{T} 01732 862841
FELICITYBOWDEN@HOTMAIL.COM
WWW.HEADSTRONGPHOTOGRAPHY.CO.UK

HEDWARD PHOTOGRAPHY
ELIZABETH STREET
WAKEFIELD WF1 5NE
{T} 07791 384178
CONTACTUS@HEDWARD.COM
WWW.HEDWARD.COM

HELEN BARTLETT PHOTOGRAPHY
28 LEE TERRACE
BLACKHEATH
LONDON SE3 9TZ
{T} 0845 603 1373
INFO@HELENBARTLETT.CO.UK
WWW.HELENBARTLETT.CO.UK

HELEN JONES PHOTOGRAPHY
9 MILTON COURT
PARKLEYS
RICHMOND TW10 5LY
{T} 020 8541 1158
ENQUIRIES@HELENJONESPHOTOGRAPHY.CO.UK
WWW.HELENJONESPHOTOGRAPHY.CO.UK

HOTSHOTSPHOTOGRAPHY
147 MILLHOUSE LANE
MORETON
WIRRAL CH46 6EF
{T} 0151 677 8393
BERNARD@HOTSHOTSPHOTOGRAPHY.CO.UK
WWW.HOTSHOTSPHOTOGRAPHY.CO.UK

HUBNER PHOTOGRAPHY GLASGOW
3/1 74 BUDHILL AVENUE
GLASGOW G32 0PH
{T} 0141 5787442
INFO@JACEKHUBNER.COM
WWW.JACEKHUBNER.COM

IAN M. BUTTERFIELD
2 TENNYSON CLOSE
HEATON MERSEY
STOCKPORT SK4 2ED
{T} 0161 431 5508
IAN@2FIELDS.CO.UK
WWW.IMB.BIZ/PAGE.PHP?PG=PORTFOLIO

IAN PARSFIELD PHOTOGRAPHY
193 LANGLEY WAY
WEST WICKHAM
KENT BR4 0DN
{T} 07723 915938
IAN.PARSFIELD@GMAIL.COM
WWW.IANPARSFIELD-PHOTOGRAPHY.COM

IAN PHILLIPS-MCLAREN
BARNSBURY, ISLINGTON
LONDON
N1 1BX
{T} 07889 861654
IAN@IANPHILLIPS-MCLAREN.COM
WWW.IANPHILLIPS-MCLAREN.COM

IAN WATSON
123 MOSS-SIDE RD
SHAWLANDS
GLASGOW G41 3UP
{T} 0141 616 6557
IANWATSONPICS@MAC.COM

IDOL IMAGES
THE STUDIO
3-5 BAKEHOUSE HILL
DARLINGTON DL1 5QA
{T} 01325 488385
ALLISON@NEREPRESENTATION.CO.UK

IMAGE PHOTOGRAPHIC
54 SHEPHERDS BUSH ROAD
LONDON
W6 7PH
{T} 020 7602 1190
DIGITAL@IMAGEPHOTOGRAPHIC.COM
WWW.IMAGEPHOTOGRAPHIC.COM

INDRACCOLO PHOTO
187 QUEENS CRESCENT
CAMDEN
LONDON NW5 4DS
{T} 020 7485 8193
INFO@INDRACCOLOPHOTO.CO.UK
WWW.INDRACCOLOPHOTO.CO.UK

INNERLIGHT STUDIO
547 CABLE STREET
LIMEHOUSE
LONDON E1W 3EW
{T} 020 7780 9838
INFO@STEPHANIERUSHTON.COM
WWW.STEPHANIERUSHTON.COM

ISABELLA PANATTONI
SW15
{T} 07833 734117
INFO@ISABELLAPANATTONI.COM
WWW.ISABELLAPANATTONI.COM

JACK BLUMENAU PHOTOGRAPHY
72 HIGH STREET
ASHWELL
HERTFORDSHIRE SG7 5NS
INFO@BLUMENAUPHOTOGRAPHY.CO.UK
WWW.BLUMENAUPHOTOGRAPHY.CO.UK

JACK LADENBURG
78 PROTHERO ROAD
LONDON SW6 7LZ
{T} 07932 053743
INFO@JACKLADENBURG.CO.UK
WWW.JACKLADENBURG.CO.UK

JAMES PEARSON PHOTOGRAPHIC
47 CASBY HOUSE
DICKENS ESTATE
LONDON SE16 4SX
{T} 07932 375549
JAMESPEARSON71@MAC.COM
WWW.JAMESPEARSONPHOTOGRAPHIC.COM

JAMES WALKER PHOTOGRAPHY
54POLSLOE ROAD
EXETER EX1 2DS
{T} 07977 924058
JAMES@JMWPHOTOGRAPHY.CO.UK
WWW.JMWPHOTOGRAPHY.CO.UK

JANIE RAYNE PHOTOGRAPHY
AVENUE STUDIOS
SYDNEY CLOSE
LONDON SW3 6HW
{T} 07973 541780
JANIERAYNEPHOTO@GMAIL.COM
WWW.JANIERAYNE.COM

JK PHOTOGRAPHY
17 DELAMERE RD
WIMBLEDON
LONDON SW20 8PS
{T} 07816 825578
JKPHOTO@YAHOO.COM
WWW.JK-PHOTOGRAPHY.NET

JOHN CLARK PHOTOGRAPHY
(STUDIO LOCATION)
79 FAIRFIELD ROAD
LONDON E3 2QA
{T} 020 8854 4069
JOHN@JOHNCLARKPHOTOGRAPHY.COM
WWW.JOHNCLARKPHOTOGRAPHY.COM

JOHN MACLEOD
27 BLACKIEMUIR AVENUE
LAURENCEKIRK
AB30 1DX
{T} 07506 708133
JCDMACLEOD@GMAIL.COM

JOHN NICHOLS STUDIO
868 WILMSLOW ROAD
MANCHESTER M20 5NL
{T} 0161 4462002
868ONLINE@GMAIL.COM

JOHN TUDOR PHOTOGRAPHY
ARMLEY
LS12 2QY
{T} 07841 113574
INFO@JOHNTUDORPHOTOGRAPHY.COM
WWW.JOHNTUDORPHOTOGRAPHY.COM

JON CAMPLING HEADSHOTS
206 ELLISON ROAD
NORBURY
LONDON SW16 5DJ
{T} 020 8679 8671
PHOTO@JONCAMPLING.COM
WWW.JONCAMPLINGHEADSHOTS.COM

JONATHAN BALL PHOTOGRAPHY
61 CRESCENT ROAD
N22 7RU
{T} 07742 636185
INFO@JONATHANBALLPHOTOGRAPHY.COM
WWW.JONATHANBALLPHOTOGRAPHY.COM

JONATHAN BOSWORTH PHOTOGRAPHY
FLAT 5 BOW BELL TOWER
PANCRAS WAY, BOW
LONDON E3 2SN
{T} 07739 738570
JONBOSWORTH@HOTMAIL.CO.UK
WWW.JONATHANBOSWORTH.CO.UK

JONATHAN LITTLEJOHN
14 PANMURE PLACE
EDINBURGH
EH3 9JJ
{T} 0131 2295079
LITTLEJOHNJONATHAN@HOTMAIL.COM
GROUPS.MSN.COM/JONATHANLITTLEJOHN

JONATHAN NUNN
KENNINGTON PARK ROAD, LONDON
SE11 5TS
{T} 07788 427843
INFO@JONATHANNUNN.COM
WWW.JONATHANNUNN.COM

JOSEPH STORY
MANCHESTER M15 5AX
{T} 07515 474851
JOSEPHSTORYIMAGES@GOOGLEMAIL.COM
WWW.JSTORYPHOTOGRAPHY.COM

JOSHUA MILLAIS PHOTOGRAPHY
85 HIGHLEVER ROAD
LONDON W10 6PW
{T} 020 8960 5957
JOSH@JOSHUAMILLAIS.COM
WWW.JOSHUAMILLAIS.COM

JOTH SHAKERLEY
15 CREDITON ROAD
LONDON
NW 10 3DT
{T} 020 8964 5823
JOTHSHAKERLEY@YAHOO.CO.UK
JOTH SHAKERLEY.COM

JULES LAWRENCE PHOTOGRAPHY
{T} 07939 157142
JULES@JULESLAWRENCE.CO.UK
WWW.JULESLAWRENCE.CO.UK

JULIA WATES PHOTOGRAPHY
THE LODGE, RIVERVIEW GARDENS, BARNES,
BARNES, LONDON
SW13 8QY
{T} 020 8741 4667
JULIAWATES@HOTMAIL.COM
WWW.JULIA-WATESPHOTOGRAPHY.COM

JULIAN MATTHEWS PHOTOGRAPHY
7 THE MOUNT
KIPPAX
LS25 7NG
{T} 0113 2877394
JMPHOTOGRAPHY1@BTINTERNET.COM

KAIZ AGENCY
44 TIDESIDE COURT
HARLINGER STREET
LONDON SE18 5SW
{T} 07739 562713
INFO@KAIZAGENCY.COM
WWW.KAIZAGENCY.COM

KARCZMARZ STUDIOS
HOMESDALE ROAD
BR2 9LD
{T} 07932 582544
KARCZMARZ.STUDIOS@GOOGLEMAIL.COM
WWW.NEXTCAT.COM/STAN_KARCZMARZ

KARL WEBER PHOTOGRAPHY
3 MAJOR TERRACE
SEATON
DEVON EX12 2RF
{T} 01297 21227
KARL.WEBER@VIRGIN.NET
WWW.KARLWEBER.CO.UK

KARLA GOWLETT
THE LONDON COLISEUM
ST. MARTINS LANE
LONDON WC2N 4ES
{T} 07941 871271
INFO@KARLAGOWLETT.CO.UK
WWW.PHOTOPERSPECTIVE.CO.UK

KELLY YOUNG PHOTOGRAPHY
BR3 4LW
{T} 020 8650 3705
KELL.YOUNG@NTLWORLD.COM

KERRY SKINNER PHOTOGRAPHY
BALHAM
LONDON SW12 9RW
{T} 020 8772 9168
KERRYSKINNER@BTINTERNET.COM
WWW.KERRYSKINNERPHOTOGRAPHY.CO.UK

KEVIN JONES
31 GRAIG VIEW
MACHEN
CAERPHILLY CF83 8SD
{T} 01633 441324
PICTUREPROJONES@AOL.COM
WWW.PICTUREPROJONES.CO.UK

KIM THORN PHOTOGRAPHY
40 TREVELYAN WAY
BERKHAMSTED
HERTFORDSHIRE HP4 1JH
{T} 01442 262820
ENQUIRIES@KIMTHORNPHOTOGRAPHY.CO.UK
WWW.KIMTHORNPHOTOGRAPHY.CO.UK

KIRSTEN MCTERNAN
6 CLIVE ROAD
CANTON
CARDIFF CF5 1HJ
{T} 07791 524551
KIRSTEN@KIRSTENMCTERNAN.CO.UK
WWW.KIRSTENMCTERNAN.CO.UK

KITTYKAMERA
90B HIGH ROAD
LONDON
N2 9EB
{T} 07903 468271
KITTYKAMERA@NTLWORLD.COM

125

LATTE PHOTOGRAPHY
1 CLOS-YR-EOS, SOUTH CORNELLY
PORTHCAWL
CF33 4RJ
{T} 01656 743007
CHRIS.BBBB@TESCO.NET
WWW.LATTEPHOTOGRAPHY.IFP3.COM

LAURA DODDINGTON PHOTOGRAPHY
6 HORSELYDOWN LANE
LONDON
SE1 2LN
{T} 07966 762251
LAURADODDINGTONPHOTOGRAPHY@GMAIL.COM
WWW.LAURADODDINGTONPHOTOGRAPHY.COM

LB PHOTOGRAPHY
RH2 9HS
{T} 01737 224578
POSTMASTER@LISABOWERMAN.DEMON.CO.UK

LEGEND PHOTOGRAPHY
MCNEIL DESIGNS, 3 WESTHILL ARCADE,
HASTINGS, EAST SUSSEX
TN34 3EA
{T} 01424 430055
INFO@MCNEILDESIGNS.CO.UK
WWW.LEGEND-PHOTOGRAPHY.COM

LENKA JONES PHOTOGRAPHY
WINDSOR
SL45PS
{T} 07921 182055
LENKI13@YAHOO.CO.UK
WWW.LENKAJONESPHOTOGRAPHY.COM

LINSEY O'NEILL DESIGN
111 BRAMPTON ROAD
POOLE
DORSET BH15 3RF
{T} 01202 680312
LINSEY@LINSEY-ONEILL-DESIGN.CO.UK
WWW.LINSEY-ONEILL-DESIGN.CO.UK

LINTONLAIDLEY PHOTOGRAHER
FLAT 10
71 LOWER ADDISCOMBE ROAD
CROYDON CR0 6PS
{T} 020 8656 3079
LINTONS@HOTMAIL.CO.UK
WWW.LINTONLAIDLEY.CO.UK

LONDON HEADSHOT PHOTOGRAPHY
THE STUDIO
189 ALEXANDRA PARK ROAD
LONDON N22 7BJ
{T} 020 8349 3632
LYNNHERRICK@GMAIL.COM
WWW.HEADSHOTSLONDON.CO.UK

LOST ART LOGIC
LOST ART LOGIC
26 FREDRICK STREET
JEWELRY QUARTER B1 3HH
{T} 0121 471 2991
ANDREWBAINBRIDGE@LOSTARTLOGIC.CO.UK
WWW.MYSPACE.COM/LOSTARTLOGICLTD

HOTT AND TOTTENHAM
E2 7SH
{T} 020 7729 9181
INFO@HOTTANDTOTTENHAM.COM
WWW.HOTTANDTOTTENHAM.CCOM

LOUISE O'GORMAN PHOTOGRAPHY
HACKNEY
LONDON E9 7NG
{T} 07794 411202
INFO@LOUISEOGORMAN.COM
WWW.LOUISEOGORMAN.COM

LOUISE O'SHEA
LONDON
N44EB
{T} 07966 236188
LOUISE@LOUISEOSHEA.COM
WWW.IMAGELAND.CO.UK

LUKE VARLEY
BRIXTON
LONDON
SW9 8RR
{T} 07711 183631
LUKE@LUKEVARLEY.COM
WWW.LUKEVARLEY.COM

M.A.D. PHOTOGRAPHY
ENFIELD CHASE
ENFIELD
NORTH LONDON EN2 7HS
{T} 020 8363 4182
MAD.PHOTO@ONETEL.NET
WWW.MAD-PHOTOGRAPHY.CO.UK

MAGNUS HASTINGS
BRICK LANE
E2 6EH
{T} 07905 304705
MAGNUS@MAGNUSHASTINGS.CO.UK
WWW.MAGNUSHASTINGS.CO.UK

MARC HANKINS PHOTOGRAPHIC
7 EDGEBOROUGH COURT
UPPER EDGEBOROUGH ROAD
GUILDFORD, SURREY GU1 2BL
{T} 07809 433555
MARC@MARCHANKINS.COM
WWW.MARCHANKINS.COM

MARCOS BEVILACQUA PHOTOGRAPHY
UNIT 6
2 LANSDOWNE DRIVE
LONDON E8 3EZ
{T} 020 7683 0954
INFO@MARCOS-BOOK.COM
WWW.MARCOS-BOOK.COM

MARCUS ROSS
50 WENHAM HOUSE
ASCALON ST
LONDON SW8 4DZ
{T} 07747 758877
MAIL@MARCUSROSS.NET
WWW.MARCUSROSS.NET/

MARGARET YESCOMBE PHOTOGRAPHY
{T} 07834 524525
INFO@MARGARETYESCOMBE.COM
WWW.MARGARETYESCOMBE.COM

MARK BLOWER PHOTOGRAPHY
174 MILLFIELDS ROAD
LONDON E5 0AR
{T} 07958 463474
INFO@MARKBLOWER.COM
WWW.MARKBLOWER.COM

MARK BROME PHOTOGRAPHER
ASTON WORKS
BACK LANE
BAMPTON, OXFORDSHIRE OX18 2DQ
{T} 01993 850077
INFO@MARKBROME.COM
WWW.MARKBROME.COM

MARK EDMONDSON - PHOTOGRAPHIC ARTIST
21 NAZE LANE
FRECKLETON
PRESTON PR4 1RH
{T} 01772 490044
MARK@MEPHOTOGRAPHY.CO.UK
WWW.MEPHOTOGRAPHY.CO.UK

MARK FARRINGTON PHOTOGRAPHY
THE OLD BAKERY
TIDMARSH
READING RG8 8ES
{T} 0118 9844320
MARK@MEDIALINK.CO.UK

MARK LOVELL
10 ELM AVENUE
CHRISTCHURCH
DORSET BH23 2HJ
{T} 07802 351635
MARKLOVELL@HOTMAIL.CO.UK

MARK YOUNG PHOTOGRAPHY
FLAT 4 CARLTON HOUSE
WESTERN PARADE, SOUTHSEA
PORTSMOUTH PO5 3ED
{T} 02392 793655
CALLMEMARKSTER@GMAIL.COM
WWW.MARKYOUNGMOVIESTILLS.COM

MARTIN COYNE PHOTOGRAPHY
2 ASHBOURNE ROAD
BH5 2JS
{T} 07788 788616
MARTIN@MARTINCOYNE.COM
WWW.MARTINCOYNE.COM

MATT JAMIE PHOTOGRAPHY
N12 9LB
{T} 07976 890643
PHOTOS@MATTJAMIE.CO.UK
WWW.MATTJAMIE.CO.UK/PORTRAITS

DURHAM PHOTOGRAPHICS
4 TROUTBECK CLOSE
SPENNYMOOR
DURHAM DL16 6XN
{T} 07590 561536
MATT@DURHAMPHOTOGRAPHICS.CO.UK

MATT STEDEFORD PHOTOGRAPHY
9 BELSIZE AVENUE
LONDON
N13 4TL
{T} 07793 741604
MATTSTEDEFORD@GMAIL.COM
**WWW.STEDEFORD.COM/PHOTOGRAPHY/LON-
DONHEADSHOTPHOTOGRAPHER**

MAXINE EVANS - PHOTOS FOR ACTORS
37 TYLNEY ROAD
FOREST GATE
LONDON E7 0LS
{T} 07966 130426
MAXINEVANS@AOL.COM
WWW.PHOTOSFORACTORS.CO.UK

LUKAS PHOTOGRAPHY
WORTHING
{T} 01903 521509
LUKASPHOTOGRAPHIC@HOTMAIL.COM

MICHAEL BRYDON PHOTOGRAPHY
59 THORNTON AVE
LONDON SW2 4BD
{T} 020 8677 6064
INFO@MICHAELBRYDON.CO.UK
WWW.MICHAELBRYDON.CO.UK

MICHAEL HEDGE
24B SANDINGRAM ROAD
E8 2LP
{T} 07725 565977
MICHAELHEDGEPHOTOGRAPHY@GMAIL.COM

MICHAEL POLLARD
MANCHESTER
SK2 6BT
{T} 0161 4567470
INFO@MICHAELPOLLARD.CO.UK
WWW.MICHAELPOLLARD.CO.UK

MICHAEL WHARLEY PHOTOGRAPHY
12 HERNE HILL MANSIONS
HERNE HILL SE24 9QN
{T} 07961 068759
MICHAELWHARLEY@GOOGLEMAIL.COM
PICASAWEB.GOOGLE.COM/MICHAELWHARLEY

MICHAELWHEELERPHOTO.COM
LONDON N8
{T} 07932 756244
INFO@MICHAELWHEELERPHOTO.COM
WWW.MICHAELWHEELERPHOTO.COM

MIDDLETON MANN PHOTOGRAPHY
26 RASPER ROAD
FINCHLEY
NORTH LONDON N20 0LZ
{T} 07930 331373
MID@MIDDLETONMANN.FREESERVE.CO.UK
WWW.MIDDLETONMANN.CO.UK

MINOT STUDIOS
STUDIO Q1, LIONWORKS
55-57 WALLIS ROAD
LONDON E9 5LH
{T} 020 8986 2743
INFO@STUDIOMINOT.COM
WWW.STUDIOMINOT.COM

MURRAY KERR PHOTOGRAPHY
GLASGOW
{T} 07763 691160
MURRAYKERR@HOTMAIL.COM

MO CARRIM PHOTOGRAPHER
16 CAMPDEN HOUSES
PEEL STREET
LONDON W8 7PG
{T} 020 7460 2183
MOCARRIM@YAHOO.CO.UK
WWW.MYSPACE.COM/MOCARRIM

MYHEADSHOTS
104 HIGH STREET
GREAT MISSENDEN HP16 0BE
{T} 01494 862888
CHRIS@SONGBIRD.CO.UK
WWW.MYHEADSHOTS.CO.UK

NATALIE MUALLEM PHOTOGRAPHER
{T} 07957 631043
NATALIEMUALLEM@HOTMAIL.COM
WWW.NATALIEMUALLEM.COM

NATASHA MERCHANT
SW16 2BT
{T} 07932 618111
NATASHAMERCHANT@MAC.COM
WWW.NATASHAMERCHANT.COM

NEAL CRISCUOLO PHOTOGRAPHY
WILDPEAR STUDIO
70 HILL STREET
RICHMOND TW9 1TW
{T} 020 8819 1222
INFO@NEALCRISCUOLO.COM
WWW.NEALCRISCUOLO.COM/

NEIL FORTESCUE
4 FENN CLOSE
FRATING
ESSEX CO7 7GB
{T} 07791 520724
NEIL@NEILFORTESCUE.COM
WWW.NEILFORTESCUE.COM

NICHOLAS DAWKES PHOTOGRAPHY
6F WESTCOTT ROAD
KENNINGTON
LONDON SE17 3QY
{T} 07787 111997
NICHOLASDAWKES@YAHOO.CO.UK
WWW.NICHOLASDAWKESPHOTOGRAPHY.CO.UK

NICK GREGAN PHOTOGRAPHY
UNIT 3, 10A ELLINGFORT ROAD
LONDON FIELDS
LONDON E8 3PA
{T} 020 8533 3003
INFO@NICKGREGAN.COM
WWW.NICKGREGAN.COM

NKPHOTOGRAPHER
5 MARIAN COURT
ROBIN HOOD LANE
SURREY SM1 2SB
{T} 07782 202072
NINA@NKPHOTOGRAPHER.COM
WWW.NKPHOTOGRAPHER.COM

NOEL SHELLEY PHOTOGRAPHY
32 HUNSDON ROAD
OXFORD
{T} 07762 661662
NOELSHELLEY@HOTMAIL.COM
WWW.NOELSHELLEY.COM

OLYDEN JOHNSON PHOTOGRAPHY
SUITE 22,CONTINENTAL HOUSE
497 SUNLEIGH ROAD
ALPERTON, MIDDLESEX HA0 4LY
{T} 07739 172399
OJ@OLYDEN.COM
WWW.OLYDEN.COM

PAUL BARRASS PHOTOGRAPHY
LONDON FIELDS, HACKNEY
LONDON E8 3PA
{T} 020 8533 1492
PAUL@PAULBARRASS.CO.UK
WWW.PAULBARRASS.CO.UK

PAUL CABLE PHOTOGRAPHY & DESIGN
246 EASTERN AVENUE
ILFORD
ESSEX IG4 5AB
{T} 07958 932 764
INFO@PAULCABLE.COM
WWW.PAULCABLE.COM

PAUL SPENCER CLAMP PHOTOGRAPHY
15 VALLANCE GARDENS
HOVE
E. SUSSEX BN3 2DB
{T} 01273 323782
PAULSPENCERCLAMP@YAHOO.CO.UK
WWW.PSCPHOT.COM

PAUL STONE PHOTOGRAPHY
95 PRINCES RD
ROMFORD
ESSEX RM1 2SP
{T} 07504 270896
PAULJAMESHENRY@MSN.COM
WWW.PAULSTONEPHOTOGRAPHY.COM

PEPE ESCUREDO PHOTOGRAPHY
2 MINUTE WALK FROM PICCADILLY CIRCUS
WEST END W1F 9EL
{T} 07956 175 863
INFO@TALENTSHOTS.CO.UK
WWW.TALENTSHOTS.CO.UK/2HEADSHOTS

PETER BOYD PHOTOGRAPHY
HUDDERSFIELD
HD1 4TX
{T} 07793 200186
INFO@PBPHOTO.CO.UK
WWW.PBPHOTO.CO.UK

PETER PAWAN PHOTOGRAPHY
WICKHAM ROAD
SE4 1PL
{T} 07786 543834
PPAWAN@ME.COM

PETER SIMPKIN
N10 2AS
{T} 020 8883 2727
PETERSIMPKIN@AOL.COM
WWW.PETERSIMPKIN.CO.UK

PHIL CROW
12 NORTHFIELD ROAD
LINCOLN
LN2 3FF
{T} 07787 155852
ENQUIRY@PHILCROW.COM
WWW.PHILCROW.COM

PHILIP HUNTON PHOTOGRAPHY
THE STUDIO, SINCLAIR COURT
BRUNSWICK VILLAGE
NEWCASTLE UPON TYNE NE13 7DS
{T} 0191 2361017
INFO@PHILIPHUNTON.CO.UK
WWW.PHILIPHUNTON.CO.UK

PHILIPPA STRANDBERG PHOTOGRAPHY
218 GLOUCESTER ROAD
CROYDON
CR0 2DJ
{T} 020 8689 7405
INFO@PHILIPPASTRANDBERG.COM
WWW.PHILIPPASTRANDBERG.COM

PICTURES INC LTD
{T} 07810 888 373
PAUL@PICTURESINC.CO.UK
WWW.PICTURESINC.CO.UK/ACTORS

PICTURESBYBISH
FLAT 2
3 PINK LANE
NEWCASTLE UPON TYNE NE1 5DW
{T} 07861 667151
PICTURESBYBISH@HOTMAIL.CO.UK
WWW.PICTURESBYBISH.COM

PIERRE MARCAR
{T} 07956 485584
SHOOTME@PIERREMARCARPEOPLE.COM
WWW.PIERREMARCARPEOPLE.COM

PIOTR KOWALIK PHOTOGRAPHY
1 HYTHE ROAD NW10
LONDON
NW10 6RT
{T} 07946 323631
KPIOTR@BTINTERNET.COM
WWW.PIOTRKOWALIK.CO.UK

PRESS PHOTOGRAPHERS
6 GROVE BUSINESS PARK
ALSCOT ESTATE
STRATFORD ON AVON CV37 8DX
{T} 0870 7773037
INFO@PRESSPHOTOGRAPHERS.CO.UK
WWW.PRESSPHOTOGRAPHERS.CO.UK

PROFILE PHOTOGRAPHY
LONDON
{T} 07971 431798

INFO@PROFILE-LONDON.COM
WWW.PROFILE-LONDON.COM.

RAFE ALLEN PHOTOGRAPHY
SE4 1DZ
{T} 07980 840757
RAFEALLEN@HOTMAIL.COM
WWW.RAFEALLEN.COM

REMY HUNTER PHOTOGRAPHY
FLAT 2, 9 BELSIZE PARK
LONDON NW3 4ES
{T} 020 7431 8055
REMY_HUNTER@HOTMAIL.COM
WWW.REMYHUNTER.CO.UK

RENATA AIELLO PHOTOGRAPHY
CANADIAN AVENUE
LONDON
SE6 3BP
RENATA@RENATAAIELLO.COM
WWW.ACTORSPHOTOGRAPHY.CO.UK

RETRORUBBER
WHINCHMORE HILL
N21 3PG
{T} 07530 217836
BRIAN@RETRORUBBER.NET

RIC BACON PHOTOGRAPHY
MUSWELL HILL, LONDON
N10 3HN
WWW.RICBACON.CO.UK

RICHARD DUTKOWSKI FBIPP FMPA
THE PHOTOGRAPHIC STUDIO
158 WHITCHURCH ROAD

CARDIFF CF14 3NA
{T} 029 2062 1665
ENQUIRIES@DUTKOWSKI.CO.UK
WWW.DUTKOWSKI.CO.UK

RICHARD GALLAGHER
{T} 07748 430022
DICKIE.GALLAGHER@GMAIL.COM
WWW.DICKIEGALLAGHER.CO.UK

RICHARD WILLIAMS PHOTOGRAPHY
AYLESBURY
BUCKINGHAMSHIRE
HP20 2JR
{T} 07710 780152
RICHARD.WILLIAMS@10BY8.COM
WWW.10BY8.COM

RIVER STUDIO
305 THE CUSTARD FACTORY, GIBB STREET
DIGBETH, BIRMINGHAM
WEST MIDLANDS B9 4AA
{T} 0121 6244777
INFO@RIVERSTUDIO.CO.UK
WWW.RIVERSTUDIO.CO.UK

ROB BOOKER PHOTOGRAPHY
LEEDS
WEST YORKSHIRE
LS6 1SE
{T} 0113 2120818
CONTACT@ROBBOOKER.CO.UK
WWW.ROBBOOKER.CO.UK

ROB POWELL PHOTOGRAPHY
9 BURDITH AVENUE
MANCHESTER

M14 7HX
{T} 07900 511778
POWELLROBJ@HOTMAIL.COM

ROB SAVAGE PHOTOGRAPHY
N10 2AH
{T} 07901 927597
CONTACT@ROBSAVAGE.CO.UK
WWW.ROBSAVAGE.CO.UK

ROBERT GOOCH
ESSEX RM19 1QW
{T} 07976 965577
INFO@ROBERTGOOCH.COM
WWW.ROBERTGOOCH.COM

ROBERT WORKMAN PHOTOGRAPHER LTD
32 WEST KENSINGTON MANSIONS
BEAUMONT CRESCENT
LONDON W14 9PF
{T} 020 7385 5442
BOB@ROBERTWORKMAN.DEMON.CO.UK
WWW.ROBERTWORKMAN.DEMON.CO.UK

ROCKWELL MEDIA UK
FLAT 3,58 ABBOTSFORD STREET
BLACKNESS
DUNDEE DD21DA
{T} 01382 434711
ROCKWELLCM@BLUEYONDER.CO.UK
WWW.ROCKWELLMEDIA.CO.UK

ROGER MOORE PHOTOGRAPHY
CAPPADOCIA
SA33 6SR
{T} 07816 085415
ROGERMOOREPHOTO@AOL.COM

133

ROLFE MARKHAM PHOTOGRAPHY
FLAT 1
23 PUTNEY HILL
LONDON SW15 6BE
{T} 020 8788 1176
ROLFE@ROLFEMARKHAM.CO.UK
WWW.ROLFEMARKHAM.CO.UK

RORY BUCKLAND PHOTOGRAPHY
BIRMINGHAM & BRIGHTON
B9 4AA
{T} 07887 897749
INFO@RORYBUCKLAND.COM
WWW.RORYBUCKLAND.COM

ROSIE COLLINS PHOTOGRAPHY
{T} 07958 486051
ROSIE@ROSIECOLLINSPHOTOGRAPHY.COM
WWW.ROSIECOLLINSPHOTOGRAPHY.COM

ROSIE STILL
391 SIDCUP ROAD
LONDON SE9 4EU
{T} 020 8857 6920
ROSIE391@TALKTALK.NET
WWW.ROSIESTILLPHOTOGRAPHY.COM

ROSY CLARKE PHOTOGRAPHER
FLAT 10
7 EGERTON GARDENS
LONDON SW3 2BP
{T} 07531 171074
ROSYPHOTOGRAPHER@HOTMAIL.COM
WWW.ROSYCLARKEPHOTOGRAPHER.COM

RUTH CRAFER PHOTOGRAPHER
HIGHBURY HILL
HIGHBURY
LONDON N5 1HH
{T} 07974 088460
RUTH@RUTHO.DEMON.CO.UK
WWW.RUTHCRAFER.CO.UK

SAMCLARK PHOTOGRAPHY
AXWORTHY COTTAGE
LEWDOWN
OKEHAMPTON EX20 4EB
{T} 01566 783233
SAM@FARLAP.CO.UK
WWW.SAMCLARKPHOTOGRAPHY.COM

SARA KIRKPATRICK PHOTOGRAPHY
MILTON KEYNES/LONDON
MK14 5EE
{T} 07736 041545
SARA@SARAKIRKPATRICK-PHOTOGRAPHY.CO.UK
**WWW.SARAKIRKPATRICK-
PHOTOGRAPHY.CO.UK**

SARAH ROESINK PHOTOGRAPHY
LONDON SE16 3EN
{T} 07775 730298
SARAH.ROESINK@GMX.DE
WWW.SARAHROESINK.NET

SCALLYWAGS
90-92 LEY STREET
ILFORD
ESSEX IG1 4BX
{T} 07974 173153
PHILIP@SCALLYWAGS.CO.UK
WWW.SCALLYWAGS.CO.UK

SCHOOL OF ART
34 ST OSWALDS PLACE
LONDON SE11 5JE
{T} 020 7793 9315
AFRANCK@BTINTERNET.COM
WWW.ALEXFRANCK.COM

SCORCHING IMAGE PHOTOGRAPHY
283 - 287 BEXLEY ROAD
NORTHUMBERLAND HEATH
ERITH, KENT DA8 3EX
{T} 0870 4321338
DAVE.WISE@SCORCHINGIMAGE.COM
WWW.SCORCHINGIMAGE.COM

SHAMBHALA
{T} 07930 101299
SHAMBHALA.PHOTO@GMAIL.COM
WWW.PHOTO.NET/PHOTOS/SHAMBHALA

SHAMEFUL PHOTOGRAPHIC
8 OAKFIELD COURT
91 KINGS AVENUE
LONDON SW4 8EQ
{T} 020 8678 9591
PADDY@SHAMEFULPHOTOGRAPHIC.COM
WWW.SHAMEFULPHOTOGRAPHIC.COM

SHEARD PHOTOGRAPHY
LONDON
SW2 1JW
{T} 07817 769666
INFO@SHEARDPHOTOGRAPHY.CO.UK
WWW.SHEARDPHOTOGRAPHY.CO.UK

SHEILA BURNETT
20A RANDOLPH CRESCENT
LONDON W9 1DR
{T} 020 7289 3058
SHEILAB33@NTLWORLD.COM
WWW.SHEILABURNETT-PHOTOGRAPHY.COM

SHOOT THE MOON PHOTOGRAPHY
CONCEPT HOUSE
NAVAL ST
MANCHESTER M4 6AX
{T} 0161 2057417
ELAINE@SHOOT-THE-MOON.CO.UK
WWW.STMPHOTOGRAPHY.CO.UK

SHORELINE IMAGING
17 QUEEN STREET
SY1 2JX
{T} 07817 232686
INFO@SHORELINEIMAGING.CO.UK
WWW.SHORELINEIMAGING.CO.UK

SHOT BY THE SHERIFF PHOTOGRAPHY
ED WAREHOUSE
1 ZENORIA STREET
LONDON SE22 8HP
{T} 0800 0377703
PHOTOS@SHOTBYTHESHERIFF.CO.UK
WWW.SHOTBYTHESHERIFF.CO.UK

SHOTID
19 GLENMOOR ROAD
OFFERTON
CHESHIRE SK1 4EB
{T} 0161 3550869
JAY@SHOTID.CO.UK
WWW.SHOTID.CO.UK

135

SIMON ANNAND
17 WINSTON ROAD
LONDON
N16 9LU
{T} 020 7241 6725
SIMONANNAND@BLUEYONDER.CO.UK
WWW.SIMONANNAND.COM

SIMON WHITEHEAD PHOTOGRAPHY
23 THE MALL
CLIFTON
BRISTOL BS8 4JG
{T} 0117 9047216
SIMON@GALLERY2C.COM
WWW.GALLERYZC.COM

SJS PHOTOGRAPHY
47 COLIN PARK ROAD
LONDON
NW9 6HT
{T} 07733 107146
STUART@SJSPHOTO.COM
WWW.SJSPHOTO.COM

SMALL SCREEN SHOWREELS
17 KNOLE ROAD
DARTFORD, LONDON DA1 3JN
{T} 020 8816 8896
HEADSHOTS@SMALLSCREENSHOWREELS.CO.UK
WWW.SMALLSCREENSHOWREELS.CO.UK

SOPHIE BAKER
1 BROOKFIELD, 5 HIGHGATE WEST HILL
5 HIGHGATE WEST HILL
LONDON N6 6AS
{T} 020 8340 3850
SOPHIEBAKER@TOTALISE.CO.UK

STAN GAMESTER PHOTOGRAPHY
90 MAYFAIR
READING
BERKSHIRE RG30 4RD
{T} 0118 9419427
INFO@STANGAMESTER.COM
WWW.STANGAMESTER.COM

STEFAN LACANDLER
51 CHURCH LANE
E17 9RJ
{T} 07949 757457
STEFAN@LACANDLER.COM
WWW.LACANDLER.COM

STEPHANIE DE LENG
7 BEACH LAWN
LIVERPOOL L22 8QA
{T} 0151 476 1563
DELENG@BLUEYONDER.CO.UK
WWW.STEPHANIEDELENG.CO.UK

STEPHANIE GIBBONS PHOTOGRAPHY
9 GODOLPHIN PLACE
LONDON W3 7NB
S.GIBBONS@LIVE.CO.UK
WWW.SMGPHOTOS.CO.UK

STEVE JOHNSTON PHOTOGRAPHY
LONDON
SW12 0HE
{T} 07775 99 1834
INFO@CASTINGPHOTO.CO.UK
WWW.CASTINGPHOTO.CO.UK

STEVE MORGAN
FERNHILL
HEBDEN BRIDGE HX7 7AB
{T} 07798 553272
STEVE@STEVEMORGANPHOTO.CO.UK
WWW.STEVEMORGANPHOTO.CO.UK

STEVE ULLATHORNE PHOTOGRAPHY
LONDON
SE19 1SB
{T} 07961 380 969
STEVE@STEVEULLATHORNE.COM
WWW.STEVEULLATHORNE.COM

STEVEBRAYPHOTO
TW3 2EU
{T} 020 8755 4156
INFO@STEVEBRAYPHOTO.CO.UK
WWW.STEVEBRAYPHOTO.CO.UK

STUART ALLEN PHOTOGRAPHY
LONDON W5 4XD
{T} 07776 258829
INFO@STUARTALLENPHOTOS.COM
WWW.STUARTALLENPHOTOS.COM

STUART CLARKE IMAGES
266A EAST BARNET ROAD
EAST BARNET
HERTFORDSHIRE EN4 8TD
{T} 07771 864 874
STUARTCLARKE@HOTMAIL.COM

STUART MCALLISTER
{T} 07947 820514
INFO@SMCALLISTER.CO.UK
WWW.SMCALLISTER.CO.UK

STUDIO ONE
ENFIELD
EN2 6NS
{T} 020 7193 8940
INFO@STUDIO1-LONDON.CO.UK

STUDIO SHOTS
12 PAINTHORPE TERRACE
WAKEFIELD
WEST YORKSHIRE WF4 3HH
{T} 07796 681935
INFO@STUDIO-SHOTS.CO.UK
WWW.STUDIO-SHOTS.CO.UK

STUDIO TIME PHOTOGRAPHERS
STUDIO 25
10 MARTELLO STREET
LONDON E8 3PE
{T} 020 7241 2816
INFO@STUDIOTIMEPHOTO.COM
WWW.STUDIOTIMEPHOTO.COM

STUDIOIV
26 IVY ARCH ROAD
WORTHING
WEST SUSSEX BN14 8BX
{T} 01903 251060
GLEN@STUDIOIV.CO.UK
WWW.STUDIOIV.CO.UK

SUKEY PARNELL
29 DYNE ROAD
LONDON NW6 7XG
{T} 020 7328 5760
SUKEY@SUKEYPARNELL.COM
WWW.SUKEYPARNELL.COM

Actors' Handbook 2009-10

SUZANNAH LEA PHOTOGRAPHY
HASLEMERE,
SURREY GU27 1QA
{T} 07702 839995
INFO@SUZANNAH-LEA-PHOTOGRAPHY.COM
WWW.SUZANNAH-LEA-PHOTOGRAPHY.COM

T.I.S.M.ART
7 FINDON CLOSE, WANDSWORTH
LONDON SW18 1NQ
{T} 07963 628274
ARTIFACTS10@AOL.COM

TEARSHEET PHOTOGRAPHY LIMITED
HENLEY-ON-THAMES
{T} 07917 808 284
BRENDAN@CORSAIRFILMS.COM
WWW.TEARSHEETPHOTO.COM

THE CASTING DUO
1 LEWES ROAD
POLEGATE, EAST SUSSEX BN26 5JE
{T} 01323 482292
THE-CASTING-DUO@HOTMAIL.COM
WWW.THE-CASTING-DUO.COM

THE LIGHT STUDIOS
COOPER HOUSE
2 MICHAEL ROAD
FULHAM SW6 2AD
{T} 020 7610 6036
INFO@LIGHTSTUDIOS.NET
WWW.LIGHTSTUDIOS.ORG

TIME MEDIA PRODUCTION
218-220 WHITECHAPEL ROAD
LONDON E1 1BJ

{T} 07876 666 060
SHAH@TIMEMEDIAPRODUCTION.COM
WWW.TIMEMEDIAPRODUCTION.COM

TITUS POWELL
EALING W5 2DZ
{T} 07970 972675
TITUSPOWELL@GMAIL.COM
WWW.TITUSPOWELL.COM

TM PHOTOGRAPHY
SUITE 14 & 15, MARLBOROUGH BUSINESS CENTRE
96 GEORGE LANE LONDON
LONDON E18 1AD
{T} 020 8530 4382
INFO@TMPHOTOGRAPHY.CO.UK
WWW.TMPHOTOGRAPHY.CO.UK

TOBY AMIES PHOTOGRAPHY
20 EATON PLACE
BRIGHTON
SUSSEX BN2 1EH
{T} 07739 108563
STUDIO@PICTUREMAKER.PLUS.COM
WWW.TOBYAMIES.COM

TOBY MERRITT PHOTOGRAPHY
21 BALDWYN GARDENS
LONDON W36HJ
{T} 07956 439595
TOBY@TOBYMERRITT.CO.UK
WWW.TOBYMERRITT.CO.UK

TONY PREECE PHOTOGRAPHY AT STUDIO 49
STUDIO 49 STATFORD WORKSHOPS
BURFORD ROAD, STRATFORD

LONDON E15 2SP
{T} 07939 139097
TONY.PREECE@GMAIL.COM
WWW.TONYPREECE.COM

TRACEY GIBBS PHOTOGRAPHY LTD
54 OLDFIELD ROAD
SALFORD M5 4LZ
{T} 0161 743 0008
INFO@TRACEYGIBBS.CO.UK
WWW.TRACEYGIBBSPHOTOGRAPHY.CO.UK

URBANI PHOTOGRAPHY
103 LIDGET STREET
HUDDERSFIELD
WEST YORKSHIRE HD3 3JR
CONTACT@URBANIPHOTOGRAPHY.COM
WWW.URBANIPHOTOGRAPHY.COM

UTOPIAN PHOTOGRAPHY
FLAT 2/1, 6 COLEBROOKE ST
GLASGOW G12 8HD
{T} 0797 6623880
CHRIS@UTOPIANPHOTOGRAPHY.COM
WWW.UTOPIANPHOTOGRAPHY.COM

VINCENT ABBEY PHOTOGRAPHY
6 LYNTON ROAD, CHORLTON
MANCHESTER M21 9NQ
{T} 0161 860 6794
VABBEY@YAHOO.COM

WWW.VINCENTABBEY.CO.UK
VINCENZO PHOTOGRAPHY
ENFIELD
NORTH LONDON
ENFIELD TOWN EN1 1PZ

{T} 07962 338289
INFO@VINCENZOPHOTOGRAPHY.COM
WWW.VINCENZOPHOTOGRAPHY.COM

WILL ROBINSON PHOTGRAPHY
54 STOKENEWINGTON HIGH ST,
LONDON N16 7PB
{T} 07843 436709
WILLNOTCOMPUTE@GMAIL.COM
WWW.WILLNOTCOMPUTE.CO.UK

WOLF MARLOH
VAUXHALL
LONDON SW8 5NA
{T} 020 8299 9707
HEADSHOTS@10X8.COM
www.10x8.com/

WOW PHOTOGRAPHY
THE STUDIO, 4 BAINES LANE
HINCKLEY LE101PP
{T} 07825 131608
WOWPHOTOGRAPHY@BTINTERNET.COM
WWW.WOW-PHOTOGRAPHY.CO.UK

YELENAVG PHOTOGRAPHY
EXETER EX4 2PU
{T} 07855 584336
YELENA_VG@YAHOO.CO.UK
WWW.GEOCITIES.COM/YELENA_VG

ZACHARY HUNT PHOTOGRAPHY
117 FAR LAUND BELPER
DERBYSHIRE DE56 1FN
{T} 08456 834551
CCP@ZACHARYHUNT.CO.UK
WWW.ZACHARYHUNT.CO.UK

Showreels

With broadband connection speeds improving and DVDs cheap to reproduce, showreels have become an increasingly important way to market yourself. A showreel provides "moving image evidence" of what you are like as a performer. Without it, a casting director or agent can only assess you on the strength of your CV and photograph, which by their two-dimensional nature can only provide part of the picture.

When it comes to all types of screen casting, nothing is more helpful to those casting than being able to see you on camera. So much so, that increasingly casting professionals will only call a person in to audition if they have seen their showreel beforehand. The showreel makes up a key third of your marketing or "job application" package.

Content

Showreels are usually created from a collection of past work, showcasing your range as an actor. Ideally your showreel will consist of clips from broadcast work. However, if you don't have sufficient clips from your body of work you could consider getting a showreel made for you from pieces shot specifically for the showreel. Many of the leading showreel companies now offer 'shoot from scratch' services in which they'll work with you to shoot your choice of scenes. If you have some previous material but not all of it is usable, showreel producers can also help you combine this with material shot from scratch. Some also offer script consultation and direction which are worth considering to ensure you choose suitable material and to get the perfect performance.

TOP PREPARATION TIP

The following process is definitely worth doing: it will save you valuable time and money in your showreel edit and will also help your thought processes when it comes to finalising your clips. Having identified your clips, log where they are on the individual DVDs or tapes, eg: 'Gladiator Clip 3 – starts at: 10 mins and 2 secs, finishes at: 10 mins and 25 seconds'. If you're using VHS, reset the time counter before finding the clip.

CHOOSING YOUR BEST CLIPS

In boxed sections in this chapter the Actor's One-Stop Shop (www.actorsonestopshop.com) provides expert advice on how to approach compiling your showreel:

You're looking for clips which will best show you off. They should show some range, you should be clearly visible within them, and as much as possible they should show you speaking.

Working on the basis of, say, an end four-minute product, when looking through your past work you should keep in mind that essentially you're looking for around eight 30-second clips.

Any clip longer than 30 seconds will feel drawn out. If you're doubtful about this, try watching three or four reels in succession, and you'll quickly notice that 30-second clips feel the 'right length'. In fact, the real rule of thumb is between 10 and 30 seconds. This variable clip length ensures that your end reel will feel pacey, as the viewer is not lulled by the predictability of exactly 30-second clips throughout.

Now, because material, like life, doesn't fit neatly into predetermined chunks, you might find that in reality you have a great clip which is, say, one minute long that you would like to use. The answer in this case is to split the scene into two 30-second segments – and then maybe show one part at the start of the reel and the other towards the end.

This brings us to another key point. When creating a showreel you should not be 'trying to tell a story', ie the running order of the clips should not be dictated by a narrative sequence. It's fine, in other words, if you have two segments of a particular film - one from the start and the other from the end of the film – to reverse the order in the actual showreel.

This is because when creating a showreel the main thrust is to show-off your various performances, not the original films.

When thinking about scripts and scenes it's generally better to concentrate on scenes showing you playing characters you are likely to be cast as. So rather than trying to show your entire range in a showreel, focus on portraying these characters – play to and showcase your existing strengths. Too much versatility makes it difficult for a casting director to picture you in the role, so put your best character forward.

Always use the services of a professional company; there is an art to putting together a professional looking showreel. A showreel that looks like it was cobbled together by a friend won't do you any favours. It really is worth going to the expense of using a professional company which specialises in showreels for actors.

Before deciding on a company, try to view samples of their work to give you an idea of the quality of the finished product. As ever, if you can get personal recommendations from other actors you know, so much the better.

Make the showreel informative and entertaining as this will help maintain a casting director's attention. The first 30 seconds of your showreel are the most important. It's often sensible to start with a brief collage of the work about to be shown, ensuring the casting director gets a quick overview of your talent right from the start.

Alternatively, you might consider opening with a still of your headshot or a long close up, over which you can place your name. At all points in your showreel it should be clear that the focus is on you as it is you who is being showcased, not the other actors. With this in mind, include plenty of close-ups.

Length
Your showreel should ideally be three to four minutes long, with the maximum length of each clip not exceeding 60 seconds, ideally only 30 seconds and of varied length (see box on p101). Try not to exceed six minutes in length; casting directors don't have the time to watch a mountain of showreels from start to finish. Better a pacey three-

SHOT-FROM-SCRATCH REELS

When opting for filming a reel from scratch, the number of scenes you choose to film will largely be dictated by your budget. However, given that the name of the game is to incorporate as quickly as possible some actual past work – even if only of a low-budget nature – we'd advise opting for just one or two scenes. Typically, each would be around one to two minutes long. The advantage here is that as the scenes are being shot specially for you, the focus of any scene will be on you. For this reason, it's perfectly acceptable to present even just one scene to agents and/or casters.

You want something that looks credible on camera – as though it might have been 'lifted' from a fuller-length film or TV production. You should select material on the basis of role-type – ie choose a script which will allow you to portray the kind of character you might reasonably be cast as. Modern scripts work best and generally you should avoid well-known ones or theatre pieces. The former will distract the viewer by inviting comparison with the more famous portrayal of that script, while the latter will usually require skilful adaptation for camera.

Do not be afraid to write something especially for the purpose, or perhaps to get a friend to. If you opt for a monologue, ensure, nevertheless, that there is interaction with the listening character, and that it's believable why the other character is non-speaking. An option might be to give the 'listener' one or two feed/ interjectory lines – which, incidentally, will also help your performance.

If going for two scenes, make sure they are not only a character contrast, but a visual contrast – by filming in two different-looking locations and changing your outfit – not to mention your 'co-star'. It may sound like an obvious tip, but learn you lines thoroughly. Being on camera can be nerve-wracking enough without having to scrabble for your lines.

Think also about your appearance. Overall, unless the character you are playing dictates otherwise, you should be well-groomed and look your best on camera.

143

COPYRIGHT

Given that an actor's showreel is intended for the personal promotion of the actor and not intended to be sold for commercial gain or broadcast, it's not usually expected to secure copyright clearance – and in fact the diversity of the source material involved would in any case tend to make it impractical.

But you should be tactful in any dealings with potential employers, so it often doesn't go amiss to let people know you're collating work for your showreel anyway – and, especially on a low budget film, it's a good idea to let it be known from the outset that one of the key reasons you'll be working on the production is because you'd like a copy of it 'for your showreel' (it may even prompt them to be more honourable about ensuring you get a copy of the end work!).

If you have the opportunity, do check with the broadcaster's rights department – just because you were in a programme or film doesn't mean you have automatic rights to take an extract for viewing in a different format.

minute reel than a five-minute one which seems to drag. Keep it clean, keep it simple and keep it relevant.

Format

If you are considering creating a new showreel, you'll want to end up with both a DVD (or CD-ROM) version of your showreel which you can post to casting directors and a 'streamed' version which you can upload to your website or to websites which offer a hosting service.

The DVD version of your showreel will look pretty standard – but take the time to ensure the box and DVD come with personalised designs which have your name and contact number clearly visible. As most showreel companies will charge you for subsequent copies of your DVD, take the price of DVD duplication services into account when selecting a service provider.

actorexpo

The UK's only tradeshow dedicated
to advancing the careers
of actors and performers.

London and Scotland.

Industry Exhibitors. Classes. Live Performances. Networking.
Visit the website to book tickets. Classes sell out fast.

www.actorexpo.co.uk

THE ACTOR ATTAINMENT SOCIETY

SUPPORTING TALENTED ACTORS
WHO HAVE A PASSION TO SUCCEED

The Actor Attainment Society connects the actor and the industry in an atmosphere designed to support, educate and inspire you in your career development.

Our intimate seminars, led by an industry professional, offer strong advice to put you ahead of the game and open doors to new opportunities.

PREVIOUS GUEST EXPERTS INCLUDE

JOHN CANNON
Casting Director, BBC

NICK MORAN
Film Actor, Writer & Director

LISA BRYER
Film Producer

ILENKA JELOWICKI
Casting Director, MAD DOG CASTING

CHRISTOPHER NICHOLSON
Director & Writer

ASHLEY MADEKWE
Television Actress

★ INTERACTIVE SEMINARS £35 - Q&A SEMINARS £20 ★

As a member of the society you will also receive access to our online members area which offers exclusive articles, discounts, a discussion forum, downloads and more.

FOR FURTHER INFORMATION AND TO APPLY FOR MEMBERSHIP VISIT

www.actorattainment.com

SUPPORTED BY

Koval Studio Photography
www.piotrkowalik.co.uk
07946323631

CCP Actor Testomonials.

"Jon takes the time to get to know you, consulting with you on each stage of the process, allowing you to influence what happens. Relaxed, enjoyable and the end result is a professional headshot that looks like you!"

"Really loved my pictures from Jon. You get to see the pictures on a screen as you go and can change what you're doing accordingly. Highly recommended ...oh, and a great price too."

"Jon is an excellent photographer with a real talent for getting the best from his subjects. He is extremely generous with his time and great value for money, offering a fantastic overall service."

"Really happy with the whole experience. Very friendly atmosphere and as Jon is an actor himself he really knows what is required. Has a "don't like don't pay" policy as well which means you cant lose."

- 100% RISK FREE
- 150+ Digital Shots
- Reluctant/First time sitters very welcome
- FULL SIZE preview `as-we-shoot`
- Sessions available weekdays evenings and weekends

- SW16. Loft Studio
- 2Hr Session
- 5 hand prepped images included
- All Images online the same day
- FREE CD of ALL Images

www.JonCamplingHeadshots.com

020 86798671   photo@joncampling.com   07941 421 101

Changing   Reception   Studio

Jonathan Bosworth Photography
07739 738 570
contact@jonathanbosworth.co.uk

Martin Coyne | Photography
Studio and Location headshots

T 07788788616   **E** martin@martincoyne.com   **W** www.martincoyne.com

'really natural' - *The Independent*

Helen Bartlett | Photography   www.helenbartlett.co.uk

Alumni:
Judi Dench
Laurence Olivier

MA ACTOR TRAINING AND COACHING

Harold Pinter
Cameron Mackintosh
Julie Christie
Michael Grandage
Zöe Wanamaker
Gael Garcia Bernal
Graham Norton
Vanessa Redgrave
Catherine Tate
Deborah Warner
James Nesbitt

Expert in combining academic and vocational study since 1906, Central is a major driving force behind the best emerging talent in the dramatic arts, performance and media industries.

Full-time or part-time study for actor training at Central enjoys international renown. MA Actor Training and Coaching is the only course of its kind in the UK to address the teaching and coaching of acting in a range of environments. The course develops skills as a specialist actor trainer, working with practitioners at Central and elsewhere.

THE CENTRAL SCHOOL OF
SPEECH AND DRAMA
UNIVERSITY OF LONDON

For further information about all courses call 0870 389 1327, email enquiries@cssd.ac.uk, or see www.cssd.ac.uk

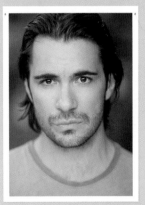
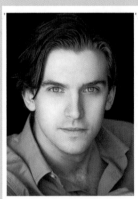

Streamed or internet showreels should be in wmv (Windows Media Video) or QuickTime format, and a typical file size for a two- to three-minute showreel should be around 6Mb.

Usually a showreel editing facility will be able to handle all the regular formats but check with them beforehand if you have a more untypical format eg VHS-NTSC (used in the United States).

Your contact details should be clearly visible at the start and end of the showreel and on all packaging. Where possible try to include your headshot on the CD cover or DVD case.

WHAT TO DO ONCE YOU'VE GOT YOUR REEL

Be aware that once you've put together your new showreel, you are now the proud owner of a powerful marketing tool. Don't rest on your laurels: get out there and make it work for you! Your basic task is to ensure that as many people as possible see it. Besides any agents you may approach with it, on your list of recipients should be anyone who's ever cast you, shortlisted you, or shown any interest in you as an actor. Casting directors, producers, directors, heads of production companies – you should consider anyone who may have casting influence.

In addition, any job application you make should include your new reel – whether or not the job advert requests it.

Go global with it: get it out on the net. There are various web directories which, for a basic charge, will allow you to have an online reel. You can even email it (but do ensure it's properly 'streamed' first or you might provoke angry reactions from casters whose mailboxes you've overloaded).

Keeping your reel current is a good idea. Apart from the obvious benefit of keeping your presentational material fresh, regular updating has the added advantage of giving you the perfect 'excuse' to keep in touch with casters on an ongoing basis.

Costs

Editing previous material is likely to be charged by the hour (probably between £40 and £80 ph), which is why getting your material organised properly important is vital – see the box on p140.

If you need material shot from scratch, it will probably cost a few hundred pounds for each scene – make sure you know where you stand on this before proceeding with a showreel company, and discuss all the details with them. Ideally you won't want to film too many new scenes, in the hope that you'll soon have new material from real work that can be spliced into a updated showreel in due course.

Given that the costs for producing a showreel are high, it's vital that you choose a company with suitable experience of working with actors, and that the end results present you in the best possible way.

A-Z of showreel providers

ACTION SHOWREELS
UNIT 10A
ALSTON WORKS
BARNET, HERTS EN5 4EL
{T} 0845 2575829
INFO@ACTIONSHOWREELS.CO.UK
WWW.ACTIONSHOWREELS.CO.UK

ACTORS AND EDITS
KINGSTON-UPON-THAMES
{T} 020 8979 9185
EDITING@COMPLETINGTHESQUAREPICTURES.COM
HTTP://COMPLETINGTHESQUAREPICTURES.COM/ACT
ORS&EDITS.HTML

ACTORSSHOWREELS.COM
LONDON
SE22 9JQ
{T} 07891 211624
INFO@ACTORSSHOWREELS.COM
WWW.ACTORSSHOWREELS.COM

AFFORDABLE SHOWREELS
COLEBECK MEWS
LONDON
N1 2YA
{T} 020 7359 6487
SHOWREELS@ALBERTOBONA.COM

ARENA PRODUCTIONS
{T} 07836 560236
STUDIO@ARENAPRODUCTIONS.CO.UK
WWW.ARENAPRODUCTIONS.CO.UK

ASPIRE PRODUCTIONS
34A POLLARD ROAD
MORDEN
SURREY SM4 6EG
{T} 0800 0305471
DARREN@ASPIREPRESENTING.COM
WWW.ASPIREPRESENTING.COM

BLANK CANVAS MEDIA
SUITE A1, 5TH FLOOR, GRESHAM HOUSE
53 CLARENDON ROAD
LONDON WD17 1LA
{T} 0845 094 0352
JOHN@BLANKCANVASMEDIA.CO.UK
WWW.BLANKCANVASMEDIA.CO.UK

BRAWIMAGES.COM
40 NEW STREET
STONEHOUSE ML9 3LT
{T} 01698 793363
JIM@BRAWIMAGES.COM
WWW.BRAWIMAGES.COM

BROWNIAN MOTION PICTURES LTD
161 LEIGHAM COURT ROAD
STREATHAM HILL
LONDON SW16 2SE
{T} 020 8677 6059
JEFF@BROWNIANMOTION.CO.UK
WWW.BROWNIANMOTION.CO.UK

147

CJB Media
5 Old Church Close
South Cornelly
BRIDGEND CF33 4SG
{T} 01656 751279
CHRIS@CJBMEDIA.CO.UK
WWW.CJBMEDIA.CO.UK

DREXL8: The production house
5 Lincoln Court
Hampton
TW12 3JZ
{T} 020 8941 5778
DREXL8@LIVE.CO.UK

DV2Broadcast
3 Carolina Way
Salford Quays
MANCHESTER M50 2ZY
{T} 0161 736 5300
INFO@DV2BROADCAST.CO.UK
WWW.DV2BROADCAST.CO.UK

EditBeyond
58 Brooksby Street
58 Brooksby Street N1 1HA
{T} 07772 759036
CONTACT@EDITBEYOND.CO.UK
WWW.EDITBEYOND.CO.UK

Free Showreels
IP4 4EY
{T} 07830 161011
SHOOT50@HOTMAIL.COM
WWW.SHOOT50.BLOGSPOT.COM

Fresh DVD
{T} 07830 023275
GREG@FRESHDVD.CO.UK
WWW.FRESHDVD.CO.UK

Hi Films TV
2 St Andrew's Road
Harrogate
North Yorkshire HG2 7RR
{T} 01423 889632
H.I.F@BTINTERNET.COM
WWW.HI-FILMS.TV

HMR Productions
SW9 8RR
{T} 020 7631 2745
EDIT@HMRLTD.COM
WWW.HMRLTD.COM

I-Star Showreel
5 Prospect Place
Maritime Quarter
Swansea SA1 1QP
{T} 01792 461507
STUDIO@ISTARSHOWREEL.COM
WWW.ISTARSHOWREEL.COM

Inner City Pictures
51-69 Vyner Street
E2 9DQ
{T} 07912 575845
INFO@INNERCITYPICTURES.CO.UK
WWW.INNERCITYPICTURES.CO.UK

IotaMEDIA
Unit 21 Chiltern House
Waterside

CHESHAM HP5 1PS
{T} 0845 1274600
INFO@IOTAMEDIA.CO.UK
WWW.IOTAMEDIA.CO.UK

JOY PRODUCTIONS LTD
LONDON
{T} 020 7247 5798
KEN@JOYPRODUCTIONS.CO.UK
WWW.JOYPRODUCTIONS.CO.UK

KATE LYONS PRODUCTIONS
808A KINGSWAY
DIDSBURY
MANCHESTER M20 5WY
{T} 07845 367486
KEIGHTSLYONS@AOL.COM

KATHERINE LEE EDITOR
118 MOUNTEARL GARDENS
LONDON SW16 2NW
{T} 07884 401430
CONTACT@KATHERINELEE-EDITOR.COM
WWW.KATHERINELEE-EDITOR.COM

KULCHA PRODUCTIONS
STUDIO A108
73-75 SHACKLEWELL LANE
LONDON E8 2EB
{T} 020 7688 2355
INFO@KULCHAPRODUCTIONS.COM
KULCHAPRODUCCTIONS.COM

LIMELIGHT SHOWREELS
{T} 07737 784533
REELS@LIMELIGHT-SHOWREELS.CO.UK
WWW.LIMELIGHT-SHOWREELS.CO.UK

MACHEATH PRODUCTIONS
{T} 07785 394214
ANDREW@MACHEATH.U-NET.COM
WWW.THEALCHEMYOFSCREENACTING.CO.UK

MARK KEMPNER
13 GRANGEWAY, SMALLFIELD
NEAR HORLEY
SURREY RH6 9LZ
{T} 01342 844434
MARK@TRUEVIEWEVENTS.CO.UK
WWW.MARKKEMPNER.CO.UK

MARKSMAN PRODUCTIONS
29 DARTMOUTH COURT
DARTMOUTH GROVE
GREENWICH SE10 8AS
{T} 020 8691 3649
INFO@MARKSMANPRODUCTIONS.NET
WWW.MARKSMANPRODUCTIONS.NET

MK PRODUCTIONS
{T} 07968 357521
MARK@MKPRODUCTIONS.CO.UK

MCMORINE FILMS
28 GREY STREET,
WALLSEND,
NEWCASTLE UPON TYNE, NE28 7SE
{T} 07515 824719
INFO@MCMORINEFILMS.CO.UK
MCMORINEFILMS.CO.UK

MNFILMSLTD
{T} 0800 9553132
INFO@MNFILMSLTD.COM
WWW.MNFILMSLTD.COM

MYCLIPS
FLAT1, 2 BLACKDOWN CLOSE
LONDON
N2 8JF
{T} 020 83719526
INFO@MYCLIPSDVD.COM
WWW.MYCLIPSDVD.COM

NEW REALITY LTD
46B FREEHOLD STREET
FAIRFIELD
LIVERPOOL L7 0JJ
{T} 0151 259 0779
D.ROBERTS@NEWREALITYLTD.COM
WWW.NEWREALITYLTD.COM

NINTH MEDIA
47 USHER LANE
HAXBY
YORK YO32 3LA
{T} 01904 768941
NINTHMEDIA@AOL.COM

NOISE LONDON
THE HAT FACTORY
16-18 HOLLEN STREET
LONDON W1F 8BQ
{T} 07769 686153
AIDAN@NOISELONDON.COM
WWW.NOISELONDON.COM

NOVEMBER REELS
SUITE 209. SOUTH BLOCK,
EALING STUDIOS, EALING GREEN
LONDON
W5 5EP
{T} 020 7193 6580

INFO@NOVEMBER-REELS.COM
WWW.NOVEMBER-REELS.COM

ONE VOICE PRODUCTIONS LTD
NE9 5LE
{T} 0870 9770 699
INFO@ONEVOICEPRODUCTIONS.CO.UK
WWW.ONEVOICEPRODUCTIONS.CO.UK

OVER THE WALL MEDIA
30 LEIGHVILLE GROVE
LEIGH-ON-SEA
ESSEX SS9 2HX
{T} 07773 463340
OVERTHEWALLMEDIA@YAHOO.CO.UK
WWW.OVERTHEWALLMEDIA.CO.UK

PALM TREE ENTERTAINMENT
DOUBLE LODGE
PINEWOOD STUDIOS
BUCKS SL0 0NH
{T} 07940 351152
SUZANNE@DEEVEE.NET
DEEVEE.NET/PALMTREEPOST/SHOWREELS.HTML

PELINOR
LONDON NW3 6AJ
{T} 020 7433 8080
SUPPORT@PELINOR.COM
WWW.PELINOR.COM

PERSONAL MOVIES
20 BENTHAM ROAD
BRIGHTON BN2 9XD
{T} 01273 383292
KEVIN@PERSONALMOVIES.CO.UK
WWW.PERSONALMOVIES.CO.UK/SHOWREEL

PINK LEMON MEDIA GROUP
LOWER GROUND, 8 MAZENOD AVENUE
WEST HAMPSTEAD
LONDON NW6 4LR
{T} 020 7372 1664
INFO@PLMEDIA.NET
WWW.PLMEDIA.NET

PROJECTIONPICTURES.COM
GREATER LONDON
{T} 07958 771120
IAN@PROJECTIONPICTURES.COM
WWW.PROJECTIONPICTURES.COM

REEL TALENT
IG8 0ED
{T} 07730 575483
CONTACT@REELTALENT.NET
WWW.REELTALENT.NET

REELPOTENTIAL
CHARLESTON ST
LONDON SE17 1NG
{T} 020 7703 1707
INFO@REELPOTENTIAL.CO.UK
WWW.REELPOTENTIAL.CO.UK

RETRO REELS
SALUSBURY ROAD
QUEENS PARK
LONDON NW6 6PB
{T} 07896 299 932
MAIL@RETROREELS.CO.UK
WWW.RETROREELS.CO.UK

ROUND ISLAND
ROUND ISLAND
PURFLEET-ON-THAMES
RM19 1QX
{T} 07701 093 183
MAIL@ROUNDISLAND.NET
WWW.ROUNDISLAND.NET

SCENE 2 SEEN PRODUCTIONS
{T} 07956 253861
S2S-PRODUCTIONS@HOTMAIL.CO.UK
WWW.S2SPRODUCTIONS.CO.UK

SHOWREELS FOR ACTORS
MANCHESTER M25 9GL
{T} 0161 7737670
INFO@SHOWREELSFORACTORS.CO.UK
WWW.SHOWREELSFORACTORS.CO.UK

SHOWREELZ
59 CHURCH STREET
ST ALBANS
HERTS AL3 5NG
{T} 01727 752 960
BRAD@SHOWREELZ.COM
WWW.SHOWREELZ.COM

SIGNALIZE LTD
DELTAWORKS
18 REGENT TRADE PARK, BARWELL LANE
GOSPORT PO13 0EQ
{T} 01329 221958
ENQUIRIES@SIGNALIZE.ORG
WWW.SIGNALIZECORPORATEVIDEO.COM

SILLY WEE FILMS
36 THE GLEN
TULLIBODY
FK102GD
{T} 07515 455513
FRASERCOULL@GMAIL.COM
WWW.SILLYWEEFILMS.CO.UK

SILVERTIP FILMS LTD
31 SMITHBROOK KILNS
CRANLEIGH
SURREY GU6 8JJ
{T} 01483 268578
CHRIS@SILVERTIPFILMS.CO.UK
WWW.SILVERTIPFILMS.CO.UK

SMALL SCREEN SHOWREELS
LONDON
{T} 020 8816 8896
ANTHONY@SMALLSCREENVIDEO.COM
WWW.SMALLSCREENSHOWREELS.CO.UK

SPECTRUM PRODUCTIONS
27 MILLBROOK MEW
27 MILLBROOK MEW FY8 5AU
LACCOHEE_2000@YAHOO.COM
MYSPACE.COM/RYANLACCOHEE

STOP&PLAY
187 QUEENS CRESCENT
CAMDEN
LONDON NW5 4DS
{T} 020 7485 8193
INFO@STOPANDPLAY.NET
WWW.STOPANDPLAY.NET

SUSPICIOUS SHOWREELS

2-4 PROWSE PLACE
LONDON NW1 9PH
{T} 020 7284 5860
GARY@SUSPICIOUSMARKETING.COM
WWW.SUSPICIOUSMARKETING.COM

THE ACTOR'S ONE-STOP SHOP
FIRST FLOOR, ABOVE THE GATE PUB
STATION ROAD, WOOD GREEN
LONDON N22 7SS
{T} 020 8888 7006
INFO@ACTORSONESTOPSHOP.COM
WWW.ACTORSONESTOPSHOP.COM

THE REEL DEAL SHOWREEL CO.
6 CHARLOTTE ROAD
WALLINGTON
SURREY SM6 9AX
{T} 020 8647 1235
INFO@THEREEL-DEAL.CO.UK
WWW.THEREEL-DEAL.CO.UK

TTV
205A ROYAL COLLEGE STREET
CAMDEN TOWN
LONDON NW1 0SG
{T} 0207 419 9555
TTVISUALS@MAC.COM
WWW.TTVISUALS.COM

TWITCH FILMS
22 GROVE END GARDENS
18 ABBEY ROAD
LONDON NW8 9LL
{T} 020 7266 0946
POST@TWITCHFILMS.CO.UK
WWW.TWITCHFILMS.CO.UK

Voicereels
Chapter kindly provided by Cut Glass Productions (www.cutglassproductions.com).

If you want to get into the voiceover industry (see p183), your first step will be to create a top quality voicereel to send out to agents, production companies and casting directors. This is your chance to showcase your vocal abilities, and is a powerful 'calling card'. A well put together reel makes an impression - and you won't be considered for voiceover jobs without one.

It's important to get your voicereel right. Even if you have a fantastic voice, if the reel is badly produced or directed, drags on for 10 minutes with boring material, uses the same backing music/scripts as hundreds of other showreels, or doesn't show any variation, it is likely to end up in a frustrated agent's bin!

Your voicereel should showcase your natural voice as much as possible, so it's a good idea to make the most of your natural accent and voice qualities. If a casting director wants a 'northern voice' they usually prefer it to be a genuine one. Occasionally, however, a job may call for one actor to voice several different voices – and if you do have an excellent ear for accents it might be a good idea to try these out in a single animation style piece/narration on your voicereel.

The recording session
You should feel comfortable and relaxed in your chosen recording environment. It is vital that you are given enough time to experiment with material, especially if you are recording a voicereel for the first time.

Good direction and production skills are vital. The director should gently guide you in what suits your voice, what is working for your voice, and what isn't. You might find your voice is just right for intimate, soft-sell ads and promos, but not punchy hard-sell. You may also discover your voice and delivery style is extremely well suited to documentary work. It should be a one-to-one journey – a flexible, creative process between you and the person directing the session.

Recording a voicereel isn't something that should be rushed through in a single hour, or even two. If you are in a studio that rushes you in and out of the door, you probably aren't getting enough guidance, help and direction, and it will be obvious on the finished product.

Your voicereel

Your finished voicereel should be around four minutes long. Any longer, and you will have lost the casting director's attention. It should be edited, together with music and sound effects, to show your voice to its maximum potential. Your reel should contain a mix of commercial ads, documentaries and narrations. A punchy 60-90 second 'montage' that sits at the beginning of the reel is also a good idea, to give a quick snapshot of your abilities.

If you are looking to get into radio drama at the BBC, they ask for a different kind of voicereel altogether, featuring dramatic pieces and no commercials. This should still be punchy, show your best possible vocal range, and be well produced.

Commercial opportunities

In an age of high-speed broadband, having a voicereel to hand has become an important way for an actor to market themselves. The industry has expanded so much that you don't need to be a high profile celebrity in order to get voiceover work. Digital technology has opened up endless possibilities for the voiceover artist: mobile entertainment, animations, narration, e-learning... and there are more commercials, documentaries and factual entertainment shows than ever before.

Although lucrative, the voiceover industry is a competitive industry, just like acting. If you are prepared to market yourself, have a great voice and an individual, well-produced showreel, you are several steps ahead of the competition!

A-Z of voicereel providers

APE MEDIA LTD.
49 BROADWAY
LONDON E15 4BQ
{T} 020 8522 6916
INFO@APE-MEDIA.COM
WWW.APE-MEDIA.COM

BORN IN A BARN AUDIO STUDIO
MOBBS WOOD FARM, NETTLE HILL
ANSTY
WARWICKSHIRE CV7 9JN
{T} 024 7662 1033
ENQUIRIES@BORNINABARNSTUDIO.CO.UK
WWW.BORNINABARNSTUDIO.CO.UK

CRYING OUT LOUD
118 LONG ACRE
LONDON WC2E 9PA
{T} 020 8980 0124
CALDARONEMARINA@HOTMAIL.COM
WWW.CRYINGOUTLOUD.CO.UK

CUT GLASS PRODUCTIONS
STUDIO 187, 181-187 QUEENS CRESCENT
CAMDEN
LONDON NW5 4DS
{T} 020 7267 2339
KERRY@CUTGLASSPRODUCTIONS.COM
WWW.CUTGLASSPRODUCTIONS.COM

DAVID ANGUS AUDIO
HAM HOUSE
7 LOWER ODCOMBE
BA22 8TX

{T} 01935 864376
ANGUSPENNY@SUPANET.COM

DAVID MORLEY HALE
21 POLWORTH ROAD
LONDON SW16 2ET
{T} 07790 865 175
DM_HALE@HOTMAIL.COM
UK.CASTINGCALLPRO.COM/DAVID.MORLEYHALE

DV2BROADCAST
3 CAROLINA WAY
SALFORD QUAYS
MANCHESTER M50 2ZY
{T} 0161 736 5300
INFO@DV2BROADCAST.CO.UK
WWW.DV2BROADCAST.CO.UK

HATS OFF STUDIOS
CHURCH STREET
WITNEY
OXFORDSHIRE OX29 8PS
{T} 01993 898620
MICHAEL@HATSOFFSTUDIOS.COM
WWW.HATSOFFSTUDIOS.COM

HOTREELS
52-53 MARGARET STREET
LONDON W1W 8SQ
020 7952 4362
ALEX@HOTREELS.CO.UK
WWW.HOTREELS.CO.UK

155

Actors' Handbook 2009-10

LANDMARK PRODUCTIONS
18 WILLOWBANK DRIVE
ROCHESTER
KENT ME3 8TW
{T} 07710 540401
KEN@LANDMARKWEB.CO.UK
WWW.LANDMARKWEB.CO.UK

PACIFIC AUDIO
226 WEST REGENT STREET
GLASGOW G2 4DQ
{T} 0141 248 2002
VOICES@PACIFICAUDIO.CO.UK
WWW.PACIFICAUDIO.CO.UK

PLANCK MUSIC
201-209 HACKNEY ROAD
LONDON E2 8JL
{T} 07712 828493
CJINNO@MAC.COM
WWW.PLANCKMUSIC.CO.UK

RUX MUSIC
NO 1 CLIFFORD COURT
WESTBOURNE PARK VILLAS
W2 5EE
{T} 07891 625 504
MAIL@RUXMUSIC.COM
WWW.RUXMUSIC.COM

SILVER-TONGUED PRODUCTIONS
{T} 020 8309 0659
CONTACTUS@SILVER-TONGUED.CO.UK
WWW.SILVER-TONGUED.CO.UK

SYLMERRILLION VOICES
24 ROSEHILL STREET
CHELTENHAM
GLOUCESTERSHIRE
GL52 6SJ
{T} 01242 523576
INFO@SYLMERRILLIONVOICES.CO.UK
WWW.SYLMERRILLIONVOICES.CO.UK

THE SHOWREEL
KNIGHTSBRIDGE HOUSE
229, ACTON LANE
CHISWICK W4 5DD
{T} 020 7043 8660
INFO@THESHOWREEL.COM
WWW.THESHOWREEL.COM

VOICE-OVER MASTERCLASS
4 CHURCH END
REDBOURN
ST ALBANS AL3 7DU
{T} 01582 792 633
VOICE@VOMASTERCLASS.CO.UK
WWW.VOMASTERCLASS.COM

Auditions & interviews

When attending interviews or auditions it's vital to be punctual: plan how you are going to get there, and allow extra contingency time for unexpected delays en route. The casting director may well have allocated specific time slots and the last thing you want is to miss yours. If you're a little early, you will have time to compose yourself.

Arrive well-presented and ready to perform, and introduce yourself clearly. Make eye contact with the casting director and try not to be too nervous. There are ways of dressing appropriately for a part, in such a way as to chime with what you think the character might wear, but unless it's been specifically requested, which is unusual, you should turn up as yourself rather than in costume. First impressions count and are difficult to overturn.

Preparation can really help in building confidence. Learn your lines, practice the piece again and again until you know the words backwards and inhabit the character instinctively. It's difficult to overemphasise how much familiarity with your material can help build confidence and ultimately deliver a good performance.

Under-preparing can have disastrous consequences. Not only will it make you look unprofessional, but if you go into the audition knowing you've not prepared then you may very well find your mouth drying and the words disappearing while the casting director is looking on and, if not shaking their head, then wondering why you're wasting their time.

Practise in front of your friends – in a lot of cases, you may think you have learned a monologue, but as soon as you are in that audition, you have so many distractions that it's easy to forget your lines. Practice might not make perfect but it will sure go a long way! Practice pacing yourself to avoid being breathless or too ponderous.

Auditions

In the audition you'll often be expected to have prepared two contrasting pieces, of about two to three minutes each, to show your range. You may have been given some guidance beforehand indicating the style of piece to perform, or you may have a shortlist of speeches/scenes from which you can pick. If you have free range to choose, select something with which you're familiar, a scene or speech you can contextualise and a character you know and care about. In addition to these prepared pieces you may also be asked to sight-read a scene or monologue.

If you're unsure whether or not to address your monologue to the panel or to a spot on the wall, the best thing to do is to ask. Some people hate it when you address a monologue to them, others don't mind. The key is to determine which they would prefer before you start. If they ask you not to address the monologue to them, then pick a spot on the wall a little above their heads.

Take a couple of seconds to gather yourself before you start and when you finish your monologue, don't say "that's it!", don't apologize and don't make excuses, just take a second or two to pause and the panel ought to know when you have finished.

You're bound to be nervous but try and remain relaxed and confident. The people you'll be performing to are not your enemies, they're human beings and they'll appreciate that auditions are a nerve-wracking experience. Make your nerves and energy work for you, harnessing and utilising them to focus on your performance. You may have your own techniques for steadying the nerves such as mental imagery or breathing patterns.

While directors may have pre-conceived notions of what they're looking for, or the part may demand certain physical characteristics, there are numerous cases of actors going into an audition and success-fully making a part their own with their own unique performance.

Be prepared to 'think around the scene' – understanding the motivations of the character will help you perform it, and will also help if you are invited to discuss the scene afterwards.

Auditions for musical theatre can be a somewhat different experience, from a hectic and anonymous 'open audition' for a big West End production down to a more personal presentation. For the former, don't be angry if your singing is cut short – it doesn't necessarily mean they don't like it.

If you are going for a smaller regional show, make sure you talk to director and choreographer equally. Prepare yourself beforehand with a suitable repertoire of different songs, and try to warm your voice up before the actual audition if you can. As for the dance element, the main point will be to see how you move and hold yourself. Don't wear heavy clothing!

Interviews

Do your background research in preparation for an interview. Find out about the director and as much as you can about the production. Consider other productions the director has undertaken and actors they have worked with. Have they a particular style? What do you think the character is like? Prepare yourself for any common questions such as 'Why do you think you're right for the role?'

Talk about the play or the script if you have read it. Show your enthusiasm and keenness and don't be shy about asking any questions you may have. The interview is a two-way process, providing an opportunity for you to find out more as well as for the director/tutor to assess you.

If there is more than one interviewer, address them all equally. Try not to let personalities get in the way – you're here to show your enthusiasm and skills, so there's not point in getting involved in any disagreements (not that you necessarily have to agree with everything they say – informed discussion can be very positive).

Never feel you have to fill every silence: a common mistake in interviews is to talk nervously at nineteen-to-the-dozen.

Rejection

Being considered for a part, auditioning and then not getting the part is a fact of life for an actor. Rejection is inevitable. This can be painful, especially if you were particularly set on a part for which you thought you were perfect. It's something you'll have to get used to. You certainly won't be alone.

It helps to think of it not as rejection, which can cement a negative perception, but rather to think of it along the lines of "I wasn't chosen this time, roll on next time". The reason you weren't chosen may not be to do with your audition; it could be that you weren't, in the end, physically what the director had in mind or that somebody else was absolutely ideal and shone out. Never let being turned down for a part dent your determination to get the next one!

Attending auditions – including those for which you don't get the part – helps to get your name and face out there and may lead to future recalls and auditions.

Section 4
Sources of work

Unpaid work

In acting the competition is fierce and paid work doesn't always come thick and fast, so new actors often take on unpaid roles to build their reputation, reviews and experience.

The scale and professionalism of unpaid theatre productions and films varies enormously, from a single person who is writer/director/crew with little or no experience of putting a piece together, to much more professional set-ups with full equipment, sound recordists, lighting camera people, a cast of actors, a director, writer. On unpaid productions you'll often find that it's not just the actors working for free – the crew may also be doing it as a labour of love and to learn more, expand their contacts and CV, just like you.

If you're looking to join in with an unpaid production, it will help to know that other people in the team are aiming for professional careers, too. Don't be tempted into thinking that 'amateur dramatics' will help you keep your hand in, for example: do it for fun by all means, but it is unlikely to help your career progression or boost your CV in a way that the industry will warm to.

Student films

Student films can be a great way of learning; simply by being in front of a camera, working with a script, a director and other actors. Everyone has to start somewhere and some of the people you work with on a student project may go on to be the leading lights of tomorrow.

If you're between jobs they can be a means of keeping your skills sharp and of networking with other actors and industry creatives. (It can be the kind of experience you don't get on a course or in your usual environment working with actors and technicians with whom you're familiar.)

As well as the actual on-set experiences, the film is likely to be viewed by a whole host of other people in the business, actors, teachers, directors, so it's another showcase for your talents.

The nature of the project could be anything from an end-of-year student film to a low/no budget film which may go on to get some kind of distribution or lead to members of the cast and crew gaining representation and the film reaching a wider audience (eg via a short film competition), gaining greater exposure for all involved. Ask the film-makers if they have signed up to the Protecting Actors Agreement (**www.protectingactors.org**).

Another option is to 'go it alone' with your own fringe theatre show at one of the festivals – see Section 5 for some specific advice on this.

The downside
The flip side of unpaid work is that you may find yourself traipsing halfway across the country, working with less than professional cast and crew and all for the grand reward of a copy of the finished film for your collection. A casting agent or director may look at your CV and see only a string of non-paid credits and not give you a second glance.

As with work as an extra (see the next chapter), you run the risk of being pigeon-holed and boxing yourself into a particular type of work, not making the transition from unpaid to paid, professional work. Having said this, most people recognise that you have to start somewhere and you can always omit work from your CV if you feel it won't be to your advantage to include it.

SOURCES OF UNPAID WORK

Various websites list casting calls. Mandy (**www.mandy.com**), for example, lists a wide range of primarily unpaid work and is well worth looking at on a daily basis. Casting Call Pro (**www.uk. castingcallpro.com**) provides automated unpaid casting call alerts to your email inbox for free. Shooting People (**www.shooting-people.org**) provides a daily email listing of film and TV casting calls, primarily for student or unpaid productions but with the occasional paid call. It's well worth the £30 annual subscription.

Part-time work

Part-time and temporary work can be a godsend in the acting profession. As well as helping towards the rent it gives you a greater degree of flexibility to attend those all-important interviews and auditions. The obvious drawback with part-time work is that it's not going to let you live like a king or queen.

Part-time jobs usually pay pro rata, so your income will be substantially less than if you were working full time. It's a cliché that the majority of actors take up part-time work in a bar as a waiter or hostess. Like most clichés, there's some truth in it. The shift nature of this and similar types of promotional work you help in fitting auditions around your work commitments.

As well as registering with temping and promotions agencies, a number of which are detailed below, plus corporate role-play firms (see p166), there are a number of other avenues you can pursue. Examples include market research and mystery shopping. These types of jobs often pay cash in hand and you're usually looking at between £30 to £50 per hour.

Extra work

Another classic source of part-time work is of course as an extra, 'walk on' or 'supporting' actor. Make no mistake: although there are people who earn some sort of a living doing loads of 'background' work (though they are often not professional actors), it's tiring work, time-consuming and requires keeping unusual hours. TV and film scenes with extras often start at the crack of dawn and go on for ages as a scene is retaken over and over again. You won't get the chance to hob-nob with the stars!

Having said all that, walk-on work can earn you £100 a day, which could be what gets the bills paid, and can be interesting experience particularly if you want to see what TV and film work is like.

Extra work is sometimes advertised in local newspapers, but you will find more opportunities at web directories such as StarNow (www.starnow.co.uk) or **www.starsinmyeyes.tv**. Total Talent (www.total-talent.com) is a directory where you can list your profile for free for casting directors to look at. There are also numerous specialist agencies for walk-on work. For more information and a list of such agents, see the National Association of Supporting Artistes' Agents at **www.nasaa.org.uk**.

PART-TIME WORK: USEFUL LINKS

PromoJobs Pro is a free site, listing promotional jobs and temporary work for actors, models and promotional staff
www.promojobspro.com

Offtowork offers opportunities in the hospitality industry in London and Birmingham.
www.offtowork.co.uk

N20 provides promotional, modelling and entertainer services.
www.n2o.co.uk

Murder mystery actors: professional actors always required throughout the UK for ongoing as-and-when murder mystery events.
www.knightstemplarevents.co.uk

Making Waves is one of the UK's leading youth and student marketing and PR agencies.
www.makingwaves.co.uk

Chaperonesuk is for chaperones and child minders looking for work and for people looking to hire chaperones and child minders.
www.chaperonesuk.co.uk

NOP Mystery Shopping: visit, make phone calls or internet enquiries to various establishments, posing as a prospective shopper or purchaser of some product or service.
www.cybershoppers.nop.co.uk

Roleplay & corporate training

In addition to acting for stage, screen and radio there are other professional outlets such as roleplaying and corporate training videos. Roleplaying is now commonplace in the business environment and seen by many companies as a valuable means of motivating and educating their employees, from sales reps through to CEOs and from multinational corporations to local authority departments.

There are companies dedicated to providing roleplay actors to businesses, working with the business on the brief then collaborating with the actors to develop tailored roleplay scenarios designed to help the company achieve its aims. Typically, workshops will be run by a trainer aided by actors and delivered to an audience who will usually be asked to participate. The workshops may be run with the aim of improving the morale of employees or instructing them on very specific skills which will be employed in their work, such as sales, customer support techniques or preparing for and giving presentations.

This kind of work puts you in front of an audience and requires you to get into character, improvise and interact, skills vital to the actor. And of course it can carry you through the lean times between roles. Equity doesn't cover or advise on rates for roleplay as it doesn't fall within their categorisation of professional acting work, so you'll sometimes find rates of pay are quite low.

Many businesses also find confident and outgoing actors helpful at trade shows, exhibitions and for marketing presentations to help demonstrate new products and services to the trade or the public.

A-Z of roleplay providers

Act Up
{t} 020 7924 7701
info@act-up.co.uk
WWW.ACT-UP.CO.UK
Act Up started in 1999. We are an independent organisation specialising in communication and acting training. We run short, part-time courses and bespoke, on-site training for people in business. All the trainers are established, professional actors.

ActorFactor
{t} 01626 336166
INFO@ACTORFACTOR.CO.UK
WWW.ACTORFACTOR.CO.UK
ActorFactor provides many different services; actors, facilitators, theatre skills, drama, performance, forum theatre, role play. ActorFactor uses interactive experiential simulation, such as role play, in an environment that promotes learning and development, ultimately to achieve successful change.

Barking Productions
{t} 0117 908 5384
INFO@BARKINGPRODUCTIONS.CO.UK
WWW.BARKINGPRODUCTIONS.CO.UK
Barking Productions is a highly acclaimed creative development and corporate entertainment company, run by professional actors and specializing in drama-based training. Barking Productions has worked with a wide range of clients from blue chip and public service organizations to medium and small companies.

Buzzword Films
{t} 01395 446895
info@buzzword-films.co.uk
WWW.BUZZWORD-FILMS.CO.UK
Buzzword Films is a producer and distributor of high quality interactive training films focusing on a range of important social and health issues

CragRats
{t} 01484 686451
INFO@CRAGRATS.COM
WWW.CRAGRATS.COM
CragRats deliver learning and communication programmes, working with people of all ages and disciplines to create engaging learning experiences which appeal to a range of learning styles. Established in 1989, CragRats now has over 300 professionally trained actors involved in their learning experiences.

167

CREATIVE FORUM

{T} 0845 4301308

INFO@CREATIVEROLEPLAY.CO.UK

WWW.CREATIVEROLEPLAY.CO.UK

Creative Forum offers bespoke training programmes and conference themed performances using theatre, role-play and drama techniques. The training is high impact, memorable and issue led.

DRAMATIC SOLUTIONS

{T} 0845 071 1036

ADMIN@DRAMATICSOLUTIONS.CO.UK

WWW.DRAMATICSOLUTIONS.CO.UK

Dramatic Solutions was created in 2001 when Richard da Costa and Colin Rote met working on a production of Rumplestiltskin. Understanding the power drama has to communicate and the impact it can have on the issues facing business today, they formed the company to utilise this powerful medium in corporate environments. Since then it has helped numerous businesses achieve their objectives using imaginative and memorable events and programmes focused on improving business performance.

IMPACT FACTORY

{T} 020 7226 1877

ENQUIRIES@IMPACTFACTORY.COM

WWW.IMPACTFACTORY.COM

Delivering courses on presentation skills, effective communication, team building, leadership development, public speaking, assertiveness skills, confidence and self esteem to name but a few.

IMPACT UNIVERSAL LTD

{T} 01484 660077

FEEDBACK@IMPACTONLEARNING.COM

WWW.IMPACTUNIVERSAL.COM

Founded on solid principles of quality and reliability, ImpAct on learning has established an enviable reputation for exceeding client expectations. Every training workshop, dramatic presentation or event is thoroughly researched and reviewed to ensure the client brief is accurately interpreted. ImpAct on Learning now services a diverse range of clients in the public sector. It has a committed policy of product development to meet the changing needs of its ever increasing customer base.

INTERACT

{T} 020 7793 7744

INFO@INTERACT.EU.COM

WWW.INTERACT.EU.COM

Interact is the UK's leading exponent of the use of theatre-skills in business. Interact work in close partnership with many organisations in the UK and Europe, to deliver creative solutions to training and development need.

JUST ROLEPLAYERS
{T} 020 8471 8616
HELP@JUSTROLEPLAYERS.COM
WWW.JUSTROLEPLAYERS.COM
Just Roleplayers represents an experienced team of professional actor roleplayers, with a wide cross section of experience, from law to health and from marketing to finance. Professional roleplay is a highly effective and well established method of developing communication skills which draws upon the abilities of professional actors to bring reality to roleplay training sessions.

LAUGHLINES
{T} 0845 170 1600
INFO@LAUGHLINES.NET
WWW.LAUGHLINES.NET
Our actors are available for all types of corporate work. We can take on any role-play situation and write the scripts to tailor it for your subject matter. Our work is usually comedy based, as this seems to make a bigger impact. We have many satisfied clients including Shell.

NV MANAGEMENT
{T} 01608 674181
HELLO@NVMANAGEMENT.CO.UK
WWW.NVMANAGEMENT.CO.UK
Specialists in providing professional actors for the business world and also offering an enticing range of related services including bespoke training films, streaming videos for the web, interactive seminars and much more.

PROACTIVE ROLEPLAY
{T} 020 8761 3804
ENQUIRIES@PROACTIVEROLEPLAY.COM
WWW.PROACTIVEROLEPLAY.COM
ProActive Roleplay looks to bridge the gap between the corporate training industry and the acting profession and is able to do this given the professional backgrounds of the two founder members who trained as professional actors at the Bristol Old Vic Theatre School and since graduating have combined appearing regularly as actors in theatre and television with their work in the training industry. Prior to embarking on acting careers they both built a considerable history of working in industry, ranging from public sector to private industry management.

ROLEPLAYUK
{T} 01780 761960
ACTORS@ROLEPLAYUK.COM
WWW.ROLEPLAYUK.COM
RoleplayUK's actors are trained to apply specific acting techniques developed by Sanford Meisner. These techniques examine how to react to stimuli provided and encourage a naturalistic reaction rather than a performance.

Actors' Handbook 2009-10

STEPS
{T} 020 7403 9000

MAIL@STEPSDRAMA.COM

WWW.STEPSDRAMA.COM

Founded in 1992, and originally known as Steps Roleplay, we began by providing professional role players for assessment centres and skills practice. The company has grown and developed since then and we now offer a range of drama based initiatives. The company was re-branded as Steps Drama Learning Development in 2001. We now have a senior management team of six, with support from in-house project managers as well as an administrative and accounting team. All our programmes are designed with the clients' specific learning objectives in mind and delivered by an experienced team of professional actors (all of whom are trained by Steps), facilitators, consultants and associate trainers.

THE PERFORMANCE BUSINESS
{T} 01932 888 885

INFO@THEPERFORMANCE.BIZ

WWW.THEPERFORMANCE.BIZ

We are always looking for actors who can portray authentic business roles. We welcome CV submissions from actors of all types. It is essential that you have worked in a business environment.

Theatre in Education

Theatre in Education (TIE) uses theatre to explore educational or social issues with children and young people. Specialist TIE companies often travel around the country, presenting workshops at schools, arts centres, community halls or smaller local theatres, and can provide an ongoing source of work for the suitably motivated actor. TIE programmes have traditionally covered issues such as racism or gender, but nowadays can equally focus on issues such as road safety, bullying or smoking, as well as more formal educational topics.

TIE work is likely to draw upon a wide range of skills, such as playing many different parts, singing, playing musical instruments or helping young people take roles themselves. Actual sessions can vary greatly in length, from short workshops to extended half- or full-day workshops. The touring nature of this work can also mean that it is exhausting – and a driving licence is probably a must.

In some cases teaching experience might be an asset, too – certain TIE companies look for it when recruiting, particularly when their work relates to specific aspects of the National Curriculum. Some companies (such as Oily Cart) also specialise in working with young people who have learning disabilities. You may be expected to attend a special workshop before you can be considered for joining some groups.

TIE can bring great rewards for the actor, and many end up sticking to this field for their whole careers, though if you're hoping for stardom this might not be the route, and rates of pay can be variable. Liking work with young people is of course a prerequisite.

A-Z of TIE companies

ACTIONWORK
{T} 01934 815163
INFO@ACTIONWORK.COM
WWW.ACTIONWORK.COM
Actionwork is one of the South Wests leading theatre-in-education companies and performs to schools throughout North Somerset, Somerset, the South West, England, the UK and other parts of the world. Recent international tours included visits to Japan and Malyaysia. Through theatre-in-education we can explore many different topics, social issues, and pshe programmes. All of our shows are backed up with workshops and can include lesson plans, evaluation reports and a variety of other resources.

AESOP'S TOURING THEATRE COMPANY
{T} 01483 724633
INFO@AESOPSTHEATRE.CO.UK
WWW.AESOPSTHEATRE.CO.UK
Aesop's Touring Theatre Company specialises in Theatre in Education, touring schools, art centres and theatres nationally throughout the year with plays and workshops specifically written and designed for Nursery, Infant and Junior age groups. The company aims to educate young audiences through the powers of entertainment and imagination whilst, at the same time, encouraging children to question and think for themselves. A high standard of professionalism is maintained by employing experienced actors with specialist skills and considerable enthusiasm.

ARC
{T} 020 8594 1095
NITA@ARCTHEATRE.COM
WWW.ARCTHEATRE.COM
For more than 20 years Arc has specialised in creating and performing theatre that challenges assumptions and causes real change in the way that people relate to one another at work, at school and in the community. As a pioneering organisation we were instrumental in bringing the issue of racism in football to the forefront of public awareness. The organisations that we work with are those that seek to move forward and achieve a lasting difference, whether it be in the field of diversity, inclusion, education, health, criminal justice or community cohesion.

BARKING DOG
{T} 020 8883 0034
INFO@BARKINGDOG.CO.UK
WWW.BARKINGDOG.CO.UK
Drawing on its vast experience of presenting and devising children's shows and drama, The Barking Dog Theatre company performs at around 250 schools each year. Other venues include: The

Barbican Centre, Cambridge City Festival, The Maltings St Albans, Colchester Arts Centre and many other theatres, arts centres and outdoor events.

BIG WHEEL
{T} 020 7689 8670
INFO@BIGWHEEL.ORG.UK
WWW.BIGWHEEL.ORG.UK
Big Wheel shows are funny, fresh and focused – which makes them an ideal way to deliver information. We have been presenting schools workshops since 1984. Our tried-and-tested show formats connect with the audience using contemporary pop-culture references and parody. Students have the opportunity to explore sensitive issues and consequences in a safe environment; young people facing challenging decisions and dilemmas are able to share views and consider the facts throughout the show, as well as having a fantastic, memorable time. Big Wheel shows are an example of TIE at its most effective.

BIGFOOT
{T} 0870 0114 307
INFO@BIGFOOT-THEATRE.CO.UK
WWW.BIGFOOT-THEATRE.CO.UK
Bigfoot Theatre Company is a UK wide organisation that promotes theatre arts as a tool to educate and empower children and teachers alike. We exist in order to offer quality creative learning experiences that are accessible, sustainable and far reaching.

BITESIZE
{T} 01978 358320
ADMIN@BITESIZETHEATRE.CO.UK
WWW.BITESIZETHEATRE.CO.UK
Bitesize was set up in September 1992 by Artistic Director Linda Griffiths to specialize in theatre for young people. Our aim is to produce high quality, accessible shows for a schools audience and so our annual programme of between ten and twelve productions contains a mixture of shows from new writing to Shakespeare. It includes educational shows based on National Curriculum requirements, adaptations of Classic Stories and entertaining seasonal shows.

BLACK CAT PUPPET THEATRE
{T} 01535 637359
DIANA@BLACKCAT-THEATRE.CO.UK
WWW.BLACKCAT-THEATRE.CO.UK
The Black Cat Theatre company was set up in 1985 and operates from a small village on the edge of the Yorkshire Dales. Founder member Diana Bayliss works as a solo puppeteer/performer, often in collaboration with other artists. The company provides puppet and shadow theatre performances, workshops, residencies and training in schools, theatres and community venues throughout the UK.

Blah Blah Blah!

{T} 0113 2740030

ADMIN@BLAHS.CO.UK

WWW.BLAHS.CO.UK

Based in Leeds for twenty years we have been taking theatre to young people across the country and internationally. Combining creative freedom with stark realism, our plays have provoked, captivated and communicated with hundreds of youth centre and school audiences. The company was created in Leeds in 1985 by three graduates from the Drama, Theatre and Television course at King Alfred's College, Winchester.

Box Clever

{T} 020 7357 0550

ADMIN@BOXCLEVERTHEATRE.COM

WWW.BOXCLEVERTHEATRE.COM

Box Clever is a touring theatre company which performs to over 70,000 young people per year, touring to schools, colleges and theatres across the UK. Our work is broad and contemporary, across many different disciplines including dance, film and music. Led by the writer-in-residence, Michael Wicherek, the company has a particular focus on new writing and creating pathways by which young people become active partici-pants in theatre projects, both within and outside formal education.

Bzents

{T} 01664 434565

ENQUIRIES@BZENTS.CO.UK

WWW.BZENTS.CO.UK

Bzents specialises in high quality and innovative entertainment for children, families, corporate events, summer fairs and historical events.

C&T

{T} 01905 855436

INFO@CANDT.ORG

WWW.CANDT.ORG

C&T was formed in 1988 by four Drama graduates from University College Worcester (now University of Worcester). Collar and TIE (as the company was then called) soon developed a strong reputation in Worcestershire and the West Midlands for touring plays in the grand tradition of Theatre in Education. Over the last ten years, we have been continuously developing new ideas, placing digital technologies at the heart of the drama, and giving young people a new sense of confidence that drama does connect to their experience, and that they do have a creative contribution to make to their community.

CHAPLINS
{T} 020 8501 2121
ENQUIRES@CHAPLINSPANTOS.CO.UK
WWW.CHAPLINSPANTOS.CO.UK
Touring children's pantomime company, entertaining children of all ages throughout the UK, able to perform in all venues, including schools.

CLASSWORKS THEATRE
{T} 01223 321900
INFO@CLASSWORKS.ORG.UK
WWW.CLASSWORKS.ORG.UK
Classworks was founded in 1983 as Cambridge Youth Theatre by Claudette Bryanston and Jenny Culank to provide a creative outlet for young people aged 15-25 years. The professional touring arm of the company tours at least once per year and is hosted by some of our leading national venues and arts centres, carrying the flag for the best in young people's theatre.

CRAGRATS
{T} 01484 686451
INFO@CRAGRATS.COM
WWW.CRAGRATS.COM
As education specialists we design and deliver programmes for schools and other educational environments. We use a range of creative techniques such as theatre roadshows, interactive workshops, media, competitions and awards, special events and much more to make your project powerful and unique. Working with young people is just one element of our service – we connect with teachers, parents and the wider community.

CREW
{T} 0845 260 4414
INFO@CREW.UK.NET
WWW.CREW.UK.NET
Our team are committed to bringing you the very best in educational drama. Promising consistent quality, excitement and learning in over 15 workshops CREW inject drama, humour, and life into all areas of the Primary National Curriculum. With workshops covering Victorians, Romans, healthy living and many more.

FREEDOM THEATRE
{T} 01225 851651
INFO@FREEDOMTHEATRE.CO.UK
WWW.FREEDOMTHEATRE.CO.UK
Freedom Theatre Company is a profes-sional theatre company and a registered charity based in Bath. The company is committed to excellence and integrity at all levels and is available to bring pro-fessional, live theatre to schools, prisons, churches and theatre venues across the region.

FRESHWATER THEATRE

{T} 020 8525 7622

INFO@FRESHWATERTHEATRE.CO.UK

WWW.FRESHWATERTHEATRE.CO.UK

Freshwater Theatre Company is proud to have become one of the most respected theatre-in-education companies in the UK. Over the last ten years the company has brought educational drama to thousands of children in primary and special needs schools all over London and the south east, providing unforgettable entertainment and learning.

GOLDEN EGG PRODUCTIONS

{T} 01372 451452

WWW.GOLDENEGGPRODUCTIONS.COM

Golden Egg Productions a touring theatre company for audiences age 3-18 years. It is made up of dedicated and experienced actors and theatre professionals with extensive backgrounds in young people's theatre and education. We have front line experience which enables us to know what children want and also what is most important to our customers: quality, reliability and value for money.

HALF MOON YOUNG PEOPLE'S THEATRE

{T} 020 7265 8138

ADMIN@HALFMOON.ORG.UK

WWW.HALFMOON.ORG.UK

Half Moon Young People's Theatre aims to produce and present professional theatre for and with young people that informs, challenges and shapes their artistic potential, placing these creative

experiences at the core of our policies and practices. The company principally serves London and works exclusively with young people from birth to age 17, placing a particular emphasis upon engaging those often excluded in terms of culture (ethnicity) and ability (disability).

HOBGOBLIN

{T} 0800 5300384

INFO@HOBGOBLINTHEATRECOMPANY.CO.UK

WWW.HOBGOBLINTHEATRECOMPANY.CO.UK

Hobgoblin Theatre Company is a young and dynamic group of actors committed to bringing entertaining, educational theatre into your school. We have all trained professionally and are members of Equity, as well as having extensive experience of Theatre In Education. We write all of our plays ourselves to ensure that they have a firm historical basis that directly supports the National Curriculum. Each of the hour long plays brings the past to life through vibrant characters and engaging stories, during which time the children are involved interactively through decision making and discussion.

IMPACT UNIVERSAL LTD

{T} 01484 660077

FEEDBACK@IMPACTUNIVERSAL.COM

WWW.IMPACTUNIVERSAL.COM

ImpAct on Learning is a communications and training provider using theatrical techniques. We use drama to help education providers deliver messages, to motivate or challenge students.

JACOLLY PUPPET THEATRE
{T} 01822 852346
THEATRE@JACOLLY-PUPPETS.CO.UK
WWW.JACOLLY-PUPPETS.CO.UK
Jacolly Puppet Theatre is a professional touring company based in Devon, England, which has toured widely on both sides of the Atlantic since 1977. Educational productions are mainly for primary schools and currently include environmental issues, biodiversity, road safety and bullying.

KINETIC THEATRE
{T} 020 8286 2613
PAUL@KINETICTHEATRE.CO.UK
WWW.KINETICTHEATRE.CO.UK
Kinetic Theatre Company Ltd is a professional Theatre-in-Education company touring musical plays geared to the National Curriculum for Science to Primary schools and theatres throughout the UK. Our purpose is to supplement science teaching practices in a fun, dramatic yet educational way.

KIPPER TIE
KIPPERTIE2004@AOL.COM
WWW.MOLESBUSINESS.COM
Kipper Tie Theatre was formed by writer/director Bernie C. Byrnes and writer/composer Jim Fowler in Newcastle upon Tyne. Our aim is to produce immersive, educational, exciting and above all entertaining theatre for children of all ages. Our energetic

approach, which mixes acting with dance, music and mime, is attracting increasing recognition and has led to our skills being 'loaned out' to companies producing theatre for adults.

LANTERN THEATRE COMPANY
{T} 020 8944 5794
WWW.LANTERNARTS.ORG
Lantern Theatre Company have many shows under their belts and offer a range of performances for different ages and areas of the curriculum. Recent developments have included receiving grants to perform in hospices and hospitals. Lantern Theatre Company enjoys performing in special needs schools and playschemes.

LITTLE FISH
{T} 020 8269 1123
INFO@LITTLEFISHTHEATRE.CO.UK
WWW.LITTLEFISHTHEATRE.CO.UK
Our mission is to produce high quality innovative theatre productions and drama experiences for young people in London. Through its activities, the company seeks to challenge social injustice and inspire personal and community growth and change.

LIVE WIRE PRODUCTIONS
{T} 01224 592777
INFO@LIVEWIREPRODUCTIONS.ORG.UK
WWW.LIVEWIREPRODUCTIONS.ORG.UK
Award winning Live Wire Productions, an ensemble science Theatre in Education company, was founded in 1994 and is a unique resource for schools, the community and organisations seeking to improve an understanding of basic scientific principals as a prerequisite to change in attitudes through drama. All 36 commissioned productions produced by the company to date cover a wide range of subjects where each performance is customised to the group, audience, class etc ensuring that the optimum impact is achieved and that the key messages relevant to the needs of those in attendance are delivered.

LONDON BUS THEATRE
{T} 01208 814514
KATHY@LONDONBUSTHEATRE.CO.UK
WWW.LONDONBUSTHEATRE.CO.UK
The London Bus Theatre Company is one of the leading TIE groups in the UK and can offer schools and colleges drama workshops and DVDs/videos on issues such as bullying, drugs, anti social behaviour and interview techniques. The London Bus Theatre Company converted to a CIC in July 2006 and is one of the leading Theatre in Education groups in the UK. Our funding is from LEAs, community funds and trusts as well as Police Forces

and PCTs. We are in constant demand as our work is of the highest quality and has proved to be cost effective for crime and disorder and substance misuse initiatives. BP, Umbro, KeyMed and the Co-operative group have sponsored a wide range of projects since 2001.

LOUD MOUTH EDUCATION & TRAINING
{T} 0121 4464880
INFO@LOUDMOUTH.CO.UK
WWW.LOUDMOUTH.CO.UK
Loud Mouth Educational Theatre Company use theatre to explore young people's issues and views. Our interactive education and training programmes are well researched, lively and accessible, with sessions aimed at adults as well as young people. Loud Mouth tours nationally and internationally and has gained a reputation as one of the country's premier theatre in health education companies.

M6 THEATRE COMPANY
{T} 01706 355 898
INFO@M6THEATRE.CO.UK
WWW.M6THEATRE.CO.UK
M6 Theatre Company is dedicated to the development and presentation of innovative and relevant, high quality theatre for young people. M6 uses theatre as a positive, creative and active learning medium to assist young people's understanding and enrich their imagination.

MAGIC CARPET
{T} 01482 709939
JON@MAGICCARPETTHEATRE.COM
WWW.MAGICCARPETTHEATRE.COM
Magic Carpet Theatre has been presenting shows and workshops since 1982. We tour children's theatre productions and workshops to schools all over the UK and abroad.

MONSTER THEATRE PRODUCTIONS LTD
{T} 0191 2404011
INFO@MONSTERPRODUCTIONS.CO.UK
WWW.MONSTERPRODUCTIONS.CO.UK
Monster is proud to be one of the UK's leading producers of children's theatre for the under sevens and providers of youth theatre programmes. To date we have given literally thousands of children their first experiences of theatre. Using a unique blend of puppetry, performance, interaction and live music we provide young children with an enchanted cornucopia of modern myths and visual magic to appreciate and share with their families.

OILY CART
{T} 020 8672 6329
OILIES@OILYCART.ORG.UK
WWW.OILYCART.ORG.UK
From its beginning in 1981, Oily Cart has challenged accepted definitions of theatre and audience. In particular we have created delightful, multi-sensory, highly interactive productions for the very young and for young people with complex disabilities.

ONATTI
{T} 01926 495220
INFO@ONATTI.CO.UK
WWW.ONATTI.CO.UK
Performs French, Spanish and German language plays for all UK and ROI Secondary Schools and UK primary schools.

POLKA THEATRE
{T} 020 8543 4888
ADMIN@POLKATHEATRE.COM
WWW.POLKATHEATRE.COM
Polka Theatre is one of the few venues in the UK which is dedicated exclusively to producing and presenting high quality theatre for young audiences. Since our doors opened in 1979, this unique venue has offered children a first taste of the thrilling, challenging and inspiring world of theatre. Every year, over 100,000 children discover theatre at Polka.

PROPER JOB
{T} 0870 990 5052
MAIL@PROPERJOB.ORG.UK
WWW.PROPERJOB.ORG.UK
Proper Job produces high quality theatre using the biomechanical technique. Our productions tour to community venues including schools and normally include full costume, impressive sets, lighting, music and are fully blacked out to provide a memorable experience for audience and participants. We aim to maximise the full participative potential of performance in theatre through our drama workshops exploring specific

issues such as citizenship, local democracy, stereotyping, sex and relationship theatre and substance misuse.

QUANTUM THEATRE
{T} 020 8317 9000
OFFICE@QUANTUMTHEATRE.CO.UK
WWW.QUANTUMTHEATRE.CO.UK

QUICKSILVER THEATRE
{T} 020 7241 2942
TALKTOUS@QUICKSILVERTHEATRE.ORG
WWW.QUICKSILVERTHEATRE.ORG
Quicksilver Theatre is a children's theatre company who commission and produce new plays and perform them to children the length and breadth of Britain and abroad, providing many with their first experience of live theatre.

SMALL WORLD
{T} 01239 615952
INFO@SMALLWORLD.ORG.UK
WWW.SMALLWORLD.ORG.UK
These are the sorts of things that we do: participatory theatre, arts and culture for development, performances, arts and refugees, workshops, training, puppet and mask making, facilitating participatory consultations, PLA & PRA processes, evaluating arts and development projects, intergenerational projects, processions, carnivals, consultantcy, cabaret, giants and giant shadow puppets, healthy eating and arts projects, multimedia events, installations and more.

TAG THEATRE
{T} 0141 429 5561
INFO@TAG-THEATRE.CO.UK
WWW.TAG-THEATRE.CO.UK
TAG Theatre Company is one of the major players in the children and young people's theatre sector in Scotland. TAG continues to offer an exceptionally broad range of highest quality theatre productions and participatory projects designed to engage and inspire Scotland's children and young people. Established in 1967, TAG draws upon unparalleled experience in generating memorable creative experiences for our young citizens both within and outwith the formal education sector. Each year, TAG brings outstanding professional performances to audiences in theatres and schools across the country. All our performance work is supported by fully integrated, cutting edge education programmes.

THE KEY STAGE
{T} 01342 892951
INFO@THEKEYSTAGE.CO.UK
WWW.THEKEYSTAGE.CO.UK
The Key Stage is a Theatre in Education company visiting schools across the UK. Our key aim is to make learning fun! Through comedic, exciting and fast-paced theatrical shows, The Key Stage endeavours to both educate and entertain. Every show is accompanied with detailed teachers' notes and suggested educational activities - these

can be used in conjunction with the play to enhance the learning experience as a pre or post show lesson.

THE PLAY HOUSE
{T} 0121 464 5712
INFO@THEPLAYHOUSE.ORG.UK
WWW.THEPLAYHOUSE.ORG.UK
The Play House creates opportunities for children, young people and their families to engage in high quality drama and theatre to explore and make sense of the world they live in. We do this through two touring companies – Language Alive! and Catalyst Theatre – and a range of projects such as The Healthy Living Centre and international projects like For Tomorrow.

THEATRE CENTRE
{T} 020 7729 3066
ADMIN@THEATRE-CENTRE.CO.UK
WWW.THEATRE-CENTRE.CO.UK
Theatre Centre exists to commission and present new pieces of professional theatre specifically created for young people. The company was founded in 1953 by Brian Way whose observations of the unimaginative fare offered to children by London theatres led him to explore a more innovative approach.

THEATRE IN EDUCATION TOURS
{T} 01934 815 163
TIE@TIETOURS.COM
WWW.TIETOURS.COM
Tie Tours is an international theatre and training company. We provide shows

and workshops to explore many issues including bullying racism and violence. Innovative, exciting, educational and great fun. Established in January 1995, the company has attracted many diverse talented people to its ranks. Exciting shows, amazing workshops: we have performed all over the UK to a variety of people in a variety of venues including schools, youth clubs, community centres, hospitals, open-air housing estates, parks, theatres and festivals.

THRIFT
{T} 01635 41119
OFFICE@THRIFTMUSICTHEATRE.CO.UK
WWW.THRIFTMUSICTHEATRE.CO.UK
Although Thrift root their work in theatre, the emphasis in all of their projects is the learning experience. We try to develop theatre as a medium for developing entrepreneurial activity, teaching young people that experiment is good, certainty does not matter and ways of finding creative solutions to problems. We seek to find ideas for Theatre in unusual and sometimes difficult places, being inspired by things that most people would never see or notice, anywhere & everywhere. In buildings and architecture; the sounds and rhythms of the street; colours, spaces, people walking past in a hurry.

181

Paid work

Much work in forthcoming productions will be filtered through casting directors and agents, but there are various other avenues which you can pursue to find out about auditions and what's in the production pipeline.

CASTING CALL PRO
UNIT 1, WATERLOO GARDENS, LONDON N1 1TY
{T} 020 7288 2233
INFO@CASTINGCALLPRO.COM
WWW.UK.CASTINGCALLPRO.COM
Casting Call Pro (CCP) was established in 2004 and offers an online CV service, casting alerts, peer networking, and a variety of industry guides and resources. It currently lists 20,000+ actors and is used by hundreds of production companies, casting directors and employers. Standard membership includes a profile listing in the directory and is free. Premium membership is £17+vat per month or £130 +VAT for a year.

CASTWEB
7 ST LUKES AVENUE, LONDON SW4 7LG
{T} 020 7720 9002
INFO@CASTWEB.CO.UK
WWW.CASTWEB.CO.UK
Established in 1999, CastWeb is an email-based casting breakdown service. Eligibility for subscription membership requires one of the following: "a current entry in the industry casting directory Spotlight, or membership of the actors' union Equity, or a suitable CV submitted to Castweb for approval". Monthly subscription is £17.95 + VAT, with reductions for 3/6/12 months.

EQUITY JOB INFORMATION SERVICE
GUILD HOUSE, UPPER ST MARTINS LANE,
LONDON WC2H 9EG
{T} 020 7379 6000
WWW.EQUITY.ORG.UK
Up to the minute breakdowns available to all Equity members. See also Equity, p222.

PCR
PO BOX 100, BROADSTAIRS CT10 1UJ
{T} 01843 860885
INFO@PCRNEWSLETTER.COM
WWW.PCRNEWSLETTER.COM
Something of an industry standard, PCR is a weekly newsletter listing what's in pre-production or casting. Prices range from £29 for 5 weeks to £260 for a full year. PCR also publish Theatre Report, covering fringe and repertory theatre (from £11.50 for three months), and Filmlog.

THE STAGE
47 BERMONDSEY STREET, LONDON SE1 3XT
{T} 020 7403 1818
ADMIN@THESTAGE.CO.UK
WWW.THESTAGE.CO.UK
Published weekly, The Stage carries industry news, articles and castings. Some job ads are free at the website; subscription to the newspaper (from £14 quarterly, £53 a year) gives full access.

Voiceover work

This chapter was kindly provided by James Bonallack, director of Foreign Voices (www.foreignvoices.co.uk).

How can you succeed in the voiceover business? You've got a brand new voice or showreel with a trendy mix of commercials, corporates and narratives and now you're ready to sit down behind the mic and start earning the big money. Let's start with the good news: if you're Jenny Eclair, Tom Baker or Jack Dee it's easy – your agent calls you, you turn up at the studio where people make a huge fuss of you, you voice a 30-second commercial and then when the cheque arrives you think there's one zero too many on the end. If not, much as with anything else in life, you'll get out what you put in – if you're lucky. Having a great voice is the easy bit – making money with it is a whole different story. This snapshot of the UK voiceover industry will help you make some informed decisions and perhaps avoid some painful mistakes.

Getting started is the most difficult part. People will not be beating a path to your door; you're going to have to get them interested in you and, more importantly, your voice and what you can do with it.

Three golden rules

A producer is looking for three things in a voice. First, that you have a voice that's worth paying for, which means that your voice will have certain qualities. It doesn't mean smooth or rich or sexy or hard sell or sporty or that your voice is recognizable. It doesn't mean that you can narrate or sight read effortlessly for hours. It doesn't even mean that you are studio savvy and know what the engineer wants before he does! It simply means that your voice has got a certain something that he or his client feels fits their requirement which is why your reel has got you a phonecall and which is why you are nervously pacing down a Soho side street looking for a studio with a name like Beach (if they think they're trendy) or Digital Sound and Video Mastering Ltd (if they don't care who thinks they're trendy).

The second thing the producer is expecting is that you do what it says on your demo or voiceover CV. That means if you say you narrate well

FEES FOR VOICE WORK

Here are some basic rules which will preserve your sanity and hopefully improve your bank balance. Voiceover sessions are calculated by the hour and then the half hour, half day or day rate. Never work for less than £50 an hour on any project that is of a commercial or corporate nature. This accounts for 95% of all voiceover sessions.

Jobs at the lowest end of the pay scale include voice telephony, charity work, talking books, language tapes and other semi-commercial products. Don't be misled, though: there are well paid projects out there in abundance in all of those areas.

Better paid work includes corporates, broadcast (idents, continuity, documentary talking heads and narrations), commercials for radio and TV and computer games. There are dozens of different types of paid work for voiceover artists but the top end is where you want to be. If you give your voice to a commercial or to a product that people are parting with their hard earned cash to buy then the chances are that you will be getting a buyout (common) or royalties (less and less common).

As a rule of thumb you should be happy working in a band from £130-£180 per hour depending on who you are working for and what kind of work you are doing. Again, check the internet and voiceover portals especially for more detail. Try Equity and Usefee TV (**www.usefee.tv**) especially for radio, TV and advertising usage deals.

Your approach to the client regarding rates is also important. A 'voice' that works efficiently and overlooks a modest overrun with good humour will be asked back. For their part, producers are usually very fair and honest but there are horror stories. (One company offered a voice artist £250 to do 24 internet ads. Luckily they found out from another voice just leaving the studio that the fee should have been in the region of £2500 once usage was taken into account.)

then you had better be able to narrate well. If it says you're as cheap as chips because you've only done a bit of hospital radio before you decided to become a voice actor then his expectations will be very much less. The point is don't say you're a genius if you're not – you'll be found out!

Finally, the third thing they want from you is that you can take direction. That simply means read what it says on the script unless it's obviously not correct; listen to what you are being asked to do and do it without a fuss and to the best of your abilities. As you gain experience you'll develop confidence about voicing your opinions but to begin with concentrate on getting the right result and showing willing.

Voiceover agents

One of the questions I hear most from new voices is "How do you find a voiceover agent?". Start by sending your demo to agents and anyone else who might be useful – but call first. There is virtually no chance that an agent will take you on if you send your demo in unsolicited. Your chances improve when you take the trouble to ask intelligent questions about their business and how you could be of use to them, supported by a clear voice CV and a short demo with your phone number on the CD and on the box spine.

But do you really need an agent just yet? It sounds odd but actually they are going to be a lot more interested in you if you've got some solid voicing experience under your belt before you start to pester them for representation.

Certainly a good agent will greatly improve your earnings and supply you with regular work but equally there are many voices languishing unused on agency books. I can think of one agency in particular which has 100 or more voices on its books. Their top people work regularly but the rest don't get a look in – the agent is too busy worrying about his star clients. Agencies do hire but they tend to hire by developing relationships with voices they know.

With the advent of online voiceover portals many agencies are booking voices without actually going to the trouble of representing them. The relationship builds and eventually they slot into the agency by default.

(By the way that's a two way street. Many savvy voices are now representing themselves and are represented by more than one agent to find as many outlets as possible for their voice. Having said that, the traditional model of putting all your work via one agent is under threat but still very much in place at the top of the food chain. If you have a top agent you won't want to upset them by touting for work outside of that relationship.)

Internet portals

If you're at all familiar with voiceover portals you'll instantly see the advantages. You're on the internet 24/7; you have your own URL (web address) without having to set up your own site; you can be searched by producers in various ways and you can take advantage of other online databases to send your link to potential clients. The better portals will offer free advice and information about aspects of the industry and directories of relevant contacts. Several portals are very established while the newer ones (www.voicespro.com and www.voicefinder.biz being my two favourites) have highly advanced features and appear much more functional than their older rivals.

Studios are strange places populated by sound engineers who don't see much sunlight. But remember they are your friends. They make you sound good; they help you drop in just after where you inexplicably fluffed for the fifth time and they make you come across as being better than you probably are. Learn the jargon and get a reputation for turning up early and being professional. These are the shortcuts to recommendations and repeat business. The same goes for producers and the money people who pay your invoices – network with anyone who might be useful!

As you develop your skills and find you have a good client base you might want to think about setting up a home studio, perhaps even with an ISDN capability. This is particularly useful for voices that do a lot of radio spots or who live outside London. The advantages are that you are more competitive and can save the production company time by editing your own .wav files. This makes using you convenient and in all probability very good value. The disadvantage is that you could find yourself very isolated as the business is very much one of networking in the pub after the session.

Here it is in a nutshell: be proactive and be professional. The industry is very competitive and luck and timing play a big part.

Section 5
Fringe & comedy

The Edinburgh fringe

This chapter – a guide to what to expect from the Edinburgh fringe – was kindly provided by James Aylett, a seasoned fringe performer and co-author of fringe (Friday Books, **www.fridaybooks.co.uk**):

Performing at the Edinburgh Festival Fringe can feel like both a month-long party and a prison sentence. Although it offers a melting pot for some of the most creative people across Britain and beyond to showcase brilliantly imaginative theatre, it's potentially the most demanding and exhausting way of fulfilling your desire to act. For a start the work doesn't stop at performing – the casts of fringe productions are generally required to muck in and help with pretty much everything else, from publicising the show to carrying the company keyboard up the Royal Mile.

As if that wasn't already more than a full-time job, you naturally want to try and experience some of the wealth of artistic experimentation going on in the same city. Shows run until the early hours; the bars are open until 3am and the clubs until 5am; parties happen on a nightly basis and there's no waiting around until the next afternoon for things to begin again. Is it any wonder that several hundred people go mad every year?

It's worth pointing out that Edinburgh fringe shows rarely offer huge amounts of money even to the most qualified actors, partly because the large number of Fringe shows results in a rather thin spread of the profits; an expenses-paid profit-share production is the most you can hope for, and not a bad deal when you consider even just the expense of living in Edinburgh during the fringe. The large number of shows at the fringe (some 1800 in 2006) also means that productions really have to work to get people to see them – while some of the larger Edinburgh venues can guarantee a more consistent chance of getting audiences, the old adage about many fringe shows having an audience of three people still holds true.

So why go at all? The easy answer is that if reading the above paragraphs fills you with dread, maybe you shouldn't. You'll probably hate it. But if you think you can cope with the challenges, there's a lot to love – and it remains a great place to develop your acting experience and, if you're persistent enough, to get seen. The intense atmosphere, the chance to perform a show in the same venue for a month and the need to keep focused on the task in hand all act as an invaluable training ground for budding performers of all varieties, which is why so many known actors, writers, musicians and comedians cite the fringe as a great stepping stone in their careers.

REVIEWS

One of the more realistic reasons for going to Edinburgh is to come back backed up by a couple of nice reviews. Not only do they actually help sell tickets for the show you're in, but they look terribly nice on your website and indeed your CV. And, surprisingly given the number of the shows at the fringe, most people can expect to get their show mentioned in at least one publication (whether it's a personal mention depends on the size of the cast, the quality of your performance and whether the reviewer likes the look of you).

SkinnyFest and Three Weeks are printed especially for the fringe and are the most likely chance you have of being reviewed. The Scotsman tries to get round as many shows as possible (though if you're not eligible for their Fringe First awards you're at a distinct disadvantage) and recently broadsheets better known south of the border have been increasing their coverage, notably The Guardian and The Independent.

If you're up in Edinburgh mainly for the sheer ego-boosting joy of seeing your name in print, you should focus your flyering upon the people wandering up and down the Royal Mile conspicuously wearing press passes. Unfortunately press passes seem to be quite easy to get hold of, and you often end up with a man from Plumbing Weekly coming to see your show for free without the slightest intention of recommending it to his large readership of plumbing enthusiasts.

But perhaps the biggest appeal of the fringe is simply that it has a creative atmosphere that nowhere else can match. It is three weeks of unbelievably sustained artistic activity which combines an element of competitiveness with a healthy sense of camaraderie (perhaps brought on by a joint sense of suffering) among a huge number of people who really care about what they're doing. The shows are of variable quality, but there are more risks taken and ideas tried out than in any of the big funded arts festivals (something which is usually clear when comparing the fringe to the offerings of the overshadowed Edinburgh International Festival which happens at around the same time).

Publicity

Taking a show to Edinburgh is not really about performing a show. It's about publicising a show. This becomes obvious the minute you arrive there. However early you get there, somebody will always have got there before you in readiness to shove a piece of cardboard in your face – probably taking advantage of the fact that you haven't yet learned to say no.

People flyer you everywhere, all the time. If you're acting at the fringe, the chances are you'll end up flyering as well. You can choose to make this the most miserable experience you've ever had, by treating it as a horrific duty and getting rid of your flyers with the same relish as stuffing envelopes. But this doesn't make for the best publicity, because people on the street probably decide not to go and see your show. Alternatively, by telling people all about what you are doing and why they should come to see it, you might engage their interest. It's also a better way of making friends.

There are also people who spend several hours devising clever and wacky ways to get people to take their flyers. Variations of the old "please could you hold this for a moment" then running away routine are rife. Or disguising flyers as pieces of cake. Or kidnapping and drugging people then tattooing publicity blurb onto their bodies. This is all good, clean fun, but at the end of the day you have only succeeded in foisting yet more onto them about which they are none the wiser except that whatever it's advertising is being put on by some cunning bastards.

WHAT TO SEE

Even the most avid fringe-goer couldn't hope to see every one of the shows on offer. So how do you even begin to choose? The first place to look is the fringe brochure. This handy guide lists everything that is on over the course of the festival, detailing all the vital information like locations and times, and helpfully split into different (albeit occasionally misleading) categories. Go through the brochure and circle the shows that look as though they will interest you. Then ignore it, because the show descriptions are written by the people who are putting them on, so they often lie and rarely describe the show you're going to see.

Reviews give you an idea of the quality of any given show, but they're naturally the opinions of individuals, and one man's inspired piece of cutting-edge physical theatre is another man's dance music-fuelled strobe nightmare. So ignore them as well.

People doing shows are in a pretty good position to give you a rough idea of what their show contains. But they will also be desperately trying to sell you a ticket however poor they really believe their show to be, so you can pretty safely ignore them too. A better way to find out about shows is to listen to what everyone else is talking about. Shows that are either brilliant or truly dreadful provide hours' worth of conversation, so if everyone is talking about a show, it's a fairly safe bet that it's going to be for one of those reasons. Even then, you can't be sure.

The best advice I can give is to take risks. You can stick to the big venues and the well-known names if you want (and you'll pay for the privilege) but not a single one of the most memorable shows we've seen was a sure-fire hit. The fringe is all about trying things out, and if you discover a little-known, poorly-attended piece of theatre that somehow achieves perfection then it's an experience that you could never repeat in London's West End. The chances of disappointment are high; but the risk is worth it for the times when you strike gold.

As far as the bums-on-seat-per-flyer hit rate goes, nothing beats personal contact. On the other hand, the wackier ways of getting rid of flyers can get a group noticed and offer the opportunity to have a bit of fun. But go carefully – flyering done properly (or indeed improperly) is extremely hard work (harder, some would argue, than the performing in the show itself). Try to avoid flyer-induced exhaustion or insanity, as it's a pity when the energy used up on publicity results in a drop in the quality of a performance.

The other main type of print publicity is posters, which work as follows: you put up a poster. Somebody else puts a poster up over the top of it. You put up another poster over the top of that one... and so on. The people with the most posters visible are not those who put the most posters up, but those who do it most regularly. It's that simple. The actual areas you can put posters up in are rather limited these days; since the venues themselves are now ultra-competitive, you are never going to be allowed to put up posters at any venue other than your own.

The alternative outdoor fringe box office has a place where posters can be displayed, otherwise there is only really the much-fought over poster space on the Royal Mile to use. Some pubs, cafes, bars etc are also happy for posters and flyers to be left on their premises, but it's a good idea to ask. Other surfaces may look tempting – those shiny blue fringe-sponsored bins may seem to be crying out for one of your lovely posters – but people are employed to remove them, and will. Fly-posting is illegal and some pretty hefty fines are threatened for doing it; on the other hand, the fact that the promoters of respected big-name acts are particularly guilty of fly-posting suggests that nothing at all is being done about it, which is annoying because, let's face it, it's not difficult to track down the culprits.

You might find yourself doing some actual performing as a publicity tactic, either on the street itself or on specially designed outdoor stages. This is all good and well, but again requires care, again in case you end up doing your actual show with very little energy or motivation left, and also in case you end up putting people off you altogether. Casts who go about chanting excerpts from their reviews or specially designed slogans get extremely irritating after a while – a production of A Midsummer Night's Dream which goes around greeting people "Hail, mortal!" is crying out to be culled. In any case, it is rare for anyone to successfully distil their show into a 20-minute performance which works in the open air. For this reason, the little stages, fun though they be, mainly benefit the fringe organisers and sponsors – and of course the punters, who treat the whole thing as free entertainment.

Doing the shows

After a day of draining intellectually and physically demanding work, deprived of sleep and most likely food and drink as well, performers at the Fringe have to throw themselves into the equally draining, physical and intellectual task of performing. Unless they happen to be in a morning show, in which case they have to get up frightfully early. And it's not as if the shows themselves are ever plain sailing. The fringe is full of idiosyncrasies, in addition to which each venue will add its own idiosyncrasies just because they can. Throw in a load of thespians with extra idiosyncrasies and you're in for a pretty idiosyncratic time.

One such idiosyncrasy is the way venues manage to cram so many shows into one day by having them virtually back to back. As if it wasn't already hard enough putting on a show in the distinctive high-pressure atmosphere of the fringe, people end up setting up everything for it in under five minutes at the same time as another show is getting all of its things out of the way. For shows involving a lot of props, big sets and complex technical set-ups, it is particularly nightmarish. You have to expect to pull your weight at these times, and there's no point in grumbling that you're an actor and need to get into character – everybody will be too busy to listen anyway.

Learning to keep performances fresh time after time is part of what being a professional is all about, but the extreme pressures of the fringe arguably make it even harder. Give yourself the space you need (if not in the mad rush immediately before the show, then in a suitable alternative time). Be as positive as possible during the show, and if you do have problems with somebody or something, wait until an appropriate time to share it with the world.

Tempting though it is to cope with shows by getting drunk before them, this will make everybody else very cross. Get drunk after the show. Do some voice exercises to assist you when you're competing with the orchestra of electric fans set up to cope with the fact that you are in a venue which has come to resemble a sauna (and wash your clothes occasionally). Most importantly, get some sleep.

And during any show, whether you are performing or spectating, enjoy it. It's the reason you're at the fringe, so you might as well get something out of it.

How do people live?

The fringe is essentially one big party. For many, the fringe lifestyle also mostly involves going to parties. And there are lots of parties. It's

BEYOND THE FRINGE

If you spend all your time at the fringe doing shows, you'll miss out on some of the other great things on offer. Don't do that – it's an essential part of the fringe experience to wallow in everything that's on, especially as some of them are free. The circus-like entertainments which take place along the Royal Mile throughout August are professional and sometimes awe-inspiring. Sometimes you even see scientologists (though they're not always free if you get too close).

Like many major fringe festivals, the Edinburgh fringe has a smaller but occasionally interesting international festival going on at the same time (though it's mainly located on the fringes). There are also several other types of festival running at the same time, notably the book festival, film/TV festival and art festival, all of which offer a breather from the fetid thespian cloud hanging over the city. You might even go and see the Edinburgh military tattoo if the relentless bagpipers busking Scotland the Brave don't sate your appetite for tourist-friendly clichés.

It's also rumoured that somewhere in the Edinburgh fringe there is a city, which has got bits that exist outside the month of August.

therefore important that you find out where the parties are, and if necessary work out how to crash them. If you want a quieter evening you might try crashing a performer bar instead. You might even see somebody famous.

But there are practical considerations, like having somewhere to live for the entire month. If you're cast in a fringe show it will almost certainly be somebody else's problem to find you accommodation – and if that's not part of the deal you must be aware that you'll end up forking out at least another £650 and you need to start looking in March rather than June if you don't want to be in a sleeping bag on the Meadows (a cheaper option is to blag space from other groups – if you're actually performing though, it's not such a good idea, because you're never going to perform well if you're sleeping on a kitchen table).
The sensible shows hire a flat, ideally close to the city centre and best of all within a few minutes' walk from their venue. Some groups share accommodation (particularly comedians, who tend to be there on their own anyway). Some groups share beds (particularly comedians, who need the warmth and companionship of another body at night to overcome the self-loathing that is behind their art).

As a performer you're well advised to check out the exact deal here as well – groups on a budget have a tendency to cram several people into one bedroom, which can increase the risk of tension and, in extreme cases, madness; people need time on their own, and this may be difficult in a cramped flat.

Some accommodation is drab, some is palatial. Quite a lot in Edinburgh seems to be somewhere in between – either a well appointed flat nestling halfway up a damp dingy staircase that looks just like the one in Shallow Grave, or an enormous apartment carved out of Georgian townhouses that nonetheless is a little rundown, with peeling paint, appliances that need encouragement, and a strange box room that has no obvious purpose (although groups on a budget will ask somebody to sleep in it). And why would you prefer large-yet-seedy over unassuming-but-well appointed? Because they're great for parties, of course.

197

What not to go to the fringe for

The fringe is not about famous people. So it's a shame that so many think it is about famous people, or at least becoming a famous person. Yes, it has its success stories, and is still the place that agents, casting directors and talent scouts hang out in the hope of finding the next Tom Stoppard or Stephen Fry. However, with the sheer number of performances at the fringe, getting an agent to see you in a show is every bit as difficult as it is in an ordinary London fringe theatre. If you happen to be planning to go to the Edinburgh fringe in the hope of finding fame and fortune, now is the time to reconsider. It will just be an expensive route to disappointment.

If you go to the fringe in the hope of finding an agent, you must be prepared to write to anyone who looks in the slightest bit promising, and you should do it well in advance of the fringe; if you're lucky they'll at least be sending a representative up to Edinburgh for a few days so they may be able to fit you into their schedule. The same goes for casting directors, and you can expect the same politely-worded but infuriating rejection letters from them both.

You might also hope to get seen by a talent scout; the problem is, you never really know where they're going to be or who they are, and they tend to visit shows that are doing quite well or that really interest them – just like any ordinary punter. You'll know who they are if they come to your show and like it, but that doesn't help you get them to your show in the first place. Your best bet is to hang around a big venue to see if you can spot anyone with a clipboard or a special pass, then flyer them with your most charming pitch. The only downside is that you may end up spending a long time flyering the boiler man.

It does happen, though – people get spotted at the fringe. There are people whose careers are launched by that one fortunate time when a casting director couldn't get a ticket for Paul Merton so went to see them in Bacmeth – the Dyslexic Tyrant instead, discovered their talent and cast them in a big television drama which propelled them into the limelight and won them a Golden Globe for the second series. It just doesn't happen to very many people.

And yet...

If I have said nothing else of importance, it is that it's okay, and indeed fun, doing shows to an audience with four people in it. It may be that your hard work is rubbished by the press and sinks into obscurity within minutes of the final performance. But you have given those four people an experience that they will take away with them for better or for worse. It's not fame – but it's a tiny bit of recognition on the broad canvas of the arts.

I was once given a flyer for a one-woman show by two breathless, excited girls. They explained that they weren't involved in the show in any way, but had been to see it and liked it so much that they had taken a stash of flyers to hand out to other people. They had been the only two people in the audience, and they felt it ought to be seen by many more.

Later that day, I saw the woman actually performing the show in costume looking pissed off and bitter, trying to give out flyers. Of course she looked pissed off and bitter – she was only getting two people in her audiences and that is why she wasn't happy.

But the two breathless girls were happy.

Stand-up comedy

As a new act in 2001, Hils Barker (**www.hilsbarker.com**) made it to the final of So You Think You're Funny?, Channel 4's national stand-up competition. She went on to co-write groundbreaking sketch show Radio9 for Radio 4 (aired in 2004–2006), and has appeared in and written for BBC TV comedy such as The Message, The Late Edition and The Comic Side of Seven Days. She is also a stand-up on the London and national circuit and here brings advice 'from the coal face'.

People come at stand-up from so many different areas of life it feels presumptuous to describe how to go about it. Why people do it is maybe more interesting. It's got me thinking that being a comedian is not so much a job, more of a condition and it's just a question of when you accept the fact, throw out your social life and start hanging out at clubs called things like 'BrouHaHa' and 'Primrose Hillarity'. I did my first gig at a biker's pub in Islington called the 'Purple Turtle'; it wasn't so much stand-up, more a monologue of five minutes of 'jokes' that I had written, delivered firmly to the back wall and at high speed so no-one could heckle. But I loved it, and after that I was hooked. The first gig raised more questions than it answered: "Where can I do this again?" "How can I do it better?", "Who names these clubs?"

Other questions might be: what are you looking to achieve through doing stand-up, and is it possible to earn a living from it? As hinted above, it's different for everyone. Comics vary so much in style that someone who is perfect for one club may go down terribly in another, and understanding that this doesn't make you crap is really important. Similarly, some comics are live stand-ups through and through; others will want to move into TV and radio, writing or sketch comedy. All of them, though, are probably motivated by having ideas and opinions that they want to 'get out there'.

It's possible to make a great living from stand-up if you're regularly playing all the bigger clubs, such as the Comedy Store, Jongleurs or the Glee, and even if you're not, there are so many clubs at the moment that you can earn a living if you're any good and you gig frequently. Having said that, it can take a good few years to get to either level, because obviously when you start out no-one will pay an inexperienced comedian, and often it costs you money to travel to gigs and do try-out spots for promoters. But as with acting, no-one gets into it because they think it's going to make them any money. You do it for the sheer fun and because you like showing off.

Open mic spots

The first step towards getting started is probably to buy your local listings guide (in London it's Time Out, Glasgow and Edinburgh The List, and so on), get familiar with the comedy section and start turning up at clubs. Go and watch comedy at all levels, from open mic nights to the Comedy Store. It will inspire you, make you laugh, give you an idea of how to shape your material, and also, you start meeting people.

Find out who runs the clubs where you can get yourself a five-minute spot, and either call them or talk to them on the night. In Time Out, you can tell more or less which clubs are for newer acts – they normally have a lot more than the standard three or four comics on the bill, or there'll be a thing saying 'interested acts should call'.

After you've done your first few open spots, I think it's massively encouraging to know that assuming you're in any way funny (and you must be, or you probably wouldn't be interested in doing it in the first place) anything is possible through hard work and fanatical dedication. I use those words advisedly; you can start getting a lot of stage time just by being the one who turns up, and there really will be a lot of new acts who turn up obsessively. I know I did when I started out, and it's true that you don't really make much progress as a comic otherwise. The best way to improve is by turning up at gigs as many nights per week as you can spare, either to get on the bill or just to watch.

It might sound dull but when you really want to play the gigs, nothing works better than a bizarre combination of quasi-stalking tactics and hardcore diary management. (Once you're up and running, with any luck you can get an agent who is brilliant enough to do all that for you.) You could also do one of the various comedy courses on offer (see box overleaf).

201

COMEDY WORKSHOPS

I did a sort of comedy workshop when I started out, where new acts and people who were thinking of starting stand-up, brainstormed ideas once a week. It was fun, but not a very professional approach, and I know there are courses which cover everything from choosing your comedy persona, to joke-writing techniques, networking and so on. That can be really useful, but it can also be a bit prescriptive. A lot of people think it's better if your comedy persona emerges organically from the kind of material you write, rather than slamming a style onto a new act, which can ring pretty false. Also, don't assume that everyone who runs a course (or indeed a gig) is in it for the love of comedy. Most are, but if you're going to get advice from someone, make sure you think they're a like-minded person.

The advantages of the comedy course are that you meet people straight away who are also trying to do what you're doing, so you've got an instant network to talk through ideas with, bitch about stuff, and celebrate / commiserate with. There are so many gigs, especially the early ones, where all you want to do afterwards is analyse every last detail with another comedian.

Good and bad gigs

Don't set too much store by reviews, whether they're negative or positive. There may be reviewers or promoters who think you're shit one minute then brilliant the next, or vice versa. But it's worth reminding yourself that every wonderful comedian who is now a household name or widely accepted as a genius has been through that process, and has had nights where people think they're terrible. As a student at the Edinburgh festival in 1998, I saw one of my favourite stand-ups, a hilarious person, get booed off stage at a gig. I remember mentioning it, shocked, to a stand-up acquaintance, who was starting to do pretty well. His reaction was simply, "And?... Bad gigs happen to everyone."

Up until that point, it just hadn't occurred to me that people probably got better as comedians via a brutal learning curve. I mean, it kind of had, but I'd mainly seen comedy videos and not much of the real live thing. In a way, though, it was liberating to learn that even when you've sort of made it you can still have bad nights. I think it was this piece of knowledge – that comics can watch other comics having a bad gig, but still know that the person on stage is a good comedian – that made me think it might be possible to give stand-up a try.

Agents
It's probably best to wait for an agent to come to you, but you can definitely hurry that along by emailing them and asking them to come and watch you gig, or by entering as many stand-up competitions as possible. There are no rules, though. There are some comics who have been gigging for ten years who don't have or need an agent. If you want to write and perform stuff for TV it can help, but then so can writing material and sending it to script editors and producers at Radio 4 or BBC 7.

It's also worthwhile thinking about what you have as a comic that is unique (remember your personality, which onstage may be a persona, can be just as important as your material, and make audiences buy into weird ideas or even average jokes). If you have long hair and write jokes like Bill Bailey, great, but that major breakthrough may be postponed until Bill Bailey retires. Unless you're a woman, in which case, brilliant; a career as 'the female Bill Bailey' is all set to go.

Also 'as a woman' though, you've got to get used to every reviewer or random person at a party saying, "So, is it hard/different/interesting being a female stand-up?" If you can learn a sarcasm-free answer to that, and the unisex one – "Where do you get your material from?" – and make it look spontaneous every time, you've probably mastered the hardest part. Welcome to the gang…

A-Z of fringe & comedy festivals

This is by no means a comprehensive list of the many arts festivals that take place around Britain and Ireland, but focuses instead on fringe festivals where new productions are likely to be welcomed, as well as events that feature comedy and street theatre. Remember that some of the smaller festivals can come and go over time. It's best to contact organisers a good six months before the actual festival if you're hoping to be involved.

ABERDEEN INTERNATIONAL YOUTH FESTIVAL
CUSTOM HOUSE
35 REGENT QUAY
ABERDEEN AB11 5BE
{T} 01224 213800
INFO@AIYF.ORG
WWW.AIYF.ORG
MONTH: AUGUST
Youth orchestras, choirs, music groups, dance and theatre groups can apply to take part in the festival by sending an application form and a recording of a recent performance. Groups must be of amateur status and made up of young people not over the age of 25 years.

ARTSFEST (BIRMINGHAM)
{T} 0121 464 5678
MAIL@ARTSFEST.ORG.UK
WWW.ARTSFEST.ORG.UK
MONTH: SEPTEMBER
The UK's largest free arts festival features strong elements of street theatre and comedy, and potential participants with these skills are invited to make contact via forms available at the website.

ARUNDEL FESTIVAL FRINGE
WWW.ARUNDELFESTIVAL.ORG.UK
MONTH: AUGUST-SEPTEMBER
Established fringe festival alongside the official Arundel Festival (www. arundelfestival.co.uk). Contact via the form at the website.

ASHBOURNE FESTIVAL
PO BOX 5552
ASHBOURNE
DERBYSHIRE DE6 2ZR
{T} 01335 348707
INFO@ASHBOURNEARTS.COM
WWW.ASHBOURNEARTS.COM
MONTH: JUNE-JULY
2007 saw the festival's first comedy night, so there could be opportunities in that area in the future,

BATH FRINGE FESTIVAL
ADMIN@BATHFRINGE.CO.UK
WWW.BATHFRINGE.CO.UK
MONTH: MAY-JUNE
Provides a banner for fringe events alongside the main Bath festivals, and arranges some of the bookings.

BELFAST FESTIVAL AT QUEEN'S
25 COLLEGE GARDENS
BELFAST BT9 6BS
{T} 028 9027 2600
G.FARROW@QUB.AC.UK
WWW.BELFASTFESTIVAL.COM
MONTH: OCTOBER-NOVEMBER
Ireland's largest international arts festival, with many theatre and comedy acts. Fringe events have been run in the past.

BEWDLEY FESTIVAL
SNUFF MILL WAREHOUSE
PARK LANE
BEWDLEY
WORCESTERSHIRE DY12 2EL
{T} 01299 404808
ADMIN@BEWDLEYFESTIVAL.ORG.UK
WWW.BEWDLEYFESTIVAL.ORG.UK
MONTH: OCTOBER
Festival featuring drama, comedy, music and visual arts, with a range of fringe events.

BRIGHTON FESTIVAL FRINGE
12A PAVILION GARDENS
CASTLE SQUARE
BRIGHTON BN1 1EE
{T} 01273 260804
INFO@BRIGHTONFESTIVALFRINGE.ORG.UK
WWW.BRIGHTONFESTIVALFRINGE.ORG.UK
MONTH: MAY
It could be a performance, a show, an exhibition, an event, a gig or an open house – more than 500 events take place each year. Full guide for participants at the website.

BROUHAHA INTERNATIONAL STREET FESTIVAL (MERSEYSIDE)
THE ALIMA CENTRE
35 SEFTON STREET
LIVERPOOL L8 5SL
{T} 0151 709 3334
INFO@BROUHAHA.UK.COM
WWW.BROUHAHA.UK.COM
MONTH: AUGUST
Carnival arts organisation involved in events around the country and focused on its own carnival in Liverpool.

BURY FRINGE FESTIVAL
12 GREEN LANE
GREAT BARTON
BURY ST EDMUNDS IP31 2QZ
SECRETARY@BURYFRINGE.COM
WWW.BURYFRINGE.COM
MONTH: APRIL
See www.buryfringe.com/fringeforum for information for performers.

Bury St. Edmunds Festival
Angel Hill
Bury St. Edmunds
Suffolk IP33 1XB
{T} 01284 757630
INFO@BURYFESTIVAL.CO.UK
WWW.BURYFESTIVAL.CO.UK
Month: May
Not a fringe festival per se, but includes a comedy strand. See also Bury Fringe Festival.

Buxton Festival Fringe
124 Brown Edge Rd
Buxton SK17 7AB
{T} 01298 71368
INFO@BUXTONFRINGE.ORG.UK
WWW.BUXTONFRINGE.ORG.UK
Month: July
Provides an opportunity for artists to perform or exhibit in an environment that is low cost and an atmosphere that is receptive. Performers make their own arrangements with venues and pay an entry fee.

Cambridge Fringe Festival
TWFCC
Fourwentways, Little Abington
Cambridge CB1 6AP
{T} 01223 323 522 OR 01223 837 891
INFO@CAMFRINGE.COM
WWW.CAMFRINGE.COM
Date: July-August
An open access festival, welcoming professionals, semi-professionals and amateurs alike.

Canterbury Festival
Christchurch Gate
The Precincts
Canterbury CT1 2EE
{T} 01227 452853
INFO@CANTERBURYFESTIVAL.CO.UK
WWW.CANTERBURYFESTIVAL.CO.UK
Month: October
International arts festival which also has a fringe.

Chelsea Festival
The Crypt
St Luke's Church
Sydney Street
London SW3 6NH
{T} 020 7349 8101
INFO@CHELSEAFESTIVAL.ORG
WWW.CHELSEAFESTIVAL.ORG
Month: July
Has a small programme of comedy events.

Dublin Fringe Festival
Sackville House
Sackville Place
Dublin 1
{T} +353 1 817 1677
GRAHAM@FRINGEFEST.COM
WWW.FRINGEFEST.COM
Month: September
A curated fringe festival where artists must apply with examples of previous work – full details at the website.

DUBLIN THEATRE FESTIVAL
44 EAST ESSEX STREET
TEMPLE BAR
DUBLIN 2
{T} +353 1 677 8439
EMAIL: INFO@DUBLINTHEATREFESTIVAL.COM
WWW.DUBLINTHEATREFESTIVAL.COM/
MONTH: SEPTEMBER-OCTOBER
The oldest English-speaking theatre
festival in the world, reaching its 50th
anniversary in 2007. Includes 'Theatre
Olympics', a fringe-like range of extra
events. See also Dublin Fringe Festival.

EALING COMEDY FESTIVAL
020 8825 6064
EVENTS@EALING.GOV.UK
**WWW.EALING.GOV.UK/SERVICES/LEISURE/EAL
ING_SUMMER/**
MONTH: JULY
Established London comedy festival,
focusing on well-known names.

EDINBURGH FESTIVAL FRINGE
180 HIGH STREET
EDINBURGH EH1 1QS
{T} 0131 226 0026
ADMIN@EDFRINGE.COM
WWW.EDFRINGE.COM
MONTH: AUGUST
The Edinburgh Festival Fringe is officially
the largest arts festival in the world.
Hundreds of groups participate, putting
on around 2,000 different shows across
more than 250 venues. Anyone can
apply to perform.

EXETER SUMMER FESTIVAL
CIVIC CENTRE
PARIS STREET
EXETER EX1 1JJ
{T} 01392 265205
GENERAL.FESTIVALS@EXETER.GOV.UK
EXETER.GOV.UK/FESTIVAL
MONTH: JUNE
Mainly a music and dance festival, but
with a good range of comedy events too.

GRASSINGTON FESTIVAL OF MUSIC AND ARTS
RIVERBANK HOUSE
THRESHFIELD
SKIPTON BD23 5BS
{T} 01756 752691
ARTS@GRASSINGTON-FESTIVAL.ORG.UK
WWW.GRASSINGTON-FESTIVAL.ORG.UK
MONTH: JUNE
Mainstream arts festival which includes
street theatre elements.

HAY FRINGE FESTIVAL
ICE HOUSE, BROOK STREET
HAY-ON-WYE HR3 5BQ
INFO@HAYFRINGE.CO.UK
WWW.HAYFRINGE.CO.UK
MONTH: MAY-JUNE
Poetry, theatre and street performance
coinciding with the Hay Literature
Festival.

HEBDEN BRIDGE ARTS FESTIVAL
NEW OXFORD HOUSE
ALBERT STREET
HEBDEN BRIDGE HX7 8AH
{T} 01422 842684
HBFESTIVAL@GMAIL.COM
WWW.HEBDENBRIDGE.CO.UK/FESTIVAL
MONTH: JUNE
General arts festival also featuring street
theatre and comedy.

HOTBED FESTIVAL (CAMBRIDGE)
THE JUNCTION
CLIFTON WAY
CAMBRIDGE CB1 7GX
{T} 01223 249300
OFFICE@MENAGERIE.UK.COM
WWW.MENAGERIE.UK.COM
MONTH: JULY
This is the Cambridge New Writing
Theatre Festival with the aim "to
celebrate the energy and excitement
that comes from commissioning,
producing and witnessing new plays".

LONDON INTERNATIONAL FESTIVAL OF THEATRE (LIFT)
19-20 GREAT SUTTON STREET
LONDON EC1V ODR
0) 20 7490 3964
INFO@LIFTFEST.ORG.UK
WWW.LIFTFEST.ORG.UK
MONTH: JUNE
International theatre festival which has
been running every other year since
1981, as well as supporting artists
throughout the year.

LLANGOLLEN FRINGE FESTIVAL
01978 860600
CONTACT@LLANGOLLENFRINGE.CO.UK
WWW.LLANGOLLENFRINGE.CO.UK
MONTH: JULY
"If you want to put some music on, run
a workshop, get into busking, stage an
art show, organise a lecture, lead a
guided walk or anything else as part of
the Fringe e-mail us and we'll do our
best to make it happen."

MANCHESTER INTERNATIONAL FESTIVAL
131 PORTLAND STREET
MANCHESTER M1 4PY
{T} 0161 238 7300
INFO@MANCHESTERINTERNATIONALFESTIVAL.COM
**WWW.MANCHESTERINTERNATIONAL
FESTIVAL.COM**
MONTH: JUNE-JULY
This showcase for new music also
features comedy and theatre perform-
ances.

NATIONAL STUDENT DRAMA FESTIVAL
19-20 RHEIDOL MEWS
LONDON N1 8NU
{T} 0207 354 8070
INFO@NSDF.ORG.UK
WWW.NSDF.ORG.UK
MONTH: MARCH
Showcase for student drama.
Submissions are invited from students of
any subject, aged 16 or over, or if they
are directing a show within two years of
graduation.

NORWICH FRINGE FESTIVAL
01603 621935
INFO@NORWICHFRINGEFESTIVAL.CO.UK
WWW.NORWICHFRINGEFESTIVAL.CO.UK
MONTH: SEPTEMBER-OCTOBER
Started in 1998. Submission form
available at the website.

OXFRINGE
0870 803 3475 (ANSWERPHONE)
INFO@OXFRINGE.COM
WWW.OXFRINGE.COM
MONTH: APRIL
Founded in 2007 with just two events,
Oxford's fringe has grown rapidly with
nearly 150 events in 2009, including
comedy, drama, music and literature.

PULSE FRINGE FESTIVAL (IPSWICH)
01473 261142
CTAYLOR@WOLSEYTHEATRE.CO.UK
WWW.PULSEFRINGE.COM
MONTH: JUNE
Showcasing comedy and drama in the
East of England.

READING FRINGE FESTIVAL
ENQUIRIES@READINGFRINGEFESTIVAL.COM
WWW.READINGFRINGEFESTIVAL.COM
Started in 2005, the Reading Fringe is
open to everyone.

SALISBURY INTERNATIONAL ARTS FESTIVAL
87 CRANE STREET
SALISBURY SP1 2PU
{T} 01722 332241
INFO@SALISBURYFESTIVAL.CO.UK
WWW.SALISBURYFESTIVAL.CO.UK
MONTH: MAY-JUNE
International arts festival with theatre
and comedy elements.

SEDBURGH FESTIVAL OF BOOKS & DRAMA
C/O SEDBURGH BOOK TOWN LTD
72 MAIN STREET
SEDBURGH LA10 5AD
{T} 015396 20125 / 20034
BOOKTOWN@SEDBURGH.ORG.UK
WWW.SEDBURGH.ORG.UK
MONTH: AUGUST-SEPTEMBER
New festival focused around books, with
theatre elements.

STOCKTON RIVERSIDE FRINGE FESTIVAL
WWW.FRINGEFESTIVAL.CO.UK/
MONTH: AUGUST
This free music festival now has a
comedy tent.

SWANSEA FRINGE FESTIVAL
C/O THE DYLAN THOMAS CENTRE
SOMERSET PLACE
SWANSEA SA1 1RR
{T} 01792 474051
INFO@SWANSEAFRINGE.COM
WWW.SWANSEAFRINGE.COM
MONTH: SEPTEMBER-OCTOBER
"Anyone can perform, from the
established to the emerging." Details at
the website.

WEXFORD FRINGE FESTIVAL
WEXFORD CHAMBER OF INDUSTRY & COMMERCE
{T} 053 9122226

WWW.WEXFORDFRINGE.IE
MONTH: JUNE
Coincides with the Wexford Opera
Festival, and embraces comedy and
street theatre.

WINDSOR FRINGE
INFO@WINDSORFRINGE.CO.UK
WWW.WINDSORFRINGE.CO.UK
MONTH: SEPTEMBER-OCTOBER
Has been encouraging new talent in
music, dance, comedy, drama and art
since 1969.

Section 6
Living as an actor

The business of you

Naturally as an actor your focus is always going to be on your performances – that's why you're doing all this! But it's important to remember that you are also running a business. As with any self-employed person (unless you're lucky enough to have a full-time job with a theatre company you respect), whether a freelance writer, a plumber or a taxi driver, this means that there is background admin to be done, as well as the business of promoting yourself.

When you start out, acting may only take up a smallish proportion of your time, and you might have a 'day job' of some kind to tide you over – but income you make as an actor often (but not always – see below) counts as self-employment, and of course you will need to make time for applying for more acting work. In this chapter we'll provide a quick survey of some of the main issues which you should consider.

Self-employment
When you 'go it alone', it's not just a question of finding the work and banking the money: you still need to pay tax, for one thing. From a tax point of view, you may well be both employed and self-employed – it depends partly on how you are paid. In some cases you may find your tax is paid at source (PAYE) before you get the money, and historically the Inland Revenue has been keen to see 'entertainers' as a special case to be treated as employees – it means you can claim fewer expenses.

Now that self-assessment is well-established, however, it's quite likely that work where your tax isn't deducted at source will be regarded as self-employment. The most important thing to do is talk to HM Revenue & Customs – their telephone helpline staff are renownedly helpful and not at all like the intimidating 'taxman' of old. Call them on 08459 154515 to talk through the issues and register as self-employed if appropriate.

The HMRC website also has loads of advice on this subject: see **www.hmrc.gov.uk/employment-status/** for a starting point. In the section under 'special cases', you'll find that it says "entertainers who are not employed under a contract of service or in an office with emoluments chargeable to tax... as employment income are treated as employed earners provided their remuneration consists wholly or mainly of salary. If it does not, they retain their self-employed status."

If the Revenue sends you a self-assessment form (for declaring income in a particular tax year, ie 6 April in one calendar year to 5 April in the next), you may need then to fill out sections both for 'employment' and for 'self-employment'. These need to be submitted by the end of the January after the tax year in question (though that's changing to the earlier time of September in the next year or two).

Payment (for any tax not taken at source) is made in two halves in January and July 'on account' for the following tax year. As well as tax, you will need to pay National Insurance. Remember: there are fines for being late with payments. The Revenue is currently encouraging people to use its online submission service rather than the traditional paper format.

All this can get very confusing. There's a simple solution: go and see an accountant! Also, if you're a member of Equity, get hold of its 'Advice and Rights Guide' for reference.

Accountants

The most important thing is to keep records of your work and income, and the relevant dates. You don't have to become obsessed with double-entry bookkeeping (though it could help) – but keep a clear record of income and outgoings related to work. This means invoices, payslips, details of cheques, and receipts for anything work-related. In terms of the latter, promotional items such as photographs and showreels ought to be tax deductible as expenses – if you're self-employed. Don't take our word for it, however: get an accountant.

Accountants are experts at things like expenses and will almost always think of things that wouldn't occur to you however much you might have read up on the subject. You can find a list of accountants specialising in finances for actors at the end of this chapter.

As a general rule, using the services of an accountant will pay for itself: having your tax return prepared will probably cost in the region of £300, but they can usually save you that and more on tax deductable expenses. Many accountants will invite you for a free initial meeting to discuss your affairs, and you can take things from there. Take any correspondence from the Revenue with you, and details of income and outgoings.

Other finances

Given the precarious lifestyle you've chosen, it's wise to bone up on other financial issues. Do you want to take out a mortgage to buy a home, for example? It's perfectly possible, and these days lenders are much less prejudiced about the self-employed than they used to be. Nevertheless, they will want to see recent accounts, perhaps for the last three years, and several months' worth of bank statements. Make sure you have all this information well organised.

Even if you're only renting a property, letting agents are getting increasingly stern about checking up on this stuff. Often they expect a 'guarantor' (someone who will cover the payments if you default), such as a parent, even for tenants well into adult life. If you have someone suitable to cover you like this, make sure you speak to them beforehand!

Another dirty word to people in creative fields is 'pensions'. You might be young and care-free now, but how will you sustain yourself in old age (assuming you don't become the next Inspector Morse)? It's worth thinking about how to save now to avoid a crisis later on. For all of these issues, you're best off talking to an expert again. Check out **www.unbiased.co.uk** to track down an independent financial adviser (IFA) in your area.

Marketing yourself

Section 3 of this book will give you a basic grounding in creating your main self-marketing kit: CV, photograph and show/voicereel. Registering with web-based services such as Spotlight is now a key part of your armoury, too. Some, such as Casting Call Pro, also offer premium services such as providing you with your own website – a great way to update people on your work and attract more.

There's more to it, though. Plumbers can often rely on word-of-mouth alone. Taxi drivers usually have their clients standing around waiting for them. Self-employment in the creative industries isn't usually that simple, largely because there's so much competition (and you're providing a service that people 'enjoy' rather than 'need').

This means being smart: always be on the lookout for opportunities to promote yourself. This doesn't mean being overconfident or excessively pushy – rather, get talking to people, make connections, show an interest, and give people reasons to want to talk to you again. If you're looking for work in the corporate field (see p166), consider getting business cards and a letterhead printed. Remember that people take you according to how you present yourself – try to talk to them in their 'language'.

Part of being professional is being organised, too. Make sure it's easy for people to get in touch with you – phone, email – and don't give them reasons to think less of you, such as a silly outgoing answerphone message. Keep track of your appointments and make sure you're always on time for them. Also, keep a record of people in the industry that you've met and their contact details, and maybe even a diary of performances you've seen – it all helps you to feel part of something, and you never know when a name in a file might be just the connection you need to help you get work.

Beating the blues

Everyone knows the clichés about actors working in fast-food outlets when they're 'between jobs'. Hopefully this book will have given you some solid guidance to get more rewarding work than that, but if not, never despair, and always come back fighting when you've been turned down for something.

Beyond applying for acting jobs, make sure you go and see other productions, too: seeing a really good performance or production can lift your spirits and remind you just why you're in this business! Also, it's important to take time out and enjoy yourself, however well or badly work is going.

Your general well-being is vital and will make you more resilient in the face of disappointment, not to mention more dynamic as a performer. Keep yourself fit and healthy: eat well, and get plenty of exercise. Doing classes such as pilates or yoga can help here, or join a gym, or simply go swimming, cycling or running regularly. All this will help you keep your body in tone, which will show in your work. We don't want to sound like your mother here, but these things really count. Time after time studies show it's things like this that keep people happy rather than making pots of cash – not that the latter wouldn't help now and then.

Acting is a unique job that brings happiness to thousands of audiences every year, and the more positive you are in the gaps between work, the more you'll be part of a 'feedback loop' that keeps you buoyant too, and at the peak of your performance.

A-Z of accountants

BOWKER ORFORD
BASED IN: LONDON
{T} 020 7636 6391
MAIL@BOWKERORFORD.COM
WWW.BOWKERORFORD.COM
We are founder members of the Institute of Chartered Accountants Entertainment and Media Group. We have been acting for clients in the music business for over 30 years and have extensive experience acting on behalf of performers, music publishers and all related areas. As a result we have a good knowledge of copyright, royalty accounting and tax issues. We have in excess of 500 actors as clients, including many household names, and we act for a number of theatrical production companies and theatrical agents.

BRECKMAN & COMPANY
BASED IN: LONDON
{T} 020 7499 2292
GRAHAMBERRY@BRECKMANANDCOMPANY.CO.UK
WWW.BRECKMANANDCOMPANY.CO.UK
Breckman & Company, chartered certified accountants, have specialised in the Arts and Entertainment Industry for over 40 years, for both individuals and companies. We are based in the West End of London, near the heart of Theatreland.

CENTRE STAGE (LONDON)
BASED IN: LONDON
{T} 0845 603 5401
ACCOUNTS@CENTRESTAGE-ACCOUNTANTS.COM
WWW.CENTRESTAGE-ACCOUNTANTS.COM
Centre Stage is a firm of Chartered Accountants specialising in the Entertainment Industry. Our experience over many years has led us to believe that there is a need for the kind of specialism we can offer due to the many unusual aspects of the entertainment industry. For example, many actors hold down other jobs, many temporary, often during or between acting jobs, but are treated as self-employed.

CENTRE STAGE (MANCHESTER)
BASED IN: MANCHESTER
{T} 0161 655 2000
See above.

DAVID EVANS CHARTERED ACCOUNTANTS
BASED IN: NORTH WEST
{T} 01200 428460
DAVID@EVANSACCOUNTANTS.COM
WWW.EVANSACCOUNTANTS.COM
David Evans Chartered Accountants has acted for individuals and businesses involved in creative work, as well as charities involved in community arts, for over 10 years. We have a wealth of experience and expertise.

GOLDWINS
BASED IN: LONDON
{T} 020 7372 6494
INFO@GOLDWINS.CO.UK
WWW.GOLDWINS.CO.UK
For many years, we have been successfully offering specialist accounting, taxation and financial services to people in the entertainment professions right across the UK.

INDIGO
BASED IN: SUSSEX
{T} 01403 892683
INFO@INDIGOTAX.COM
WWW.INDIGOTAX.COM
At Indigo we have clients from a wide spectrum of industries. However, we pride ourselves on our knowledge of accountancy in the music or entertainment industry and many of our clients are musicians, performers, producers, writers or are otherwise involved in multimedia business.

MARK CARR & CO (HOVE)
BASED IN: HOVE
{T} 01273 778802
INFO@MARKCARR.CO.UK
WWW.MARKCARR.CO.UK
Our principal expertise is supplying accounting and taxation services to the entertainment industry. We act for actors, dancers, writers and agents among other professions within the industry.

MARK CARR & CO (LONDON)
BASED IN: LONDON
{T} 020 7717 8474
See above.

MARTIN GREENE
BASED IN: LONDON
{T} 020 8360 9126
INFO@MARTINGREENE.CO.UK
WWW.MARTINGREENE.CO.UK
As with all aspects of the entertainment industry, we work closely with lawyers on all contractual, tax planning and commercial matters. These include intellectual property exploitation and protection, recording and licensing contracts.

MGI MIDGLEY SNELLING
BASED IN: LONDON & WEYBRIDGE
{T} 020 7836 9671
EMAIL@MIDSNELL.CO.UK
WWW.MIDSNELL.CO.UK
Since our formation, we have built a strong tradition of delivering specialist services to clients associated with the entertainment industry and have a thorough knowledge and understanding of this unique industry.

SAFFERY CHAMPNESS
BASED IN: LONDON
{T} 020 7841 4000
INFO@SAFFERY.COM
WWW.SAFFERY.COM
Our specialist media and entertainment team act as enthusiastic and trusted

advisers to the creative industries sector, to both businesses and individuals operating within it. The group possesses particular experience in the fields of advertising, marketing and PR, film and broadcasting, music, publishing, sport, theatres, and talent agencies.

SLOANE & CO
BASED IN: LONDON
{T} 020 7221 3292
MAIL@SLOANEANDCO.COM
WWW.SLOANEANDCO.COM
Sloane & Co., founded in 1974 by David Sloane, is a firm of Accountants offering a wide range of financial services of particular concern to organisations and individuals working in the entertainment field.

SPENCER DAVIS AND CO
BASED IN: LONDON
{T} 020 8863 0009
INFO@ACCOUNTANCYFORMUSICIANS.CO.UK
WWW.ACCOUNTANCYFORMUSICIANS.CO.UK
Spencer Davis and Co is an accountant based in Harrow, London. We provide a full and comprehensive range of accountancy services for performing artists including musicians, actors, jugglers and fire eaters.

TAYLORCOCKS (BOURNEMOUTH)
BASED IN: BOURNEMOUTH
{T} 0870 770 8111
BOURNEMOUTHENQUIRIES@THEACCOUNTANTS.CO.UK
WWW.THEACCOUNTANTS.CO.UK

For many years we have provided specialist accounting, taxation, business and financial advice to the leisure and entertainment industry. Our knowledge and experience mean that we understand the special requirements of the sector.

TAYLORCOCKS (FARNHAM)
BASED IN: FARNHAM
{T} 0870 770 8111
FARNHAMENQUIRIES@THEACCOUNTANTS.CO.UK

TAYLORCOCKS (PORTSMOUTH)
BASED IN: PORTSMOUTH
{T} 0870 770 8111
PORTSMOUTHENQUIRIES@THEACCOUNTANTS.CO.UK

TAYLORCOCKS (PORTSMOUTH)
BASED IN: OXFORD
{T} 0870 770 8111
OXFORDENQUIRIES@THEACCOUNTANTS.CO.UK

TAYLORCOCKS (READING)
BASED IN: READING
{T} 0870 770 8111
READINGENQUIRIES@THEACCOUNTANTS.CO.UK

Section 7
Organisations & resources

Equity

Equity, formed in 1930, is the trade union for actors and the entertainment profession. Its 35,000+ members include actors, singers, dancers, choreographers, stage managers, theatre directors and designers, variety and circus artists, television and radio presenters, walk-on and supporting artists, stunt performers and directors and theatre fight directors. Equity works on behalf of actors, lobbying to secure minimum terms and conditions of employment. In addition to its ongoing campaigning for better pay and conditions, Equity offers a casting service, advice and insurance.

To qualify for membership you must have undertaken professional acting work. Subscription fees are 1% of your gross earnings (with a minimum of £125 and a maximum subscription of £2025) plus a one-off £25 joining fee. If you're on a full-time accredited drama course you're eligible for student membership (£15 per year). Outlined below are some of the main benefits of joining Equity (taken from the Equity website).

Pay & conditions
Equity negotiates minimum terms and conditions with employers across all areas of the entertainment industry. Copies of contracts and agreements are available from Equity offices for a small charge.

Help & advice
Equity can help you throughout your career, offering a range of services as well as advice. Its staff have detailed, specialist knowledge and are happy to give advice to members and their agents on contracts and terms of engagement.

Equity card
The universally recognised symbol of your status as a professional in the entertainment industry.

Legal and welfare advice
Free legal advice on disputes over professional engagements including

personal injury claims. Free advice on National Insurance, taxation, benefits, pensions and welfare issues.

Publications
A quarterly magazine is sent free of charge to all members, keeping you in touch with Equity initiatives and activities. Equity also produces a wide range of information leaflets which are always available to members.

Medical support
All members can use the British Performing Arts Medicine Trust Helpline to access advice and information on performance-related medical, psychological and dental problems.

Royalties & residuals
Equity distributes royalties, residuals and other payments to members for TV and film re-runs, video sales and sound recordings.

Registers
Equity compiles a large number of specialist registers which are made available to casting directors and employers.

Job information
Equity members can access a service giving them information on job availability across the industry.

Campaigns
Equity campaigns vigorously on behalf of its members on a wide range of national, local and specialist issues and has a strong track record of success.

Your professional name
Equity reserves your choice of professional name when you join, as long as it is not already in use by another member.

Insurance
Public liability of up to £5 million, backstage cover and accident cover are available free to all members as long as they are in benefit. Call First Act Insurance on 020 8686 5050 for more information.

Rights, copyright & new media
Equity monitors national and international developments in intellectual property rights, campaigning for adequate recognition of performers' statutory rights.

Charities
Equity runs two charities, the Equity Benevolent Fund and the Evelyn Norris Trust, which exist to help members in times of trouble. Call 020 7379 6000 for more information. Equity also supports other organisations which provide help specifically for performers.

Pensions
The Equity Pension was set up in 1997 and if a member chooses to join, the BBC, ITV companies, PACT TV companies and West End theatre producers will pay into it when you have a main part with one of them. There is a similar scheme in place for opera singers and dancers in the standing companies.

Discounts
Equity members are entitled to discounts on a range of services and goods including hotels, car breakdown recovery, ticket prices and others.

EQUITY
GUILD HOUSE
UPPER ST MARTINS LANE
LONDON WC2H 9EG
{T} 020 7379 6000
{F} 020 7379 7001
WWW.EQUITY.ORG

Spotlight

Founded in 1927, Spotlight is the current industry standard for UK actors in terms of recognition and reputation. Spotlight produces both an annual book and a CD which lists more than 30,000 actors and is used by thousands of TV, film, theatre and radio professionals. Membership also entitles you to an advice resources staffed by Spotlight. Once registered you'll appear in The Spotlight Book, published annually, and have an online profile which you can login to with a pin number to keep your details up to date.

Casting professionals can search the online database by a range of characteristics (eg credits, physical attributes and skills). Spotlight is often the first port of call for casting directors and industry professionals whether looking to cast for a particular production or a more general browse and to keep abreast of who is out there, the old hands and the new kids on the block. It is strongly recommended that you join Spotlight – not to do so can be a false economy and entry will ensure that you are in the main 'shop window' for the UK acting profession.

The Spotlight Link is a system which allows industry professionals to post casting breakdowns to registered casting agents who can then submit their clients. Contacts is a directory of industry resources and professionals published by Spotlight.

Preliminary application forms can be printed off online or requested by post. Once submitted, these are then vetted. If your application is successful your online entry should appear within 21 days and your profile included in the next available offline directory. You don't need to have an agent but "Spotlight only accepts entries from artists who have recognised training and/or professional acting experience". Costs vary depending on when you join. Please contact Spotlight for current rates.

THE SPOTLIGHT
7 LEICESTER PLACE
LONDON WC2H 7RJ
{T} 020 7437 7631
INFO@SPOTLIGHT.COM
WWW.SPOTLIGHTCD.COM

Casting Call Pro

Established in 2004 and now with 20,000+ professional actors and 10,000+ casting professionals, Casting Call Pro has quickly become one of the largest networking resources for the UK acting industry. Actors can create a comprehensive online profile which displays credits, physical characteristics and skills, photos and, where applicable, links to their Imdb entry and Spotlight page.

Once listed in the directory, actors can be searched and contacted by casting directors. Using cutting edge software, Casting Call Pro employs sophisticated searching and matching technology to provide casting professionals with actors who fit their requirements.

The site also has a section for casting alerts where agents can place character breakdowns. The team at Casting Call Pro then alert actors who fit the bill via email to the new casting. Actors can then apply via the site, sending a covering letter direct to the casting director and an automated link to their online Casting Call Pro profile. A tracking system allows them to see when their application has been viewed. This also logs all views from casting professionals searching the directory, giving real time reporting to the actors.

Membership includes entry into the actors' database, searchable by industry professionals, and access to resources and directories including photographers, theatres, drama schools, peer networking tools, substantial discounts on key services (eg headshot sessions for £65 + VAT), and a host of online resources for the actor.

Minimum requirements for registration
(Members must meet at least one of these criteria)
• Equity membership
• training at an accredited drama school
• three professional credits.

Subscription fees

Standard membership gives actors a listing in the directory and is free. The optional premium package allows members to access paid casting alerts, upload up to 20 photographs, showreel and voicereel clips, create a castingcallpro email address (eg mattbarnes@casting-callpro.com) and their own URL (web address). Please contact them for current rates.

CASTING CALL PRO
UNIT 1 WATERLOO GARDENS
MILNER SQUARE
LONDON N1 1TY
{T} 020 7700 0474
INFO@CASTINGCALLPRO.COM
WWW.UK.CASTINGCALLPRO.COM

A-Z of useful organisations

THE ACTOR ATTAINMENT SOCIETY
48 DOWNS COURT ROAD
PURLEY
SURREY CR8 1BB
{T} 07893 456 832
WWW.ACTORATTAINMENT.COM
The Actor Attainment Society runs
seminars throughout the year to help
the working actor in their career
development. Our exclusive seminars
connect the actors with the industry in
an atmosphere designed to educate,
inspire and empower you and your
career development. Each session is led
by an industry expert who offers first-
hand support and advice to put you
ahead of the game.

ACTORS' BENEVOLENT FUND
6 ADAM STREET
LONDON WC2N 6AD
{T} 020 7836 6378
{F} 020 7836 8978
OFFICE@ABF.ORG.UK
WWW2.ACTORSBENEVOLENTFUND.CO.UK
The role of the Actors' Benevolent Fund
is to care for actors and theatrical stage
managers unable to work because of
poor health, an accident or frail old age.
The fund has been in place for over
120 years.

ACTORS' CHARITABLE TRUST
AFRICA HOUSE
64 KINGSWAY
LONDON WC2B 6BD
{T} 020 7242 0111
ROBERT@TACTACTORS.ORG
WWW.TACTACTORS.ORG
TACT helps the children of actors under
the age of 21 with grants, advice and
support.

ACTOREXPO
AIM HIGH EVENTS LTD
SUITE 2, B106 FAIRCHARM TRADING ESTATE
8-12 CREEKSIDE
LONDON, SE8 3DX
{T} 0208 320 2111
INFO@ACTOREXPO.CO.UK
WWW.ACTOREXPO.CO.UK
ActorExpo is the UK's biggest trade
show dedicated to advancing the
careers of actors and performers. Due to
its popularity the event has expanded
and now takes place in both London and
Edinburgh on an annual basis. The show
is a unique opportunity for actors and
performers to get insider knowledge
from experts and to essential practical
career advice. The Expo offers:
educational programmes, keynote
speakers, live performances plus plenty
of networking opportunities. 2008
exhibitors included companies such as
Casting Call Pro, Spotlight, The Stage,

PCR and Equity. Edinburgh date: 27 June 2009; London date: 3 October 2009.

AGENTS' ASSOCIATION
54 KEYES HOUSE
DOLPHIN SQUARE
LONDON SW1V 3NA
{T} 020 7834 0515
{F} 020 7821 0261
ASSOCIATION@AGENTS-UK.COM
WWW.AGENTS-UK.COM
The largest professional trade organisation of its kind in the world. Our member agents represent and book all kinds of performers, celebrities and musicians within all areas of the light entertainment industry.

ARTSLINE
54 CHALTON STREET
LONDON NW1Ê1HS
{T} 020 7388 2227
{F} 020 7383 2653
ADMIN@ARTSLINE.ORG.UK
WWW.ARTSLINE.ORG.UK
Artsline is a disabled led charity established twenty-five years ago to promote access for disabled people to arts and entertainment venues promoting the clear message that access equals inclusion.

BECTU
373-377 CLAPHAM ROAD
LONDON SW9 9BT
{T} 020 7346 0900
{F} 020 7346 0901
INFO@BECTU.ORG.UK
WWW.BECTU.ORG.UK
BECTU is the independent union for those working in broadcasting, film, theatre, entertainment, leisure, interactive media and allied areas. The union represents permanently employed, contract and freelance workers who are primarily based in the United Kingdom.

BRITISH ACADEMY OF DRAMATIC COMBAT
3 CASTLE VIEW
HELMSLEY
NORTH YORKS YO62 5AU
WORKSHOPCOORDINATOR@BADC.CO.UK
WWW.BADC.CO.UK
The BADC is the longest established stage combat teaching organization in the United Kingdom. The BADC also enjoys international recognition as a provider of excellence in teaching quality, curriculum design and assessment rigour. The BADC is dedicated to the advance of the art of stage combat in all forms of performance media.

BRITISH ARTS FESTIVAL ASSOCIATION
2ND FLOOR
2B CHARING CROSS ROAD
LONDON WC2H 0DB
{T} 020 7240 4532
INFO@ARTSFESTIVALS.CO.UK
WWW.ARTSFESTIVALS.CO.UK
BAFA is a vibrant membership organisation covering the widest span of arts festivals in the UK. These include some of the large international cultural events such as the Edinburgh International Festival and Brighton Festival through to small dynamic festivals such as the Winchester Hat Fair and the Corsham Festival in Wiltshire.

BRITISH COUNCIL
10 SPRING GARDENS
LONDON SW1A 2BN
{T} 020 7930 8466
{F} 020 7389 6347
GENERAL.ENQUIRIES@BRITISHCOUNCIL.ORG
WWW.BRITISHCOUNCIL.ORG
The organisation was set up in 1934 to promote a wider knowledge of the United Kingdom abroad, to promote the knowledge of the English language, and to develop closer cultural relations between the United Kingdom and other countries.

CASTING DIRECTORS GUILD
{T} 020 8741 1951
WWW.THECDG.CO.UK
The Guild is a professional organisation of casting directors in the film, television,

theatre and commercials communities in the UK who have joined together to further their common interests in establishing a recognised standard of professionalism in the industry, enhancing the stature of the profession, providing a free exchange of information and ideas, honouring the achievements of members and standardisation of working practices within the industry.

BRITISH FILM INSTITUTE (BFI)
BELVEDERE ROAD
SOUTH BANK
LONDON SE1 8XT
{T} 020 7255 1444
LIBRARY@BFI.ORG.UK
WWW.BFI.ORG.UK
The BFI promotes understanding and appreciation of Britain's rich film and television heritage and culture.

CONFERENCE OF DRAMA SCHOOLS (CDS)
THE EXECUTIVE SECRETARY
P O BOX 34252
LONDON NW5 1XJ
{T} 020 7722 8183
{F} 020 7722 4132
INFO@CDS.DRAMA.AC.UK
WWW.DRAMA.AC.UK
The Conference of Drama Schools comprises Britain's 22 leading drama schools. CDS exists in order to strengthen the voice of the member schools, to set and maintain the highest standards of training within the vocational drama sector, and to make it

easier for prospective students to understand the range of courses on offer and the application process. Founded in 1969, the 22 member schools offer courses in acting, musical theatre, directing and technical theatre training.

CONSERVATOIRE FOR DANCE AND DRAMA (CDD)
1-7 WOBURN WALK
LONDON WC1H 0JJ
{T} 020 7387 5101
{F} 020 7387 5103
INFO@CDD.AC.UK
WWW.CDD.AC.UK
The Conservatoire for Dance and Drama (CDD) is a new higher education institution, founded in 2001. It was established to protect and promote some of the best schools offering vocational training in dance, drama and circus arts. The CDD offers courses in acting, stage management, classical ballet, theatre directing, contemporary dance, lighting, costume and scenic design. Entry to the schools is very competitive but they seek students who have the talent, skill and determination to succeed regardless of their background.

COUNCIL FOR DANCE EDUCATION AND TRAINING (CDET)
OLD BREWER'S YARD
17-19 Neal Street
LONDON WC2H 9UY
{T} 020 7240 5703
{F} 020 7240 2547
INFO@CDET.ORG.UK
WWW.CDET.ORG.UK
Founded in 1979, the Council for Dance Education and Training is the national standards body of the professional dance industry. It accredits programmes of training in vocational dance schools and holds the Register of Dance Awarding Bodies – the directory of teaching societies whose syllabuses have been inspected and approved by the Council. It is the body of advocacy of the dance education and training communities and offers a free and comprehensive information service, Answers for Dancers, on all aspects of vocational dance provision to students, parents, teachers dance artists and employers.

DRAMA ASSOCIATION OF WALES
THE OLD LIBRARY
SPLOTT
CARDIFF CF24 2ET
{T} 029 2045 2200
{F} 029 2045 2277
ALED.DAW@VIRGIN.NET
WWW.AMDRAM.CO.UK/DAW
Founded in 1934 and a registered charity since 1973, the Association offers a wide and varied range of services to Community Drama. Among others, members include amateur and professional theatre practitioners, educationalists and playwrights.

THE DRAMA STUDENT MAGAZINE

TOP FLOOR
66 WANSEY STREET
LONDON SE17 1JP
{T} 020 7701 4536
EDITOR@THEDRAMASTUDENT.CO.UK
WWW.THEDRAMASTUDENT.CO.UK

The Drama Student Magazine launched in January 2009 as the first and only publication dedicated to drama students in the UK. Covering the entire journey, from auditioning for vocation training, right through to graduation, each quarterly issue is packed with inspiring interviews, articles and news that are sure to assist students in their chosen career path. Embarking on a career in the industry as an actor or behind the scenes is an exciting time and The Drama Student aims to be at the forefront of that passion, delivering a publication with enthusiasm and substance.

FOUNDATION FOR COMMUNITY DANCE

LCB DEPOT
31 RUTLAND STREET
LEICESTER LE1 1RE
{T} 0116 253 3453
{F} 0116 261 6801
INFO@COMMUNITYDANCE.ORG.UK
WWW.COMMUNITYDANCE.ORG.UK

The Foundation for Community Dance is a UK-wide charity, established in 1986, to support the development of community dance, providing information, advice and guidance for dance artists, organisations, students and communities about community dance and the issues they face.

FRINGE THEATRE NETWORK

IMEX BUSINESS CENTRE
INGATE PLACE
LONDON SW8 3NS
{T} 020 7627 4920
HELENOLDREDLION@YAHOO.CO.UK
WWW.FRINGETHEATRE.ORG.UK

Fringe Theatre Network (FTN) was founded in 1986 as Pub Theatre Network when fringe venues felt the need for an organisation to support them, keep them in touch with each other and present their case on their behalf. FTN was registered as a charity in 1987 and exists to support and promote fringe theatre in London by providing services, support and a network of contacts for venues, producing companies and individuals working on the fringe and thereby to increase the viability and profession-alism of fringe theatre, and by repre-senting fringe theatre as an umbrella organisation which can act and speak on behalf of fringe theatre to statutory authorities, funding bodies, policy makers and other arts organisations.

INDEPENDENT THEATRE COUNCIL (ITC)

12 THE LEATHERMARKET
WESTON STREET
LONDON SE1 3ER
{T} 020 7403 1727
{F} 020 7403 1745

ADMIN@ITC-ARTS.ORG
WWW.ITC-ARTS.ORG
The ITC is the UK's leading management association for the performing arts, representing around 700 organisations across the country. The ITC works closely with Equity on agreements, contracts and rights for performers.

NATIONAL ASSOCIATION OF YOUTH THEATRES
DARLINGTON ARTS CENTRE
VANE TERRACE
DARLINGTON DL3 7AX
{T} 01325 363330
{F} 01325 363313
NAYTUK@BTCONNECT.COM
WWW.NAYT.ORG.UK
NAYT (National Association of Youth Theatres) supports the development of youth theatre activity through training, advocacy, participation programmes and information services.

NATIONAL COUNCIL FOR DRAMA TRAINING (NCDT)
1-7 WOBURN WALK
BLOOMSBURY
LONDON WC1H 0JJ
{T} 020 7387 3650
{F} 020 7387 3860
INFO@NCDT.CO.UK
WWW.NCDT.CO.UK
The National Council for Drama Training is a partnership of employers in theatre, broadcast and media industries, employee representatives and training

providers. The aim of the COUNCIL is to act as a champion for the drama industry, working to optimise support for professional drama training and education, embracing change and development.

NATIONAL OPERATIC AND DRAMATIC ASSOCIATION (NODA)
58-60 LINCOLN ROAD
PETERBOROUGH PE1 2RZ
{T} 0870 770 248
{F} 0870 770 2490
EVERYONE@NODA.ORG.UK
WWW.NODA.ORG.UK
The National Operatic and Dramatic Association (NODA), founded in 1899, is the main representative body for amateur theatre in the UK. It has a membership of some 2500 amateur/community theatre groups and 3000 individual enthusiasts throughout the UK, staging musicals, operas, plays, concerts and pantomimes in a wide variety of performing venues, ranging from the country's leading professional theatres to village halls.

NATIONAL YOUTH THEATRE
443-445 HOLLOWAY ROAD
LONDON N7 6LW
{T} 020 7281 3863
{F} 020 7281 8246
INFO@NYT.ORG.UK
WWW.NYT.ORG.UK
The National Youth Theatre was
established in 1956 to offer young
people the chance to develop their
creative and social skills through the
medium of the theatrical arts which
includes acting and technical disciplines.
The National Youth Theatre is now an
internationally acclaimed organisation,
providing opportunities to all young
people aged 13-21 in the UK, regardless
of background.

PERFORMING RIGHTS SOCIETY
COPYRIGHT HOUSE
29-33 BERNERS ST
LONDON W1T 3AB
WWW.MCPS-PRS-ALLIANCE.CO.UK

PERSONAL MANAGERS ASSOCIATION (PMA)
1 SUMMER ROAD
EAST MOLESEY
SURREY KT8 9LX
{T} 020 8398 9796
WWW.THEPMA.COM
The PMA is the professional association
of agents representing UK based actors,
writers, producers, directors, designers
and technicians in the film, television
and theatre industries. Established in
1950 as the Personal Managers'
Association, the PMA has over 130
member agencies representing more
than 1,000 agents.

NORTHERN ACTORS CENTRE
21-31 OLDHAM STREET
MANCHESTER M1 1JG
{T} 0161 819 2513
{F} 0161 819 2513
INFO@NORTHERNACTORSCENTRE.CO.UK
WWW.NORTHERNACTORSCENTRE.CO.UK
The NAC provides workshops for actors
and other professionals in theatre,
television, film and radio to enable them
to continuously maintain and develop
their craft once their initial training has
been completed. Areas covered include
physical, vocal, studio techniques, char-
acterisation, approaches to specific
styles, genres and authors, career
management.

SKILLSET
PROSPECT HOUSE
80-110 NEW OXFORD STREET
LONDON WC1A 1HB
{T} 020 7520 5757
INFO@SKILLSET.ORG
WWW.SKILLSET.ORG

Skillset is the Sector Skills Council for the audiovisual industries (broadcast, film, video, interactive media and photo imaging). They conduct consultation work with industry, publish research and strategic documents, run funding schemes and project work, and provide information about the challenges that face the industry. They also provide impartial media careers advice for aspiring new entrants and established industry professionals, online, face to face and over the phone.

SOCIETY OF TEACHERS OF SPEECH & DRAMA
73 BERRY HILL ROAD
MANSFIELD
NOTTINGHAMSHIRE NG18 4RU
{T} 01623 627636
STSD@STSD.ORG.UK
WWW.STSD.ORG.UK

The STSD was established soon after the Second World War from the amalgamation of two much earlier Associations formed to protect the professional interests of qualified, specialist teachers of speech and drama, to encourage good standards of teaching and to promote the study and knowledge of speech and dramatic art in every form.

THEATRICAL MANAGEMENT ASSOCIATION
32 ROSE STREET
LONDON WC2E 9ET
{T} 020 7557 6700
{F} 020 7557 6799
ENQUIRIES@SOLTTMA.CO.UK
WWW.TMAUK.ORG

TMA is the pre-eminent UK wide organisation dedicated to providing professional support for the performing arts. Members include repertory and producing theatres, arts centres and touring venues, major national companies and independent producers, opera and dance companies and associated businesses. The association undertakes advocacy on behalf of members to authorities to promote the value of investment in the performing arts. The association also facilitates facilitating concerted action to promote theatre-going to the widest possible audience.